STUDIES IN MEDIEVAL
AND RENAISSANCE
LITERATURE

Canto is an imprint offering a range of titles, classic and more recent, across a broad spectrum of subject areas and interests. History, literature, biography, archaeology, politics, religion, psychology, philosophy and science are all represented in Canto's specially selected list of titles, which now offers some of the best and most accessible of Cambridge publishing to a wider readership.

STUDIES IN MEDIEVAL AND RENAISSANCE LITERATURE

BY C. S. LEWIS

COLLECTED BY WALTER HOOPER

CAMBRIDGE
UNIVERSITY PRESS

PUBLISHED BY THE PRESS SYNDICATE OF THE UNIVERSITY OF CAMBRIDGE
The Pitt Building, Trumpington Street, Cambridge CB2 1RP, United Kingdom

CAMBRIDGE UNIVERSITY PRESS
The Edinburgh Building, Cambridge CB2 2RU, UK http://www.cup.cam.ac.uk
40 West 20th Street, New York, NY 10011-4211, USA http://www.cup.org
10 Stamford Road, Oakleigh, Melbourne 3166, Australia

Printed in Great Britain at the
University Press, Cambridge

Library of Congress catalogue card number: 66–12749

First published 1966
First paperback edition 1979
Reprinted 1980, 1989, 1995
Canto edition 1998

ISBN 0 521 64584 0 paperback

CONTENTS

Preface, by Walter Hooper   *page* vii

1   *De Audiendis Poetis*   1

2   The Genesis of a Medieval Book   18

3   Imagination and Thought in the Middle Ages   41

4   Dante's Similes   64

5   Imagery in the Last Eleven Cantos of Dante's *Comedy*   78

6   Dante's Statius   94

7   The *Morte Darthur*   103

8   Tasso   111

9   Edmund Spenser, 1552–99   121

10   On Reading *The Faerie Queene*   146

11   Neoplatonism in the Poetry of Spenser   149

12   Spenser's Cruel Cupid   164

13   Genius and Genius   169

14   A Note on *Comus*   175

Additional Editorial Notes   182

Index   187

PREFACE

When Professor C. S. Lewis died on 22 November 1963, he left few unpublished manuscripts; and that in spite of the astonishing fertility of his pen. He managed throughout his life to meet pub-lishers' dead-lines and see most of his works in print. As I had become Lewis's private secretary before his retirement from Cam-bridge, his brother, Major W. H. Lewis, has kindly allowed me to publish his literary remains.

Many people will have heard Lewis read papers which have not appeared in print. I note in his pocket diaries the numerous occa-sions for which he prepared learned addresses. Yet so few survive today. This is because those manuscripts which he did not intend to publish immediately were often turned over and used for writing other books and essays—all in his tiny, beautifully regular handwriting. And, as Lewis habitually kept his desk-tops tidy, they usually ended in the wastepaper basket. Several of the studies in this volume, such as the one on Tasso, survive, I suspect, only because they burrowed their way into his college 'files'—several large desk drawers into which he threw used envelopes and odd memoranda. Yet the fertility of his genius allowed him to throw so much away, and still to publish an extraordinary number of books, essays, poems and book reviews, as can readily be seen from my bibliography of his writings in *Light on C. S. Lewis* (1965). This present volume is composed of all the studies in medieval and renaissance literature I have been able to find and which Lewis, for various reasons, never published in his lifetime. I have also chosen to reprint seven related essays which are difficult for some readers to come by. The order in which I have placed the pieces this volume contains is the chronological order of the subjects they discuss.

'*De Audiendis Poetis*' was written as an introductory chapter to a book Lewis began several years before his retirement. Some of it recalls passages in his essay 'The Anthropological Approach' as well as parts of *The Discarded Image*. Yet the aim of this book is not like that of either work; it is, as he says, to 'cure errors of misapprehension' and even in this single chapter his purpose is clear.

Again, in 'The Genesis of a Medieval Book', we have only the first chapter of a proposed work. His first subject is Laȝamon's *Brut*, which was becoming increasingly dear to Lewis. This is one of the last pieces he wrote. He knew that the Early English Text Society edition of the *Brut* was in preparation, but had to rely on Madden's edition of 1847. Rather than replace his quotations with those of the E.E.T.S. edition so far available, I have decided to print Lewis's study just as it stands.

The two consecutive lectures, 'Imagination and Thought in the Middle Ages', amount almost to a précis of *The Discarded Image*. Lewis's approach is not the same, however, and herein lies the difference—these lectures were specially prepared for, and delivered to, an audience of scientists at the Zoological Laboratory, Cambridge, on 17 and 18 July 1956. Instead of emphasizing the literary sources—these he hardly mentions—Lewis's purpose was to construct a clear and simple image of the universe as the men of the Middle Ages understood it. It is, in fact, a 'map' for those who want to see their way about, but who have read no medieval literature and for whom even a longer introduction would be a surfeit.

'Dante's Similes' was read to the Oxford Dante Society on 13 February 1940 and 'Imagery in the Last Eleven Cantos of Dante's *Comedy*' was read to the same society on 9 November 1948.

'Dante's Statius' is reprinted from *Medium Aevum* (xxv, no. 3, 1957) with the permission of the editors.

'The *Morte Darthur*' is an unsigned review (7 June 1947) of Professor Vinaver's *Works of Sir Thomas Malory*, reprinted by permission of *The Times Literary Supplement*. Judging from the handwriting, I should guess that Lewis wrote the essay on 'Tasso' in the 1940's.

It is to Harcourt, Brace and World Inc. that I owe permission to reprint 'Edmund Spenser, 1552–99' which originally accompanied Lewis's selections from *The Faerie Queene* and *Epithalamion* in *Major British Writers* (vol. 1, 1954). In his correspondence with the late William Borst, editor of the Harcourt, Brace and World college department, Lewis speaks of his own satisfaction with the article and his concern that readers should remember that Spenser is primarily a romancer *à longue haleine*. Students, he complains, 'are too carefully shielded from the rumour of worlds they have not yet broken into' by being led to read only the 'dear old show-pieces' from *The Faerie Queene,* selections which leave the reader content to adventure no further. In his own choice of selections Lewis attempts to quarry from the poem those passages which he feels reproduce its real characteristics: 'leaving the first appearances of characters as unprepared as Spenser leaves them'. As a consequence, one is tantalized and asks for more. With this in mind, one can better appreciate Lewis's discussion of what he calls 'polyphonic narrative' in the essay reprinted here. 'On Reading *The Faerie Queene*' was originally entitled 'Edmund Spenser' and is reprinted by permission of the Oxford University Press from *Fifteen Poets* (1941).

'Neoplatonism in the Poetry of Spenser' is a review-essay of Dr Robert Ellrodt's book of the same title and is reprinted from *Etudes Anglaises* (XIV, no. 2, 1961) by permission of its editors. I include it here because, as with all of Lewis's reviews, his own contribution is noteworthy. There is certainly a marked similarity between some of his most recent thinking about Spenser's poetry (as I see from his Cambridge lecture notes) and his criticism of Dr Ellrodt's book. And, judging from my conversation with Lewis, I gather that, had he enjoyed a longer retirement, he might have written a book-length study of Spenser's poetry based on his Cambridge lectures. Happily, there does survive a further draft of one passage from his notes. It is 'Spenser's Cruel Cupid', a study of *Faerie Queene,* III, xi, 48 which Lewis was discussing with Dr Alastair Fowler a few months before his death. Lewis himself spoke of the piece as exemplifying an *iconographical* approach which he was finding fruitful with Spenser.[1]

'Genius and Genius' is reprinted from *The Review of English Studies* (XII, no. 46, 1936) by permission of its editors and 'A Note on *Comus*' is reprinted from the same source (VIII, no. 30, 1932) by permission.

I mentioned desk-tops above. Lewis could write anywhere, even when conditions were unfavourable. During term he usually worked in his college rooms, but on vacation and week-ends he wrote in one of his two studies at The Kilns, his home in Oxford. As could be expected, his papers were in no particular order: I found the pages of

---

[1] Lewis's Cambridge lecture notes on Spenser are now being freely edited by Dr Alastair Fowler. It is expected that they will be published soon.

'Spenser's Cruel Cupid' in three different places. This arrangement also meant that part of Lewis's library was invariably in the other place. He almost always quoted from memory; I have compared the quotations in these studies with the texts he used and have needed to make a number of minor corrections. As Lewis did not himself prepare these papers for publication, I have used my judgement also in correcting and regularizing the spelling and punctuation.

We all wonder, I suppose, what Lewis would have written had he lived longer. I spoke of the two introductory chapters in this volume and of Lewis's growing delight in the Arthurian legend. This brings me to his plans for retirement. Lewis asked several times what I should like him to write. I wanted him to finish his novel on Menelaus, but he could not see his way after the first few chapters. Then I suggested that he might do a translation of Laȝamon's *Brut*: this he liked, although it meant, he said, waiting for the new E.E.T.S. edition to appear. Meanwhile he had other ideas—and here I hope I shall be forgiven for digressing a little.

One morning in August of 1963 we were discussing our plans for Christmas and Lewis reminded me that he neither gave nor *received* Christmas gifts. Then almost immediately he expressed a desire to write something on the Arthurian legend—if only he owned a copy of the *Vulgate Version of the Arthurian Romances*. 'I have all seven volumes', I said. 'Have you?' he asked, his eyes twinkling. 'Yes,' I said, 'Would you like them?' There was a very long pause. 'After what I have just said,' he fumbled, 'would you—*could* you part with them?' It gave me great pleasure to see the noble Arthurian volumes on his shelves and I continue to imagine what golden visions might have sprung from them.

I should like to thank Dr and Mrs Austin Farrer, Mr Colin Hardie, Dr J. E. Stevens, Dr Alastair Fowler and Mr Daryl R. Williams for their valuable assistance and encouragement in the preparation of this volume. And it is to Major W. H. Lewis that I owe the honour of being allowed to collect these, his brother's last studies in medieval and renaissance literature.

W.H.

Oxford
St Matthias's Day 1965

NOTE

Asterisks refer to the Additional
Editorial Notes on pages 182–6

'DE AUDIENDIS POETIS'

There are more ways than one of reading old books. A choice between two of them is well expressed by Mr Speirs[1] when he denounces as 'discouraging' the notion 'that before the modern reader can properly appreciate a medieval poem he must first have somehow put himself back' into the age when it was composed. For thus he will be seeking not 'what the poem *means*', but 'what it once meant' and will become 'concerned less with reading and responding to a poem than with reading and researching outside it'.

That anything which takes us outside the poem and leaves us there is regrettable, I fully agree. But we may have to go outside it in order that we may presently come inside it again, better equipped. (We have to go outside some medieval poems pretty often to look up hard words in a glossary or dictionary.) And what we find inside will always depend a great deal on what we have brought in with us. Mr Speirs modestly under-rates all the knowledge of history, all the imaginative and emotional adjustments, which he himself uses when he reads an old book. A man who read the literature of the past with no allowance at all for the fact that manners, thought, and sentiments have changed since it was written, would make the maddest work of it. Finding that Nausicaa does the washing, though her father seems to be in easy circumstances, he would think he was reading a version of Cinderella. In the *Knights Tale* the action of Theseus, who condemns two prisoners of war to a dungeon for life, would strike him as an atrocity. The battles of Romance, fought in peacetime between knights who had no quarrel—and what might the very word *knights* mean to such a reader?—would seem to him a picture of lunacy.

This is, of course, only to say that the reader of medieval poetry must already be a man of general education. But the point is that what we call 'general education' includes a quite considerable

[1] *Medieval English Poetry: The Non-Chaucerian Tradition* (1957), p. 48.

knowledge of the past and a considerable mental adjustment to it. Some substitution of what the work may be supposed to have meant in its own day for what it would mean to us if we now read it with nothing but modern feelings and ideas, is therefore unavoidable. It is made by everyone; even, in their degree, by children of ten and by the uneducated. We are all so used to this substitution that we make it almost unconsciously. The only question is how far the process should go. Are we to rest content with 'putting ourselves back' into the attitudes of the old author just so far as general education permits, and indeed forces, us to do: or are we to go on and put ourselves back as completely as, with labour and patience, we can?

I am asking, of course, which we should do as lovers of literature. In so far as we are historians, there is no question. When our aim is knowledge we must go as far as all available means—including the most intense, yet at the same time most sternly disciplined, exercise of our imaginations—can possibly take us. We want to know—therefore, as far as may be, we want to live through for ourselves—the experience of men long dead. What a poem may 'mean' to moderns and to them only, however delightful, is from this point of view merely a stain on the lens. We must clean the lens and remove the stain so that the real past can be seen better.

But among lovers of poetry the question admits two answers. You may do which you please. There are two ways of enjoying the past, as there are two ways of enjoying a foreign country. One man carries his Englishry abroad with him and brings it home unchanged. Wherever he goes he consorts with the other English tourists. By a good hotel he means one that is like an English hotel. He complains of the bad tea where he might have had excellent coffee. He finds the 'natives' quaint and enjoys their quaintness. In his own way he may have a pleasant time; he likes his winter-sports in Switzerland and his flutter at Monte Carlo. In the same way there is a man who carries his modernity with him through all his reading of past literatures and preserves it intact. The highlights in all ancient and medieval poetry are for him the bits that resemble—or can be so read that they seem to resemble—the poetry of his own age. Thus when modernity was Romanticism (for modernity naturally changes) the great thing in Sophocles was the nightingale chorus in the *Coloneus*;

and Dante meant the *Inferno* and the *Inferno* meant Paolo and Francesca and Ulysses: and what really mattered about Villon was just the Old Frenchness, so archaic, so wistful. This sort of reading is well reflected in the successive schools of translation. A while ago the classics were made to sound like the Authorised Version or the Pre-Raphaelites; now they are to be stark and slangy and ironic. And such reading has its reward. Those who practise it will have certain enjoyments.

But there is another sort of travelling and another sort of reading. You can eat the local food and drink the local wines, you can share the foreign life, you can begin to see the foreign country as it looks, not to the tourist, but to its inhabitants. You can come home modified, thinking and feeling as you did not think and feel before. So with the old literature. You can go beyond the first impression that a poem makes on your modern sensibility. By study of things outside the poem, by comparing it with other poems, by steeping yourself in the vanished period, you can then re-enter the poem with eyes more like those of the natives; now perhaps seeing that the associations you gave to the old words were false, that the real impli-cations were different from what you supposed, that what you thought strange was then ordinary and that what seemed to you ordinary was then strange. In so far as you succeed, you may more and more come to realize that what you enjoyed at the first reading was not really any medieval poem that ever existed but a modern poem made by yourself at a hint from the old words. But that is an extreme case. Sometimes, by luck, your first shot may not have been so wide. Not all things at a given date in the past are equidistant from the present.

I am writing to help, if I can, the second sort of reading. Partly, of course, because I have a historical motive. I am a man as well as a lover of poetry: being human, I am inquisitive, I want to know as well as to enjoy. But even if enjoyment alone were my aim I should still choose this way, for I should hope to be led by it to newer and fresher enjoyments, things I could never have met in my own period, modes of feeling, flavours, atmospheres, nowhere accessible but by a mental journey into the real past. I have lived nearly sixty years with myself and my own century and am not so enamoured of either as to desire no glimpse of a world beyond them. As the mere tourist's kind of holiday abroad seems to me rather a waste of Europe—there is more to be got out of it than he gets—so it would seem to me a waste of the past if we were content to see in the literature of every bygone age only the reflexion of our own faces—*zum Ekel find' ich immer nur mich?*

But if I left it at this I should seem to be demanding as much austerity in one direction as Mr Speirs perhaps would approve in the other. Actually, the two approaches can to some extent be combined. We come to see the old texts with a sort of double vision. Most of us, I fancy, when we read Virgil's Fourth Eclogue, see simultaneously—or with oscillations so rapid as to give the effect of simultaneity—the poem as it may have been for the Romans and the poem as it came to be in Christian times. But this double vision, the reward of some ripeness, is different from acquiescence in our first illusions.

> A man that looks on glasse,
> On it may stay his eye;
> Or if he pleaseth, through it passe,
> And then the heav'n espie.*

If he pleaseth. This is quite different from mistaking the flaws or blurrings of the glass for real clouds or hills.

The worst method of all, in my opinion, would be to accept the first impression that the old text happens to make on a modern sensibility and then apply to this the detailed methods of 'practical' criticism. That is to make the worst of both worlds. If you are content that the Heraclitus epigram should mean to you what it meant to Cory, if you are content, with Hopkins, to find sprung rhythm in *Piers Plowman*, best enjoy these phantoms lightly, spontaneously, even lazily. To use the microscope, yet not to focus or clean it, is folly. You will only find more and more mares' nests. You are passing from uncorrected illusions to positively invited illusions. The critic who said (of medieval poetry, as it happens) 'one cannot find what is not there' was unduly optimistic. Here, as elsewhere, untrained eyes or a bad instrument produce both errors; they create phantasmal objects as well as miss real ones.

The sort of problems that arise when we begin to read medieval poetry in the way I like best may be illustrated from a textual variant in the fourteenth-century *Sir Orfeo*. Orfeo, after he has lost Dame Heurodis, is wandering in the forest. There he often catches a glimpse of 'Þe king o fairy wiþ his rout' hunting. Repeatedly the chase goes past him: and vanishes. It goes past with a sound: and the three MSS describe the sound thus:

> A. Wiþ dim cri and bloweing
> B. With dunnyng and with blowyng
> C. Wyth dynne, cry, and wyth blowyng.

Leaving aside all question as to which is the correct reading, which do we like best? I agree with the poem's last editor[1] that the *A* reading is 'certainly more poetical'. But when I ask why it seems so to me, I find, first, that the scales are, for my sensibility, weighted against *B* and *C* by the mainly disagreeable associations of *din* in Modern English. But those considerations are modern; I must try to discount them. And next, I realize where my pleasure in *dim* comes from. For me this is 'properly' (as the grammarians say) a word describing a degree of light; its use to describe a degree of sound is therefore a metonymy. These transferences from one of our senses to another delight my modern taste. But there is some evidence that *dim* in fourteenth-century English applied to the audible quite as 'properly' as to the visible, in which case a metonymy would not have been felt.[2] My scales have perhaps been weighted in favour of *dim* as well as against *din*. There are indeed other grounds for preferring *A*. It gives a finer conception and perhaps a more interesting rhythm. But its apparent superiority as mere language probably did not exist in the Middle Ages.

In that passage we might easily have found what was not there. In the following, we might miss what is. Langland thus describes the Incarnation:

> Loue is the plonte of pees and most preciouse of vertues;
> For heuene holde hit ne myȝte so heuy hit semede,
> Til hit hadde on erthe ȝoten hym-selue.

---

[1] A. J. Bliss, *Sir Orfeo* (1954).
[2] Cf. Chaucer, C.T. A 2432–3, 'a murmuringe Ful lowe and dim'; Gower, C.A. v, 4967, 'A vois which cride dimme.'

Was neuere lef up⁄on lynde lyghter ther⁄after,
As whanne hit hadde of the folde flesch and blod ytake.[1]

(Piers Plowman, c. II, 149–53)

On any reading, no doubt, the passage is one of most daring in⁄tensity. It ascribes weight to the immaterial and painful tension (almost physiological and sexual) to Omnipotence. It makes spirit grow *lighter* by assuming a load of earth. But the crowning audacity escapes us unless we realize how gay, homely, and thoroughly secular 'lef up⁄on lynde' is. Women are laughingly advised to be as 'light as leef on linde' (*Clerkes Tale*, E 1211). In the *Bouge of Court* that disgraceful confidence trickster Harvy Hafter comes up to the dreamer 'leaping light as lynde' (stanza 33).* And *light* in Middle English, we must remember, refers at least as 'properly' and as often to cheerfulness, frivolity, and nimbleness of movement, as to small⁄ness of weight. Hence the effect is almost as if Langland had said that Love, incarnate, became 'as merry as a lark' or 'as busy as a bee'. (In the next line he will be telling us it was as sharp as a needle.) The real poetry of the phrase depends on its being a good deal less 'poetical' (in the graver and more demanding sense) than the uninstructed modern reader would probably take it to be; on its being this, yet uttered with the deepest reverence and gratitude.

The error we might have made in reading the passage from *Sir Orfeo* was linguistic in a fairly narrow sense. A really good glossary or dictionary would have set us right about *dim* and *din*, as about many other words which are misleading precisely because they survive in modern English. (*Against, comedy, complexion, constellation, danger, I dare say, feeling, fellow, free, girl, law, religion, sad,* and *wait,* are all notorious pitfalls.) What we might have missed in the passage from *Piers Plowman,* on the other hand, can be supplied only by a fairly wide reading of medieval English literature; whether our own, or that vicarious reading which is offered to us by the quotations of 'parallels' in good commentaries. Those who speak with contempt of editors and their notes often show much ingratitude.

[1] Love is the plant of peace and the most precious of powers, for heaven could not contain it, it felt so heavy, until it had poured itself out on the earth. After that, no leaf on a lime⁄tree was lighter (gayer, more mobile) than it, when it had taken flesh and blood from the clay.

The aim of this work is mainly to prevent, or cure, errors of yet a third kind. They may first be revealed to a teacher by a mistake in his pupil's translation which is itself merely lexical; but it is symptomatic of a far wider misapprehension. Thus only a careless student will render the line from *Pearl* 'Fro spot my spyryt þer sprang in space' (61) as 'From that place my spirit sprang in space'. The conscientious man would have found out what *in space* really meant (in a space of time, presently). To be sure, the correction of this error even on the philological level will be most fruitful; the pupil who learns that *space* usually meant a temporal rather than a local extension and that *space* as a concrete (the abyss, the vacuity in which all material objects exist) cannot be traced earlier than Milton, will have learned something worth knowing—especially about Milton. But a far greater light dawns upon him when he comes to realize that this modern meaning of *space* could not have existed in the fourteenth century because the thing meant did not exist for the human mind. The drama of existence was not performed against any such forbidding backcloth. There was no abyss. Man looked up at a patterned, populous, intricate, finite cosmos; a builded thing, not a wilderness; 'heaven' or 'spheres', not 'space'. The readjustments he will find himself compelled to make when he has thoroughly grasped this will lead him on to reckon with the presence of that very different conception behind almost every stroke of the medieval chisel, brush or pen.

Later in the same *Pearl* the poet says that if any man in the body had 'suffered the favour', *abiden þat bone*, which was given him in his vision, then, though all the learned men in the world had him under their care,

His lyf were loste *an-vnder mone* (1092)

'his life were lost beneath the moon'. Similarly Nature, in Chaucer's *Phisiciens Tale*, says

ech thing in my cure is
Under the mone, that may wane and waxe. (C.T. C 22-3)

The modern reader might take 'under the moon', like our modern 'under the sun', as an entirely vague synonym for everywhere or anywhere, and the whole of Chaucer's second line for padding. In reality they are of an almost scientific precision. He might misunderstand Dante's reference to 'the Love that moves the sun' (*Paradiso*, XXXIII, 145). Donne's 'So thy love may be my loves spheare' (*Aire*

7

and Angels, 25) can be grossly misunderstood. The exact reason why 'Fortune may non angel dere' (*Monks Tale*, C.T. B 3191) or why Hamlet's lunacy will not be noticed in England (III, i, 168) may escape us. All these possible misinterpretations of single lines, however, are not the most serious danger. They will be corrected, for a careful reader, by the notes. What we really have to fear is a slighter, but more continuous and in the long run more impoverishing, blindness to the full implications of apparently innocent passages. In the language of the old poets it is not the obviously 'hard' words that betray us; it is the seemingly easy words which will make sense (but not the sense the poet intended) if we take them in their modern meanings. So in their images. If *influence* occurs in an explicitly astrological passage we shall not go wrong; but unless we have our whole imagination so impregnated with the old point of view that reference to it has become habitual, we shall almost certainly fail to respond to the metaphorical uses of *influence* (say, in Milton). In our own language the metaphorical use of this word is the only one, and the metaphor is thoroughly dead. In the older writers it is glitteringly alive. So again, when Chaucer exhorts his young readers to return 'hoom' from worldly vanity (*Troilus*, V, 1837), or when Frank says in *The Witch of Edmonton* 'All life is but a wandring to finde home' (IV, ii, 31),* we may see in this no more than a pious metaphor at all times very natural to a Christian and familiar in the Hymn-Books. But we shall have missed something.

It is on these grounds that I think it worth while to spend some labour on 'putting ourselves back' into the universe which our ancestors believed themselves to inhabit. What their work means to us after we have done so appears to me not only more accurate (more like what they intended) but also more interesting and nourishing and delightful. But I have no special wish to make converts. I write for those, whether few or many, who, like me, care to know more of this theatre and this play than can be seen from the particular row and seat of the mid-twentieth century.

Even this, however, does not sufficiently define my endeavours. There are two possible approaches to medieval literature which I shall not adopt, and readers who favour either of them are entitled to ask why. These are the theological and the anthropological.

8

There are some who see all medieval literature primarily, if not exclusively, as exposition of medieval Christian doctrine. The Middle Ages would have been pleased to be taken in this way, but would have known that the compliment was undeserved. *Troilus* is for Chaucer something to be repented of. And this approach can become baneful when it leads critics to equate the edificatory value of a work with its value as literature. From the premise (perhaps true) that *Piers Plowman* is a great sermon, I think, some have wrongly drawn the conclusion that it is a great poem. (That it contains great poetry, no one doubts; that is a distinct proposition.) If I say little about this error it is because I anticipate that most modern readers will be in no danger of excessive leniency to it. If I were addressing only my 'even-Christians' I might sing a very different tune.

About the anthropological approach two questions arise, one of fact, and one of relevance. On the question of fact I say nothing. The claims made by Professor Loomis and others for a mythical origin behind many objects, people, and situations in romance—and for a ritual origin behind the mythical—may be true or false. It would be natural to suppose that some were the one and some the other. I may believe that Gawain's property of growing stronger as the sun ascended[1] is causally linked, through many intermediate stages, with a story about a sun-god. I need not also believe that if someone who 'on a mor lay', someone 'sleeping rough' on a mountain side, is said to have drunk spring water, this has a connexion with well-worship.[2] A pint of beer or glass of wine is hard to come by on a *mor*.

The question of relevance, however, is one I have a view on. When we are discussing the meaning not of books but of single words, we sometimes meet a stupid person who produces an etymology with the air of one settling the whole affair; as if the earliest recorded meaning of the word (or of its remotest ancestor) necessarily threw any light on its meaning in a particular passage a thousand years later. In reality it might or might not. It is an equally gross error to suppose that the ritual or myth from which some ingredient in a romance or poem originated necessarily throws any light on its meaning and function in that romance or poem. Let us for argument's sake assume that every story in which a father fights his son is

---

[1] Malory IV 18, XX 21.   [2] J. Speirs, *op. cit.* pp. 62-3.

causally connected with some myth and ritual of the Eniautos Daimon. Then take four concrete pieces of literature in which such a combat occurs: the *Hiltebrantslied*,* *Henry VI* (Pt 3, II, v, 54–93), *Sohrab and Rustum*, and *On Baille's Strand*. What is common to all four is the pathos and irony of the human situation; a thing certainly independent of, perhaps even blunted by, the mythical association. They have no other resemblance. The *Hiltebrantslied* gives us that irony and pathos and nothing else. Arnold's poem gives us these, romantically, seen from an almost infinite distance, seen with a double vision at once Homeric and Victorian, blended with his own sad lucidity, filled with the charm of strange, remote places; it is a very complex poem. In Shakespeare the episode serves a crudely didactic purpose: there are the wounds of the civil war, thus stings the Serpent of Division. In Yeats's play we first get the full mythical excitement. *Et pour cause*. He is a modern. He is (besides being an Occultist and a spokesman of the Celtic revival), like us, an amateur of myth. But not especially of the Eniautos Daimon. I cannot, for the life of me, see what light the Daimon has cast on any of the four. After I have heard of him they do to me neither more nor less nor other than what they did before. And they do different things. What is common to them is not, from the literary point of view, important. What matters is the differences: the difference between *Du bist dir, alter Hun, ummet spaher*[1] and 'O pity, God, this miserable age' and 'Right for the Polar Star past Orgunje' and ''Twas they that did it, the pale, windy people'. Similarly with Malory's Gawain. What does it matter whether his peculiar gift has a solar origin or not, when, in this story, the gift itself is utterly unimportant and leads to nothing? It throws not the least light either on the frivolous Gawain (Tennyson's Gawain) of the earlier books or on the serious Gawain of the later blood-feud. By concentrating on it or its mythical origins you will not increase your enjoyment or understanding of one single sentence in the rest of the prose *Morte*. The Gawain we actually meet in a book has nothing divine and (but for those two passages) nothing solar about him.

Granted then (if only for purposes of argument) the mythical origins, it is a further question what literary relevance they have, if

---

[1] *Hiltebrantslied*, 37–8. You're very clever, you old Hun.

any, in this or that literary work; a question to be decided, in each case, on its merits. Some feel that such origins have on occasion carried with them into the concrete poem or romance something qualitative, some emotional flavour, which preserves the feeling of the myth, which in its turn preserves the feeling of the ritual. Anthropologists may describe to us what modern savages do; they may conjecture what our ancestors did. But what it all felt like from within, what the ritual meant to those who enacted it, we do not know. None of us have, as believing pagans, participated in a pagan fertility ritual. That old blend of religion, agriculture, sex, drink, tragedy, and buffoonery, cannot be recovered; at any rate, not by external observation. We cannot get inside it; not directly. But if that experience had infused its quality into some other thing which we can get inside, then this other, more penetrable, thing would now be the only medium through which we can get back to the experience itself. Such a 'more penetrable thing' might be provided by a work of plastic or literary art which we can still appreciate. If so, our response to the work will in some measure introduce us to the inwardness of the rite. Let us suppose that Bercilak in *Gawain and the Green Knight* really is derived from Jack in the Green, and Jack from the Eniautos Daimon (both suppositions seem to me quite probable). I have never met a Jack in the Green, still less worshipped the Daimon. I don't know what it felt like to do so. But I know very well what it is like to meet Bercilak in the poem. His impact is immensely strong; his quality unlike that of anything else. If both our suppositions are correct, then in appreciating Bercilak I may be learning quite a lot about the concrete, qualitative, inward character of the Daimon. In other words the poem is illuminating the myth; the myth is not illuminating the poem. The unknown cannot illuminate the known. What is merely conjectured or reconstructed, or at best known only from without, cannot illumine what we encounter directly and receive deeply into our emotions and imagination. Our knowledge of savage or prehistoric religions is at best only *savoir*; our knowledge of Bercilak is *connaître*, knowledge-by-acquaintance. It therefore seems to me that while anthropology might have much to gain from a sensitive reading of the literature, literary criticism can learn almost nothing from anthropology.

Anthropology works only with the bones of paganism. In art we meet them reclothed with flesh, alive. (Always, of course, on the assumption that such theories about the origins of Romance are in fact true.)

Yet the anthropological approach is clearly of great value to readers of a particular type. I never fully realized this until I read a certain passage by Mr Speirs; an invaluable passage because it shows plainly why he values anthropology so highly as an aid to literary experience and what, for him, this approach seems to be safeguarding. (That is what I should always wish to know about another man's theories; people are nearly always fighting for something they, not unjustly, prize.) He has been speaking of a certain marvellous episode in a metrical romance. I abstain from specifying either, so that no one's attention may be sidetracked by the question whether this episode or this romance would have been his own choice. He suggests for the episode a ritual origin. Then he proceeds:[1] 'But what difference, it may be asked, does that make to the poetry? It means that the episode is really more serious than simply a sport of fancy...it means that we might have to correct our way of taking these episodes as if they belonged to something of the order of a boy's adventure story —taking them, that is, too easily.' He adds that even if the medieval authors knew nothing about the ritual origins 'they surely inherited with such episodes something of the traditional reverence towards them, a sense of their mystery, a sense too of the mystery of all life'.

Let me emphasize at once my unshakeable agreement with Mr Speirs that what he calls 'our way of taking these episodes' needs to be corrected wherever it exists. The reader who sees in all the (let us call them) 'ferlies' of medieval romance mere 'sports of fancy', who equates them with such vulgar appeals to stupid astonishment as we too often meet in the *Arabian Nights*, with the halfcomic marvels of Italian epic, or with the wholly comic ones of Baron Munchausen,[2] the reader who does not respond to them with 'reverence' and 'a sense of their mystery' and even 'a sense of the mystery of all life', utterly misunderstands the best specimens of the *genre* he is reading.

[1] *Op. cit.* p. 117.
[2] I exclude 'boy's romances' because I do not, myself, share Mr Speirs's view if it is meant to apply to all of them. Neither blind Pugh tapping with his stick in *Treasure Island* nor the hall of petrified chieftains in *King Solomon's Mines* affects me as 'simply a sport of fancy'. This disagreement is irrelevant to the argument.

Once one has understood that Mr Speirs finds in his anthropological bearings a safeguard against this error, one can understand,
and sympathize with, the value he puts upon them. Nor do I think
he is fighting an imaginary danger. It is true that 'our way' of misreading the romances is very recent. In the nineteenth century, even
in the Edwardian period, a serious response to the ferlies seems to
have been easy and almost universal. Even now it is common among
the elderly. Most of my generation have all our lives taken these
things with awe and with a sense of their mystery. But a generation
has grown up which really needs the corrective that Mr Speirs is
offering. For whatever reason—a materialistic philosophy, anti-
romanticism, distrust of one's unconscious—gigantic inhibitions
have, with astonishing rapidity, been built up. The response which
was once easy and indeed irresistible now needs to be liberated by
some sort of mental *ascesis*. In working out an (anthropological)
ascesis which will do this Mr Speirs is performing a useful work.
He is 'digging again the wells that the Philistines have filled'. If the
choice, for his generation, lies between reading the romances as
frivolous or arbitrary fancy and reading them with constant reference
to *The Golden Bough*, let them by all means take the second alternative.

It must, however, be remembered that the anthropological *ascesis*
is not the only way of dealing with ferlies (whether in romances or
elsewhere). Some readers find their responses liberated by Jung's
Theory of Archetypes. Others, I believe, find it helpful to see in
every epic or romance the vestiges of real history. Those who cannot
take the Grail for what (in the romances) it purports to be, find that
they can take it either as something out of the collective unconscious,
or as something out of Celtic paganism, or as a prehistoric burning-
glass.[1] The distribution of these views does not confirm one's first
suspicion that what is common to them all is simply a dislike of
Christianity. Rather, they all supply the modern reader with
apparently rational grounds for feeling that 'more is meant than
meets the ear', that there is a great deal 'behind' the ferly, that he is
surprising a secret. Thus the sense of mystery which the ferly, un-
aided, would evoke in the mind of an older reader, but which in the
modern is inhibited, is released. He is no longer afraid of being taken

[1] Lady Flavia Anderson, *The Ancient Secret* (1953).

in. He allows himself to feel the wonder and excitement which the old poet or romancer, I believe, intended to produce, because a sop has been given to his intellect and he now believes that his reactions can be defended on extra-literary grounds. For this purpose all three approaches can probably be equally useful. Since they are not mutually contradictory, they may even be usefully combined.

But their utility, as psychological preparatives for 'softening up' the reader and restoring 'his lapsed powers', is one thing. Their truth in fact, or their power, if true, of really explaining the way the ferlies affect us, is quite another. If I cannot accept any of them myself, this is certainly not because they are repulsive to me. Rather the reverse. (I was overjoyed when, as an undergraduate, I believed, erroneously, that *brun* as an epithet for swords was a survival from the Bronze Age.) My difficulties are of another sort.

We must distinguish two propositions. *A*. That a myth be-queaths to the ferlies which descend from it a power to move us. *B*. That the idea of a ferly's being thus descended from a myth increases our receptiveness so that we are moved when we read of the ferly. In *A* the myth within the ferly works on us by its own power, as a drug mixed with our food may work. In *B* it is rather as if the knowledge or belief that something was mixed with our food pro-duced a certain reaction by suggestion; as if a sensitive person were to vomit on hearing that the stew he had eaten contained human flesh, though human flesh is not in its own nature an emetic. Now if we take *A*, I have the following difficulty. The myth or rite does not always (it may sometimes) seem to me superior or equal in interest to the romancer's ferly. The cauldron of the Celtic under-world seems to me a good deal less interesting than the Grail. The tests and ordeals—often nasty enough—through which savages, like schoolboys, put their juniors interest me less than the testing of Gawain in *Gawain and the Green Knight*. In tracing the ferly's imaginative potency to such origins you are therefore asking me to believe that something which moves me much is enabled to do so by the help of something which moves me little or not at all. If after swallowing a quadruple whisky I said 'I'm afraid I'm rather drunk', and you replied 'That's because, while you weren't looking, some-one put half a teaspoonful of Lager beer into it', I do not think your theory would be at all plausible. At this stage we may adopt a modified form of the *A* theory. We may say 'No. It is not the myth, simply by being the myth it is, that makes the ferly potent. What the myth does is to modify the way in which the romancer tells it; and that in turn modifies the way in which you read it.' This is a great improvement; not least because, in explaining a literary effect, it does allow something to the activity of a literary artist. The mythical origin is held (even if they did not know about it) to have modified the romancers' treatment because 'they surely inherited with such episodes something of the traditional attitude of reverence towards them'.[1] But does traditional reverence for his theme always compel, or enable, a writer to move us thus, or only sometimes? If always, why are all the hymns and patriotic songs not more impressive? For we surely know that the hymnodists had a traditional reverence for Christianity, and the patriotic poets for England, quite as well (to put it mildly) as we know the attitude of the medieval poets to the things they wrote about. If, on the other hand, traditional reverence produces these happy results on some occasions but not on others, there must be some cause for the difference. And that cause the *A* theory does not seem to supply. It might after all be a literary cause. The impressiveness of the ferlies in a good romance might depend not on the source from which the author received his materials, nor on his reverence for them (if he had any), but on his worth as an author.

I turn with pleasure to the *B* theory which, I feel sure, is the true one. As Mr Speirs significantly says, after reading Miss Weston and Professor Loomis and others, he 'certainly *notices* things in the romances that one might, or would, have missed'.[2] This can hardly mean that certain objects or episodes were simply 'blacked out' when he read the romances before he had studied the anthropologists. If it did (but the supposal is injurious to so diligent a critic), it's no great wonder that a careful reading of any book gets more out of it than a skimming. I take it he means that the anthropological preparation caused him to dwell more seriously on the ferlies, to open his sensibility for moment and significance in details which he might otherwise have regarded as trivial. If so, then the mere fact of mythical origins, which of course was a fact (if at all) long before

[1] J. Speirs, *op. cit.* p. 117.   [2] *Op. cit.* p. 103. The italics are Mr Speirs's.

Miss Weston or Professor Loomis or anyone else thought about it, clearly gave the ferlies no power to stir his imagination; it was his believing, and thinking about, the fact which did the good. In other words, this is not like the drug mixed in the food: it is like the effect of being told 'you have eaten human flesh'.

Unfortunately the power of such a statement to produce nausea in a sensitive person would not in the least depend on its being true. It is enough that he should believe it. In the same way, all the beneficial effects produced on our reading of the romances by a belief in the process 'from ritual to romance' would operate equally well if that belief were false. Indeed, not even a belief is required. The mere surmise will do. It is the same with the Jungian arche- types, and with the (euhemeristic) theory of buried history. You only have to say 'Perhaps...who knows?' Perhaps, behind this odd detail in the romance there opens a dark backward and abysm of time—who knows if this is only a veil which hides immemorial paganism, with all its ecstasies and horrors—how if this were the unobtrusive mouth of a shaft by which I can descend (*ibant obscuri*) to the true underworld, the living darkness, of the collective human psyche? Anyone but a dull clod is moved by such conjectures. If we believe that the disguise is intentional of course the pleasure is increased. We have penetrated a mystery, undergone an initiation.*

But the very thing which perhaps makes such beliefs so acceptable to some (the *surmises* we can all enjoy) is just what awakes my scepticism. What we are doing when we thus feel excitement, wonder, and even awe at the idea of such hidden depths behind myths or romances seems to me far too like what goes on in the myths and romances themselves. I do not mean like it in being untrue; I mean like it in quality. We are wandering in a tangled forest of anthropology as the knights wander in a literal forest. We are going down to dark ancient things like Orpheus or Aeneas. We have to depend on cryptic signs, are confronted with what would be meaningless unless *The Golden Bough* (or Merlin or a hermit) explained it. Above all, anything may turn out to be far more important than it looks. I enjoy this, but the enjoyment is suspiciously like that I get from the myths and romances themselves. Jung's theory of myth is as exciting as a good myth and in the same way. Mr Speirs's analysis of a romance is for me itself romantic. But I have an idea that the true analysis of a thing ought not to be so like the thing itself. I should not expect a true theory of the comic to be itself funny. Of such theories one feels, for the first moment, 'This is just what we wanted'. And so, in one sense, it is. It is just what our emotions craved; a licence to prolong and perhaps to intensify the very mood which, in some of us, the romance or myth had already aroused and, in others, was beginning to arouse until the inhibitions stepped in—to be deliciously dispelled by this apparently scientific sanction. But whether it is in another sense 'just what we wanted', whether it satisfies our intellectual desire, as psychologists, to understand our experience, or as critics to diagnose the art by which an author evoked it—that is a different matter. I remain open to conviction but so far unconvinced.

A satisfactory theory of ferlies and their effect is, I believe, still to seek. I suspect that it will not succeed unless it fulfils two conditions. In the first place, it will have to be sure it has exhausted the possibilities of purely literary diagnosis before it looks further afield. A comparison of ferlies which do, and those which do not, succeed, will be involved. We shall have to try to discover whether narrative structure, or language, or preparation, or the total atmosphere of the work in which they occur, or the immediate content of the ferlies themselves, has usually most to do with it. But literary art can never be solely responsible for the effect of literature, for literature can never be pure like music. It has to be 'about' something, and the things it is 'about' bring their own real-life quality into the work. If roses did not smell sweet Guillaume de Lorris could never have used a rose to symbolize his heroine's love. An onion would not do instead. The second condition, therefore, is that the theory should deeply study the ferlies as things (in a sense) in the real world. Probably such things do not occur. But if no one in real life had either seen, or thought he saw, or accepted on hearsay, or dreaded, or hoped for, any such things, the poet and romancer could do nothing with them. As anthropologists we may want to know how belief in them originated. But it will illuminate the literary problem more if we can imagine what it would feel like to witness, or to think we had witnessed, or merely to believe in, the things. What it would feel like, and why.

THE GENESIS OF
A MEDIEVAL BOOK

In this chapter I shall first consider two early medieval texts and then say something about a remarkable characteristic which they have in common. They illustrate it all the more clearly because they are, in every other respect, extremely different. The one is a poem, the other a tract; the first full of heroic action and open air, the second entirely subjective and allegorical. Yet both can be shown to have come into existence by the same sort of process. It is a process wholly foreign to modern literature, but normal in the literature of the Middle Ages. It is almost the first thing we must grow used to and allow for in our medieval reading.

1. LAȝAMON'S 'BRUT'

It is easy to explain why Laȝamon's *Brut* has few readers. The only text[1] is almost unobtainable; the poem is long; much of its matter is dull. But there are very good reasons for overcoming these obstacles. One is that Laȝamon is much easier than most Middle English poetry: far easier than Dunbar or *Pearl* or *Gawain*, yet not flattering the beginner, as Chaucer does, with a deceptive appearance of easiness. But secondly—and this is the reason most to my mind—the *Brut* is well worth our attention in its own right. The dull passages are a legacy from its known sources; its vividness, fire, and grandeur, are new. And sometimes—rarely, I admit—it reveals, in a flash,

---

[1] Ed. F. Madden, 3 vols. 1847. The reader who has no access to this edition can nevertheless learn a good deal about the *Brut* from the (undated) Everyman volume *Arthurian Chronicles* by Eugene Mason which contains a close prose translation of *Brut* 12802–28651 (from the usurpation of Vortigern to the last battle of Arthur) and of the corresponding part of Wace's *Geste*. [Since Lewis wrote this the first volume of a complete new edition of the *Brut*, edited by G. L. Brook and R. F. Leslie for the E.E.T.S., has been published (1963). At the same time, *Selections from Laȝamon's 'Brut'*, edited by G. L. Brook with an Introduction by C. S. Lewis, appeared in the Clarendon Medieval and Tudor Series.—W.H.]

imaginative power beyond the reach of any Middle English poet whatever.

As everyone knows, the ultimate source of Laȝamon's subject-matter is Geoffrey of Monmouth's *Historia Regum Britanniae* (1147). It was a foundation quite unworthy of the structure raised upon it. Geoffrey is of course important for the historians of the Arthurian Legend; but since the interest of those historians has seldom lain chiefly in literature, they have not always remembered to tell us that he is an author of mediocre talent and no taste. In the Arthurian parts of his work the lion's share falls to the insufferable rigmarole of Merlin's prophecies and to the foreign conquests of Arthur. The latter are, of course, at once the least historical and the least mythical thing about Arthur. If there was a real Arthur he did not conquer Rome. If the story has roots in Celtic Paganism, this campaign is not one of them. It is fiction. And what fiction! We can suspend our disbelief in an occasional giant or enchantress. They have friends in our subconscious and in our earliest memories; imagination can easily suppose that the real world has room for them. But vast military operations scrawled over the whole map of Europe and excluded by all the history we know are a different matter. We cannot suspend our disbelief. We don't even want to. The annals of senseless and monotonously successful aggression are dreary enough reading even when true; when blatantly, stupidly false, they are unendurable. Whether Geoffrey intended all this stuff as political propaganda for our continental empire or merely as a sop to national vanity, we neither know nor care. It is either way deplorable, and it is what Geoffrey chiefly wants to tell us about Arthur. He has of course included better things, but his own contribution is a mere disfigurement. The decided contempt which it gives me for Geoffrey has the paradoxical effect of making me readier to believe that the *Historia* is filled with valuable deposits of tradition, both legendary and historical. Wherever I meet anything that I think good as story or probable as history (and I meet both fairly often) I feel sure that Geoffrey did not make it up.

After Geoffrey came Wace, the Norman, who was born in Jersey and made Canon of Bayeux by Henry II. He died, perhaps, about 1175. He is remembered by everyone for his account of

Taillefer riding before William the Bastard's army at Senlac and singing the Song of Roland; this comes in his *Roman de Rou*. In 1155 he retold Geoffrey's matter in octosyllabics as the *Geste des Bretons*, which we, following the manuscripts, know as the *Roman de Brut*. He certainly did not regard himself as a writer of what we should call romance. His attitude to his material is rather that of a historian to an unreliable, yet by no means worthless, document. He thinks it is partly true, partly false. He is anxious to avoid errors. He has even been at the pains of investigating a fountain in Broce-liande where the fays were said to appear, and his comment (in the *Roman de Rou*) on the negative result of the experiment is well known: 'Wonders I sought but I found none; a fool I returned, a fool I went.' But in another way he is not in the least like a historian. He feels perfectly free to touch up his original, describing, as if he had been an eyewitness, scenes he never saw and supplying vivid details from his own imagination.

After Wace, Laȝamon, whose *Brut* was probably written before 1207. He tells us he was priest at Ernleȝe (now King's Arnley) on the Severn. It *com him on mode*,[1] came into his head, to relate the noble deeds and origin of the *Engle*. He travelled far and wide[2] and secured these books as his sources: the 'English book' made by Bede (i.e. the Anglo-Saxon version of the *Ecclesiastical History*), a book by 'Seint Albin and the feire Austin', and a book by a 'French Clerk' called Wace.[3] The second item in this catalogue is puzzling. It is generally taken to be Bede's Latin original of the very same book which, in Anglo-Saxon, makes Laȝamon's first item. I find it difficult to be content with this theory, but the question is not very important since Laȝamon actually makes extremely little use of Bede in any shape or form. Wace is the only one of his three authors who really counts. Perhaps when the poet mentioned all three books in his poems—for those days, and for a man in his humble station, they were a costly library, which he *leofliche bi-heold*[4]—he expected to use them much more than he actually did.

[1] 11.

[2] Whether only in England or also abroad, his language (29) does not make clear. The delightful passage on *muglinges* (29593-8) suggests that he had visited the continent and been twitted on coming from an island where men have tails.

[3] 11-41.   [4] Lovingly beheld, 47.

But we cannot next proceed, as we used to do with Chaucer and *Il Filostrato*, to get a text of Wace, collate it with the English *Brut*, and thus try to isolate Laȝamon's original work. It is generally accepted that Laȝamon worked from a redaction of Wace, con-taminated by other versions of the story. And it seems clear to me, as to others, that he was in touch with real Welsh or (less often) English traditions. Thus he knows, and could not learn from Wace, the name of Arthur's helmet *Goswhit* (21147) and his shield *Pridwen* (21152), and of the smith Griffin who made his spear (23783). In a passage peculiar to himself (13562-90) he gives to the Pict who murdered King Constance the name Gille Callæt, which is un-known to both Wace and Geoffrey. It is too good a name for a Pict to have been invented by a writer so unphilological as Laȝamon, who elsewhere cheerfully gives the names Ethelbald and Ælfwald to two 'Britons' who revolted against 'Gracien'. The passage in which he does so (12253 *seq.*) is also significant. No one else relates this revolt; but Laȝamon's very clear localization of it in East Anglia—no county patriotism would tempt him thither—suggests that a historical tradition of some far later rebellion may underlie it. There are, too, places where Laȝamon unexpectedly agrees with Geoffrey against Wace. At 1275 his *pritti dawes* confirms Geoffrey's figure, and our text of Wace reads *trois jors*. This might be a mere accident. More importantly, at 14050 Laȝamon and Geoffrey both tell us that Lindesey was the fief given by Vortigern to Hengest, and Wace—in our *textus receptus*—does not. Since Laȝamon is generally thought to have made no use of Geoffrey, and certainly does not mention him, this passage suggests a source, probably British, common to both. It is certainly difficult not to suppose Welsh poetry behind the following prophecy about Arthur:

> Of him scullen gleomen godliche singen.
> Of his breosten scullen æten aðela scopes.
> Scullen of his blode beornes beon drunke.[1]   (18856-61)

Geoffrey, doubtless from the same source, had said 'His deeds will be meat to their tellers',[2] but Laȝamon gives more.

---

[1] Of him shall minstrels sing finely. Of his breast noble poets shall eat; on his blood, heroes be drunk. (N.B. My line-numbering is that of Madden, who prints, and numbers, each half-line as a line.)*   [2] *Actus ejus cibus erit narrantibus* (vii, 3).

We thus know neither what (exactly) Laȝamon's MS of Wace contained nor from what other sources, oral or written, he supple-mented it. I believe, myself, that many, or even most, of those passages peculiar to the English *Brut* which I shall mention are in fact Laȝamon's own. But I must not assume this. In order to avoid committing myself I shall therefore speak no more of Laȝamon but simply of the *Brut*, of the text itself. Who, or how many people, or in what proportions each, made it what it is, is a question I cannot answer. This inability of course frustrates our curiosity as scholars, and it puts out of use our characteristically modern critical habits. There is no question here of finding the single author, totally responsible for his work of art, and expressing his unique personality through it. But this frustration is instructive, and it is fortunate that the text which meets us at the very threshold of Middle English poetry should so clearly render the modern approach impossible. If criticism cannot do without the clear separation of one work from another and the clear unity of the indi-vidual author with the individual text, then criticism of medieval literature is impossible.

The metre of the *Brut* has often been described and I shall not deal with it at length. Sometimes for a line or so it conforms to the classical Anglo-Saxon pattern:

> æðela inwurðen,
> wihte wal-kempen, on heora wiðer-winnan.[1]   (776–8)

At the opposite extreme we get

> He makede swulc grið, he makede swulc frið
> monien laȝen gode, þe lond swuððen stode.[2]   (4254–7)

Internal rhyme had appeared in *Maldon* and was (like consonance) regular in certain Old Norse metres: the real novelty is the absence of alliteration. To an ear trained on *Beowulf*, a text which oscillates thus may at first be as repulsive as 'monkish hexameters' were to the Humanists. But one grows reconciled to it in the end; and not, I think, only because one's standards have been lowered by habitua-tion. The types of classical Old English half-line are, after all,

[1] To be valiant—tough death-warriors—against their enemies.
[2] He made such peace, he made such order, many good laws, that thereafter the land was steady.

blocks of pure speech rhythm. So are the half-lines of the *Brut*'s
new rhymed (or consonanced, or assonanced) lines. Hence they lie
down together not uncomfortably. There is no real parallel to the
jarring effect we should get if alcaics were suddenly introduced
among elegiacs or octosyllabics amid blank verse. There is, too, a
tendency for one norm or the other to predominate over fairly long
stretches. Battle-pieces, appropriately, often keep close to the old
metre. The new, often used for pathetic, derisive or gnomic comment, has its own rustic pungency. Notice its effect in the following
where it comes after two lines of fairly pure alliterative verse:

> '...
> And 3if þu him abidest he þe wule binden,
> quellen þine leoden and þi lond a3en'.
> Ofte wes Arðure wa; neuere wurse þene þa.[1]   (20379–84)

If the *Brut* is only partially Anglo-Saxon in metre, it is almost
wholly so in style. Expressions that recall the old poets meet us at
every turn: *Godes wiðer-saka* (1808; of Gogmagog), *mid orde and mid
egge* (5202), *sæ-werie* (6205), *weorld-scome* (8323), *gumene ælder*
(12178).[2] If they are not always exact reproductions, this makes
them more interesting. It shows that the poet is not merely imitating,
as Claudian, say, imitated the Augustans, but working in a live
tradition. Hence his resemblance to his predecessors is not limited
to vocabulary. Arthur's prayer, with its accumulation of more or
less synonymous phrases (almost *kenningar*), comes in the very accents
of Hrothgar:

> Lauerd drihten crist, domes waldende,
> midelarde mund, monnen froure,
> þurh þine aðmode wil, walden ænglen.
> Let þu mi sweuen to selpen iturnen.[3]   (25567–74)

The *Brut* is Anglo-Saxon in style for the best reason: because it is
Anglo-Saxon in temper. Its outlook, its most recurrent emotions,
its sense of values, all belong to the old order.

This brings us to an instructive paradox. In the opening lines the
Brut promises to tell the history of the *Engle* (13): actually it tells that

---

[1] 'And if you await him he will make you prisoner, kill your people, and hold your land.' Often had Arthur been in woe; never worse than at that moment.
[2] God's enemy. With point and edge. Sea-weary. World-shame. Lord of men.
[3] Lord, master, Christ, prince of glory, protection of middle earth, comfort of men, by thy gracious will, prince of angels. Make thou my dream turn to good.

of the Britons when they had been conquered, killed, and dis-possessed. Even if the word *Engle* is merely a careless slip, it is no bad symbol of what is to follow. This poem, while Anglo-Saxon in style and temper, is wholly British in its conscious sympathies. For those Germanic invaders who were Laȝamon's real ancestors and whose language he wrote, the *Brut* has hardly a good word to say. They are treacherous, heathen hounds. Best deal with them as Aldolf did with Hengest when he swiped off his head, gave him good burial after his own heathen fashion (for he was after all a brave fighter) and then

bad for þere sæule þat hire neuere sæl neore.[1]   (16723-4)

We may suspect that the *Brut*'s view of the English invaders against whom Arthur fought has been much coloured by memories of a far more recent invasion. At l. 7116, significantly, it speaks of the Normans coming to England *mid heore nið crafte*.[2] But no such explanation for its British partialities is really needed. Centuries later when we no longer had cause to hate the Normans we still somehow accepted the Britons (as represented by Geoffrey) for our ancestors and delighted in this supposed link with Arthur, Cassi-belaune, Brennes, and the Trojans. The consciousness of race, or (if you prefer) the illusion of race, seems hardly to have existed. Nor is race much use to us as critics. If there was a historical Arthur he was probably a Roman. His legend is Celtic in origin. The particular handling of it which we are now considering is the adaptation, thoroughly Anglo-Saxon in spirit, of a Norman poem. Its later dissemination is the work of French poets and romancers. Its modern developments are almost exclusively English and American. We should use a very misleading metaphor if we said the legend had a Celtic 'kernel'; 'for, when he hath the kernel eate, who does not throw away the shell?' If we threw away what is not Celtic we should have left something other than the Arthurian legend which has really mattered.

From what has already been said it will be obvious that the *Brut* is a very different poem from Wace's *Geste* as we have it, and must

---

[1] Prayed for his soul that bliss should never come to it.
[2] With their evil strength (*or* cunning).

have been very different from any redaction of Wace which we can imagine. The mere language determines this. *Feollen þa fæie*[1] has a ring which nothing could have in French octosyllabics. The habitual images and attitudes of the English poem add another difference. An angel, or that early aviator King Bladud, has, not wings, but a *feðerhome*[2] (2874, 25871). Heroes may speak of their exploits in the devout manner of Beowulf himself: *godd hit me iuðe þat ich hine igripen habben*[3] (16549). Characters give one another a great deal of advice, sometimes, as may be thought, portentously, but sometimes, as in the old poetry, with magnificent weight—

> Nu þu ært al ane of aðele þine cunne.
> Ah ne hope þu to ræde of heom þat liggeð dede.
> Ah þenc of þe seoluen. Seolðen þe beoð ȝiueþe;
> for selde he aswint þe to him seolue þencheð.[4]   (17934-41)

But the differences go far beyond this kind of thing. The *Brut* is much more archaic and unsophisticated than the *Geste*. One can easily believe that Wace was familiar with real, contemporary courts and camps. But the *Brut* sees all its battles in terms of the heroic past. Strategical features are blurred or omitted. Instead, we get the war-hedge standing like a grey wood,[5] faces turning pale, many a grey-haired warrior hewn with sword,[6] broad-bladed spears broken and cloven shields[7]—

> Heowen hardliche hælmes gullen,
> falewede feldes of fæie blode.
> And þa heðene saulen helle isohten.[8]   (18316-21)

It paints its courts in equally old-fashioned colours. In the *Geste* as we have it the Roman ambassadors are true diplomats, elderly men, well-dressed, carrying olive branches, walking slowly and behaving with much dignity. In the *Brut* they are

---

[1] The fated ones fell (14038 *et passim*).
[2] Feather-jacket or swanskin.
[3] God granted me that I have caught him.
[4] Now thou alone art left of thy noble kindred. But hope not to get counsel from those that lie dead, but take heed to thyself. Good will befall thee. For seldom he fails who takes heed to himself.   [5] 16371.
[6] 4161, 4166-7.   [7] 5185-6.
[8] They hewed hardily, helms resounded, fields were discoloured with fated blood, as the souls of heathens set out for hell.

þeines ohte mid palle bi∕þehte.
Hæȝe here∕kempen, hehȝe men on wepne.[1]   (24741-4)

The Norman gaiety and lightness do not get into the *Brut* at all. There is a striking example a few lines later when Arthur consults with his lords about his answer to the Romans. It is a delightful scene in Wace. The King holds his council in a stone keep called the Giant's Tower. As they go up its spiral stair, Cador, who was a man of jokes, calls out merrily to Arthur who happens to be in front of him. This threat from Rome, he says, is welcome. We have had far too much peace lately. It softens a man. It encourages the young bachelors to spend too much time dressing, with an eye to the ladies. Gawain, overhearing this, says Cador need not bother his head about the young men. Peace after war is very pleasant. So is love. Bright eyes teach chivalry. Thus they jested. Now turn to the *Brut*, 24883-972. First, by a tiny touch, it alters the whole lighting. It cannot mention the tower without adding

An ald stanene weorc; stiðe men hit wurhten.[2]   (24885-6)

With this characteristically Beowulfian glance at the remoter past everything becomes at once darker, graver, more wintry. There is no prattle on the stairs. When everyone is seated in his place, Cador rises and expresses his view about the corrupting influence of peace in a set speech, seriously. Then Walwain *wraððede hine swide*.[3] His praise of peace has nothing to do with ladies' eyes—

God is grið and god is frið þe freoliche þer haldeð wið,
and godd sulf hit makede þurh his godd∕cunde—[4]   (24957-60)

and there is nothing sportive about his disagreement with Cador. It is a real strife, a *flit* (24966), and Arthur, as if he knew that swords might be out in a minute, has to cry out

Sitte adun swiðe, mine cnihte alle.
And ælc bi his lifen luste mine worden.[5]   (24969-72)

[1] Valiant thanes, clad in pall, high battle∕warriors, high men with weapons.
[2] An old stone work; tough men made it.
[3] Was very angry (24951).
[4] Good is peace and good is quiet for him who uses them nobly; and God Himself made it through His Deity.
[5] Sit down, I tell you, my knights all. Let each, on his life, hear what I shall say. (A literal translation of *swiðe* is impossible in Modern English.)

Equally instructive are the different eulogies which the *Geste* and the *Brut* give of Arthur. In Wace he is one of Love's lovers. He founded those courtesies which courts have followed since. He lived in great state and splendour. In the *Brut, he wes þan ȝungen for fader, þan alden for frouer*[1] (19936–7). Thus everywhere the *Brut* is heavier, more serious, more plangent than its Norman counterpart. Provided that we carefully define for ourselves the sense in which we are using the word, we may say that it is more barbaric and less civilized.

We must not misunderstand this. It has to be admitted that the *Brut* at one point (22841 *seq.*) introduces an atrocity of which Wace and Geoffrey are innocent. But it was something done in hot blood. In general the *Brut* is a kinder work than the *Geste*. It is both fiercer and more tender. The Norman courtesy can be callous, the Norman lightness can be cynical; the *Brut* is, at bottom, more sensitive. Its favourite heroes, if rough-hewn, remember the sufferings of common men. Its Brennes, as soon as he has conquered Rome, starts repairing the war damage, prevents a massacre, forbids plunder, and summons back the refugees (*flæmen*) with the assurance that they shall have peace and live under the laws of their own country (5938–69). Its Vortimer, at his accession, undertakes to emancipate all slaves (14852). Its Arthur resolves that if he conquers France,

> Auere ælche ærmen mon þe æð scal iwurðen,
> and wurchen ic wulle muchel godes wille.[2]   (23741–4)

It may, no doubt, be suspected that the sympathies of the *Brut* here reflect the humble condition of its author. But they are not confined to the poor. It dwells lovingly on Arthur's discharge of his veteran knights when he bade them go with joy and repent their sins, never carrying weapons more, but living the rest of their days religiously.[3] It extends even to Pagans—provided, of course, they are not Saxons—as in its lament for Julius Caesar

> Wale þat eæuere ei sucche mon in to eælde sculde gan.[4]   (7223–4)

---

[1] To the young he was a father, to the old a comforter.
[2] Always every poor man shall find his lot the easier, and I mean to do great God's will.
[3] 24115–24.
[4] Well-away that every any such man had to go in to Hell! (taking *helle* from Otho MS).

And to the Caesar whom it thus laments it independently attributes courtesy and chivalry in his treatment of the captured Cassibelaune (8942 *seq.*). It alone shows us Ygærne, in private, sorrowing for the lives which Uther's love for her will cost (18616 *seq.*). Its conceptions are sometimes finer than those of Wace. Androgeus, though a traitor fighting against Cassibelaune, warns his men to take the king alive and give him no wound, 'for he is my lord and kinsman' (8605).

Another distinction of the *Brut* is its love for the supernatural. It knows that a fairy smith, *on aluisc smið*, made Arthur's byrnie (21131). Wace, following Geoffrey, had peopled Loch Lomond with prophetic eagles; the *Brut* adds

> uniuele þinge.
> Þat water is unimete brade; nikeres þer badieð inne,
> þer is æluene ploȝe in atteliche pole.[1]   (21744–8)

Of another strange water it adds *alfene hine dulfen*, elves dug it (21998). It interpolates the statement that as soon as Arthur came on earth elves took and enchanted the child and gave him their gifts (19253 *seq.*). It could have learned from the *Geste* that Arthur after his last battle was carried to Avalon for the healing of his wounds and that the Britons still look for his return thence. The *Brut* likes the passage so well that it reproduces it twice (23067 *seq.*, 28610–41), making us much surer than Wace had done that Avalon is a fairy country, since Arthur is taken thither by Argante 'the queen', 'the fairest of all elves'. Let us notice, however, that the *Brut*'s marvels are not all Celtic. The fairy smith was called Wygar. The *nikeres* and their pool might have come straight out of *Beowulf*. And the word I have translated 'elves' has to do duty both for the *fées* of continental tradition and for our own more formidable *ylfe*.

So far I have been speaking of differences between the *Brut* and the *Geste* which are not necessarily differences of poetic merit. Except in the scene between Cador and Gawain, where the *Geste* is in my opinion superior, a man might reasonably prefer either. Certainly if a Gigadibs could have existed among the Normans and had deigned (and been able) to read the *Brut* he would truly have

---

[1] Unchancy things. The water is immensely wide; nikeres (aquatic monsters) bathe therein, there is play of elves in the dreadful pool.

said that it 'lacked contemporaneity'. I now turn to those of its peculiarities which seem to me to be also superiorities.

First of all, it might have been written by someone who had read Aristotle and learned that a narrative poet ought to speak as much as possible through the mouths of his characters and as little as possible through his own. Again and again where our text of Wace merely says that people issued such and such orders, or had such and such disputes, or gave one another such and such news, the *Brut* sets them talking. I should say there was twenty or even thirty times as much dialogue in it as in the *Geste*; besides prayers, soliloquies, and the like. It is often extremely vigorous. Arthur's speech (20825–98) after the submission of Childric is a good example.

But of course the author (or authors) of the *Brut* did not need to have read Aristotle. This reiterated use of the dramatic method is part and parcel of the general intensity with which it grasps all that it treats. It is far more committed, more engaged, closer to its matter, than the *Geste*. It shows us happening what the *Geste* often merely records. It knows how everyone looked and behaved: how Corineus, after his great speech on the ingratitude of Locrin, brought down his axe and shattered the stone the King stood on (2311); how Godlac, on hearing of his mistress's marriage, swooned in his chair and the courtiers threw cold well-water on his face (4516 *seq.*); how Panto-laus and his crew must have appeared after their long voyage, with their tattered clothes and their indifference to decency (6271 *seq.*). No one who has ever watched for the return of the fishing fleet after bad weather will miss the graphic reality of the following, where the two vikings watch the storm-tossed fleet of Ursula coming in:

> And swa heo leien i þan æit-londe and iseȝen þat weder stronge;
> iseȝen scipen an and an, while ma, while nan,
> þeonne feowere þenne fiue....[1]   (12033–7)

The *Brut*'s certainty as to what you would have seen if you had been present creates character. We are perhaps told of too many people

> Þeo hit up bræc hit wes god þat he spec—[2]   (5431–2 *et passim*)

---

[1] And thus they lay in the island and saw the wild weather; saw ships—one—and one—sometimes more—sometimes none—then four—then five.

[2] When it came out, what he said was good.

though it certainly brings vividly before us a certain type of slow starter. Far more interesting is the process whereby Merlin—little more than a name in the *Geste*—becomes impressive in the *Brut*. In both texts he tells Uther how to get the monoliths for Stonehenge. This is a mere necessity of the plot. The *Brut* adds

> Þus seiden Mærlin and seoððen he sæt stille
> alse þeh he wolde of worlden iwiten.[1]   (17232-5)

He is liable to such stillnesses. On another occasion, having been asked a question, he

> sæt him stille longe ane stunde,
> swulc he mid sweuene swunke ful swiðe.
> *Heo seiden þe hit ise3en mid heore a3en æ3en*
> þat ofte he hine wende swulc hit a wurem weore....[2]
>
> (17906-13)

Whether this is how wizards (what we'd call mediums) really behave, I don't know, but I think the passage would carry immediate conviction even without the line I have italicized. It is, however, the real masterpiece. Here is another. After Uther's death Wace merely tells us that the bishops and barons sent a message to Arthur calling upon him to be King. *Tantamne rem tam negligenter?* The *Brut* tells us how three bishops and seven knights sought the youth out (he was only fifteen) in Britanny, and gives their speech. Then

> Arður sæt ful stille.
> Ænne stunde he wes blac and on heuwe swiðe wak;
> ane while he wes reod and reousede on heorte.
> Þa hit alles up brac hit wes god þat he spac.
> Þus him sæide þer riht Arður þe aðele cniht,
> 'Lauerd crist, godes sune, beon us nu a fultume,
> þat ich mote on life goddes la3en halden.'[3]   (19887-99)

It will be noticed that in all these quotations there is hardly anything that could be called poetical adornment. I doubt whether the

---

[1] Thus said Merlin and then sat still as though he were going out of the world.

[2] Sat still for a long time as though he were labouring hard with a dream. Eyewitnesses said that he often turned the way a snake would.

[3] Arthur sat very quiet. Now he was pale and very drained of colour; now he grew red and was moved at heart. When it all came out, what he said was good. Thus in that place spoke Arthur the good knight: 'Lord Christ, Son of God, help us that while I live I may keep God's laws.'

poet was thinking about poetry; it sounds more as if his only object
were to make sure that we should see exactly what he had imagined.
We may even doubt how far he knew that he was working from
imagination. But the *Brut* can be good in a different vein. I spoke a
while back of its close adherence to the Anglo-Saxon type of poetry.
But in one important way it departs from that type. The simile was
almost (not quite) unknown to the Anglo-Saxon poets. It is
frequent in the *Brut*. Some of its similes are short and easily found.
Troops muster thick as the falling hail, *alse haʒel þe ualleð* (14517 *et
passim*): Ridwathlan rushes on his enemies as a *þode* or whirlwind,
carrying a dust-cloud, falls in a field (27645); at an angry meeting
many a stout Briton had *beres leches*, boar's looks (22281-2); or (less
obviously) an army advances 'as if all the earth would catch fire'
(20643-4). But besides these we find similes of the Homeric or
'long-tailed' type; fittingly, since the *Brut* is, in its manner and
temper though not in its art, the most Homeric poem in English.
One would much like to know where its long-tailed similes come
from. If they had any literary model it has been fully assimilated;
they do not read at all like the stanza-long, laboured similes in which
Spenser thought he was being Virgilian. They smell of real country
and first-hand observation. As here:

> Up bræid Arður his sceld foren to his breosten
> and he gon to rusien swa þe runie wulf
> þenne he cumeð of holte bi-honged mid snawe
> and þencheð to biten swulc deor swa him likeð.[1]   (20120-7)

A moment later—for, as in Homer, and more than in Virgil, the
similes tend to bunch—he tells his men that their enemies will fly

> swa þe hæʒe wude
> þenne wind wode weieð hine mid mæine—[2]   (20135-7)

and after that comes the longer and more complex simile of the
crane flying broken-winged from the hawks to be met among the
reeds by hounds, so that neither land nor water will now save it, for
the hour of the noble bird (*kinewurðe foʒel*) is come (20163-75). That

---

[1] Arthur hitched up his shield before his breast and began to rush like the howling (?)
wolf when it comes, all hung with snow, out of the wood, and means to get its teeth
into any beast that pleases it.
[2] As the tall wood when the mad wind tosses it with its strength.

of the goat pursued by the wolf (21301–15) is too long to be quoted.
It is remarkable for being, at the end, mortised back into the main
narrative (I think Homer never does this) by Arthur's triumphant
cry that he himself is the wolf and Colgrim the goat (21315).

It will be noticed that all these come from the Arthurian section
of the *Brut*, and it is there, I believe, that its addition to, and trans-
formations of, any possible source we know, are most continuous.
Our text of Wace reads, in comparison, like an epitome; it gives a
skeleton: nearly all the flesh is supplied by the *Brut*. This is of course
most obvious in the very long and frequent passages which have no
analogue at all in the French; but it is no less instructively seen where
the two texts are close. In the following, where Merlin's mother tells
how he was begotten, I have italicized what is peculiar to the *Brut*.

> Þa ich wes an uore *fiftene зere*,
> *þa wunede ich on bure, on wunsele mine,*
> *maidene mid me, wundre ane uæire.*
> *Þenne ich wæs on bedde iswaued mid soft mine slepen,*
> þenne com [me]* biuoren *þa fæirest þing þat wes iboren,*
> *swulc hit weore a muchel cniht al of golde idiht.*
> Þis ich isæh *on sweuene alche niht on slepe*;
> þis þing *glad me biuoren* and *glitene on golde.*
> Ofte hit me custe, ofte hit me clupte....[1]   (15700–17)

It will be apparent how much the *Brut* has shaded and softened and
beautified the story, making it both more credible and more tolerable.
The young princess is put in her right setting, with her *wunsele* and
her maids: the image of sheltered royal girlhood—sheltered, at least,
from all merely human lovers—is built up. Her own experience is
all dim, half a dream, something between sleep and waking. And
the daemon is the loveliest thing ever born.

But I have kept to the end two touches that seem to me proofs of
yet higher power. One turns on two words. We are twice told, of a
storm at sea, that the waves were like 'burning towns' (or villages):
alse tunes *þer burnen* (4578), *tunes swulche þer burnen* (11978). It may

---

[1] When I was, long since, *fifteen years old, then I lived in my bower, in my chamber of
delight, my maidens with me, wonderfully fair. When I was in bed, plunged in my soft sleep,*
then there came before me *the loveliest thing ever born—like a tall knight all decked with
gold.* This I saw *in dream each night in my sleep.* This thing *moved before me* and *glimmered
in gold.* Often it kissed me, often embraced me.

be the phrase of a longshoreman rather than a sailor; waves out at sea are less likely to give this particular appearance. But I do not think I shall ever again see a breaker coming in against the wind without remembering the burning towns. The image, so far as I know, never occurs before or after the *Brut*. It embodies a quality of eye and imagination which I believe we never meet in Langland, Chaucer or Gower. My other example is more complex. Arthur, exulting over the Saxon rout, looks down on the Avon and sees

> Hu ligeð i þan stræme stelene fisces
> mid sweorde bi-georede; heore sund is awemmed,
> heore scalen wleoteð swulc gold-faȝe sceldes,
> þer fleoteð heore spiten swulc hit spæren weoren.[1] (21323–30)

Coleridge and Wordsworth would have made this the text for a full dissertation on the esemplastic faculty. First, the imagination turns the mail-clad, hence silvery-gleaming, dead into fishes. Then, assuming the fishes as a basis, by way of a simile within a simile, it half turns them back into knights, comparing the wooden shields and spear-shafts (which would of course leave the bodies on the river bed and float on the surface) to scales and fins. And it does this not as the romantic imagination might, for its own sake, but under the influence of a strong, bitter, and probable passion.

2. 'SAWLES WARDE'

I now turn to the early thirteenth-century *Sawles Warde*. Its history begins with a well-known passage in the New Testament: 'If the master of the house knew at what time the thief was going to come he would no doubt keep watch and not allow his house to be broken into.' This passage is then used as the peg on which to hang an allegory in chapters 13–15 of a Latin prose treatise *De Anima*, possibly by Hugo of St Victor (1096–1146). It is at once twisted into an almost entirely new meaning. In Our Lord's saying the 'thief' had represented Himself, and the unknown hour was the date of the Second Coming and the Day of Judgement. In the *De Anima*, however, the *principalis fur*, the master thief, is the Devil, supported by a gang of Vices, and what the master of the house (the soul) has to

---

[1] How steel fishes lie in the stream, girt with sword; their swimming is spoiled, their scales float like gold-bright shields, their fins drift there as if it were spears.

keep watch against is temptation. It is unbelievable that the Latin author misunderstood or forgot or did not reverence the sense of the original. He obviously feels perfectly free to transform it in any way that suits his purpose, provided that, thus transformed, it is still orthodox and edifying. Very possibly he regarded himself as choosing one, instead of another, from among its multiple senses. In his allegory the master of the house is *Animus*. He rules, with the aid of *Prudentia*, *Fortitudo*, *Temperantia*, and *Justitia*, a *familia* of thoughts, senses, and volitions. *Prudentia*, as door-keeper, admits a messenger called *Timor Mortis* who describes the pains of Hell. His words move the virtues to several wholesome resolutions. Then comes another messenger called *Amor vitae aeternae et Desiderium coelestis patriae*, who, of course, describes the joys of Heaven. The author concludes by drawing, in few words, the obvious moral.

On this modest text an English Johan, of whom we know nothing except that he asks our prayers for his soul, gets to work. He produces something considerably longer than his original, and it cannot, by our standards, be classified either as a new book or as a translation. At the very outset he quotes the Dominical words from Matt. xxiv. 43; the Latin had quoted them from Luke xii. 39. It is hard to see any reason for this change and I suspect that Johan did not even know he had made it. He gives *Wit* (his equivalent for *animus*) a silly wife called *Wil*. It is she who sets the whole *familia* wrong if she is not carefully watched. The four virtues are daughters of God. *Meað* (*Temperantia*) is described as teaching *measure* which is the middle point between two evils (49)[1]—the 'golden middle way between much and little' (184). This scrap of Aristotle's ethical system had not occurred in the Latin. Nor had the clear Virgilian echo at 124, where the first visitant says of the torments of Hell, as the Sibyl had said of the same subject, that he would not tell all though he had a thousand tongues of steel and spoke till they were all worn out (cf. *Aeneid*, VI, 625). Thus what Johan adds to his original is not necessarily original itself. His loathsomely vivid account of the reptilian horrors in Hell goes far beyond anything in the *De Anima*, but is indebted to earlier vision literature.

[1] My references are to the lines in the excellent edn. of *Sawles Warde* by R. M. Wilson, Leeds School of English Language Texts and Monographs, 1938.*

But while Johan is ready to use anything that comes to hand, he also uses continuously—perhaps does not know that he is using, and cannot help using—his own imagination. The *De Anima* is not very imaginative; at point after point Johan touches it into life. In the Latin *Timor Mortis* is not described at all. In Johan, 'he is let in and looked at very hard by them all, for lank he is and lean and his face deathlike and pale and of a strange colour. Every hair seems to be standing erect on his head' (62–5). He gives his name not as Fear of Death but simply as Fear (68)—a change which, for me at any rate, makes him far more formidable. He tells how the devils will one day bring to us books in which all our sins are written; it is Johan who adds 'in black, small letters'. We learn how the damned, as in Milton, will be hurried from the extreme of heat to that of cold; Johan adds 'And they never know which of these two feels (*punched*) the worse' (110–11). He adds (not without precedent) that if there were no other pains in Hell the very sight of the devils, their faces, their voices, the torrent of insult (*schenðlac*) that they utter, would be torment enough (131–5). He rises at last into an apostrophe, all his own, which I should weaken by modernizing: *O helle, deaðes hus, wununge of wanunge of grure ant of granunge, heatel ham, ant heard wan of alle wontreaðes, buri of bale ant bold of eauereuch bitternesse, þu laðest lont of alle, þu dorc stude*... (138–41). Such a passage may have originated the fancy—for I think it is nothing more—that *Sawles Warde* is intended as verse, not prose.

Of the second messenger we learn from the Latin only that he is *pulcher et hilaris*: in Johan we see *Deaðes Sonde* actually entering and greeting the master with laughing cheer, and the whole house shining and gleaming with the light that comes from him (227–30). Later, when he is describing Heaven, a small change makes, if I may trust my own reactions, a big difference. The Latin said that the sweet smell of those regions 'surpasses all kinds of perfumes'. Johan says 'A man could live forever in the sweetness of it' (298–9). The first leaves our imagination in the barber's shop: the second suggests another world.

I believe any fair reader will find *Sawles Warde* a sappy and lively little work. As often, we must be careful to get the right view of what seem to be, or actually are, its naïveties. When Johan says that the blessed will behold God *nebbe to nebbe* (318), the daring and homely quality which we find in his words probably did not exist for him. He is simply translating the Pauline *facie ad faciem* (I Cor. xiii. 12) and might have been hard put to it to find any other rendering. Later (298–300) he tells us that God remains seated as He receives the prayers of all other saints, but stands up when addressed by the virgins. We may smile with pleasure and rejoice to find that not only the Prince of Darkness is a gentleman; or we may say, as someone said to me, that it is 'a pleasant piece of silliness'. Both reactions perhaps miss the point. It is possible to disagree with, even to hold for 'silliness', the medieval exaltation of virginity as the supreme virtue. But granted that exaltation, Johan's image is a good symbol. If he had met a real anthropomorphist, I expect he would have been quite able to explain that God was incorporeal and there-fore would not really sit down or stand up. It would not, of course, follow that in the heat of composition he consciously attended to this.

3

It will be clear that Laȝamon is not the author of the *Brut*, nor Johan of *Sawles Warde*, in the sense in which Jane Austen is the author of *Persuasion*. On the other hand, neither is simply a trans-lator. Nor is it quite satisfactory to regard Wace (in whatever text) and the *De Anima* as their 'sources' if by a 'source' we mean some-thing that stands to their work as a *novella* or a Plutarchan *Life* stands to a play by Shakespeare. They are not changing the *genre* nor the structural outlines. The truth is that these Middle English texts have come into existence by a process which is quite foreign to modern literature. The scholar's ideal of accuracy in translation, the his-torian's ideal of fidelity to a document, and the artist's ideal of originality, are all alike absent from the minds of Laȝamon and Johan. In one way they seem enslaved to their originals; it never occurs to them to break these up and melt the slivers down and forge out of them an essentially new work. But in another way their treatment of them is very cavalier. They do not hesitate to supplement them from their own knowledge and, still more, from their own imagination—touching them up, bringing them more fully to life. The impulse to do this is obviously irrepressible; I get the impression that it is not always fully conscious or voluntary. In that way it might even be true that they are sometimes most indebted to the originals where they most improve them; that the more completely they are carried away by the story or the doctrine, the more of their own they mix with it. I think we can understand this in the light of those occasions when we have remembered a good passage from a book as being even better than it was. We look it up, perhaps in order to quote it; and find that what we had seemed to remember as the master touch was never there at all. We have added it. But it was the vitality of the passage which enabled, and forced, us to do so. The author's imagination has fertilized ours. Similarly, perhaps, it is just because Wace's narrative has taken complete possession of Laȝamon's mind that he sees—and may even believe that it was Wace who showed him—Arthur's changes of colour when they came to offer him the crown.

Now even the student who has only begun his medieval reading will have met already some instances of this very curious relation between a Middle English text and an original. His attention will almost certainly have been drawn to Chaucer's handling of Boc⸗ caccio, whether in *The Knights Tale* or the *Troilus*; perhaps also to Malory's handling of his 'French book'. But he will be very mis⸗ taken if he thinks he has been learning something merely about Chaucer or Malory. He must understand how typical, in this respect, they are. Their procedure is, if not the universal, at any rate the normal, medieval procedure. The characteristic activity of the medieval—perhaps especially the Middle English—author is pre⸗ cisely 'touching up' something that was already there. And this something may itself be the 'touching up' of something earlier: as we see in the sequence Geoffrey—Wace—Laȝamon. The beginning of this process—if it had a beginning any more definite than daylight has each morning—is often lost to us. Hence we might equally well call our medieval authors the most unoriginal or the most original of men. They are so unoriginal that they hardly ever attempt to write anything unless someone has written it before. They are so rebel⸗ liously and insistently original that they can hardly reproduce a page of any older work without transforming it by their own intensely visual and emotional imagination, turning the abstract into the concrete, quickening the static into turbulent movement, flooding whatever was colourless with scarlet and gold. They can no more leave their originals intact than we can leave our own earlier drafts intact when we fair-copy them. We always tinker and (as we hope) improve. But in the Middle Ages you did that as cheerfully to other people's work as to your own. And the tinkering very often really improved them.

In my opinion all criticism should be of books, not of authors. But when we are treating the Middle Ages it often must be. For many of the texts there is no one human being who can really be called the author in the full sense. You may sometimes be able to pick out the bits added by the last writer and separate them from those which were already there in the text he touched up. You may decide that his are the best bits. But of course this does not make him responsible for that complex organization which the whole book now is. If a great painter adds a few square feet (or even inches) of his own work to the canvas of a good, but less good, artist, he certainly modifies everything else that the picture contains; but then everything else modifies what he has added. His own work, if he really is a master, presupposes all the rest, is calculated to improve *this* picture. It would not improve any other. For the total result we cannot exclusively thank either painter. So for the *Brut* we cannot exclusively thank Laȝamon; nor Chaucer for the *Troilus*. In other words, what we may call 'the Author-Book unit' will not always work for the Middle Ages. Sometimes we begin to doubt whether even the Book is the unit; when we are presented with something constantly retold, which never remains exactly the same in the re-tellings yet never becomes wholly new, it is hard to say where one Book ends and another begins.

The Ballad, which is such a troublesome phenomenon to those who approach it with the modern idea of single authorship in their minds, can thus be seen as no more than an extreme instance of that 'shared authorship'—*shared* is a safer word than *communal*—which was widespread in the Middle Ages. The Prologue and Links in the *Canterbury Tales* are probably not an instance at all. The *Troilus* and the prose *Morte* are good, central examples.

Those who find this state of affairs repellent may be reminded that we tolerate it quite easily in another art. A cathedral often contains Saxon, Norman, Early English and Perpendicular work. The effect of the whole may be deeply satisfying. Yet we have no one artist to thank for it. None of the successive architects foresaw or intended it. One suspects indeed that most of these would have prevented it if they could, that each generation left the work of its predecessors standing only because funds for demolition and total rebuilding in the new style were not forthcoming. It may be difficult, according to some theories, to call the cathedral as we now have it a 'work of art'. But it is certainly not a work of nature (though nature has by now added some beauties and destroyed others). It is the work of men, though not of a man. We may find it helpful to regard some medieval literature as we regard such cathedrals. Indeed the books may be in one way easier to accept than the buildings. Each reviser may improve or correct (and of course misunderstand) his predecessor. But at least he is not, as the architects may have been, in revolt against him. The shared authorship is more voluntarily shared.

But while this often makes criticism of authors impossible it leaves criticism of books untouched. The text before us, however it came into existence, must be allowed to work on us in its own way and must be judged on its own merits. I agree whole-heartedly with a recent critic[1] that 'it is what is made of the "story", how it is realized, the kind of significance it is made to bear, what the poem totally communicates or does, that is our object'. As historians, as critics of authors, we may want to know whether some simile in the *Brut* came first from Wace or Laȝamon; whether some speech in *Troilus* came first from Boccaccio or Chaucer. But as readers we are concerned only to receive, as critics of books we are concerned only to diagnose and evaluate, what this simile or speech contributes to the whole 'communicating and doing' of the work before us. And while we are reading or criticizing we must be on our guard against a certain elliptical mode of expression which may be legitimate for some other purpose but is deadly for us. We must not say that the Grail 'is' a Celtic cauldron of plenty, or that Malory's Gawain 'is' a solar deity, or that the land of Gore in Chrestien's *Lancelot* 'is' the

[1] J. Speirs, *Medieval English Poetry: the Non-Chaucerian Tradition* (1957), pp. 217-18.

world of the dead. Within a given story any object, person, or place is neither more nor less nor other than what that story effectively shows it to be. The ingredients of one story cannot 'be' anything in another story, for they are not in it at all. These supposedly identical ingredients are the abstract products of analysis. Within concrete literary experiences we never meet them.

3

IMAGINATION AND THOUGHT
IN THE MIDDLE AGES

1

The man of the Middle Ages had many ignorances in common with the savages of more modern times, and some of his beliefs would certainly suggest savage parallels to an anthropologist. But it would be very wrong to infer from this that he was at all like a savage. I do not only, or chiefly, mean that such a view would depress medieval man beneath his true dignity. That's as may be; some might prefer the Polynesian. The point is that, whether for better or for worse, he was different. He was in a different predicament and had a different history. Even when he thought or did the same things as savages, he had come to them by a different route. We should be quite on the wrong track if we sought the origin, at least the immediate origin, of even the strangest medieval doctrines in what some even call pre-logical thinking.

Here is an example. In a twelfth-century English poem called the *Brut* we read the following: 'There dwell in the air many kinds of creatures which shall remain there till doomsday comes. Some of them are good and some do evil.'* These beings are mentioned to account for the birth of a child for whom no human father could be detected; one of them had in fact begotten Merlin. Now, if we considered this passage *in vacuo*, we might very well suppose that the poet's mind was working just like that of a savage, and that his belief in aerial daemons sprang as directly from a tribal culture as coarse grass from uncultivated soil. In reality, we know that he is getting it all from a book, from Geoffrey of Monmouth's Latin History of the Kings of Britain, and that Geoffrey is getting it from the second-century *De Deo Socratis* of Apuleius, who, in his turn, is reproducing the pneumatology of Plato. Trace that pneumatology back for a few centuries or so and then at last you may come to

41

whatever roots it had in a culture really close to savagery and a thinking possibly pre-logical. But all that is almost as remote from the medieval English poet as it is from us. He tells us about the aerial daemons neither because his own poetic imagination invented them, nor because they are the spontaneous reaction of his age and culture to the forces of nature, but because he has read about them in a book.

Here is another. In a French poem of the fourteenth century Nature personified appears as a character and has a conversation with another personage called *Grâcedieu*. Grace-of-God would, for various reasons, be a misleading translation, so I will call her *Super-nature*. And Nature says to Supernature 'The circle of the cold moon truly marks the boundary between your realm and mine forever'.* Here again we might well suppose the savage mind at work; what more natural than to locate the houses of the gods at a reasonable distance and choose the Moon for the gate between their world and ours? Yet, almost certainly that is not what is happening. The idea that the orbit of the Moon is a great boundary between two regions of the universe is Aristotelian. It is based on a contrast which naturally forced itself upon one whose studies were so often biological and psychological, but also sometimes astronomical. The part of the world which we inhabit, the Earth, is the scene of genera-tion and decay and therefore of continual change. Such regularities as he would observe in it seemed to him imperfect; terrestrial nature carried things on, he thought, not always but 'on the whole' in the same way.* It was clear from observing the weather that this irregu-larity extended a good way upwards above the surface of the Earth. But not all the way. Above the variable sky there were the heavenly bodies which seemed to have been perfectly regular in their behaviour ever since the first observations were made and of which none, to his knowledge, had ever been seen to come into existence or to decay. The Moon was obviously the lowest of these. Hence he divided the universe at the Moon; all above that was necessary, regular, and eternal, all below it, contingent, irregular and perishable. And of course, for any Greek, what is necessary and eternal is more divine. This, with a Christian colouring added, fully accounts for the passage we began with.

Both examples—and it would not be difficult to cite more—point to the same truth, and it is a truth basic for any understanding of the Middle Ages. Their culture is through and through a bookish culture. Millions, no doubt, were illiterate; the masters, however, were literate, and not only literate but scholarly and even pedantic. The peculiar predicament of medieval man was in fact just this: he was a literate man who had lost a great many of his books and forgotten how to read all his Greek books. He works with the rather chancy selection he has. In that way the Middle Ages were much less like an age which has not yet been civilized than like one which has survived the loss of civilization. An exaggerated, but not wholly fake, model would be a party of shipwrecked people setting to work to try to build up a culture on an uninhabited island and depending on the odd collection of books which happened to be on board their ship.

Of course this is grossly oversimplified and I must immediately take notice of one complication which may have already occurred to you. Genealogically, and in some measure culturally, the medieval European had roots in the barbarian life of the north and west as well as in Mediterranean civilization. Along that line, it may be said, he had a much closer link with primitive thought than through its far-off echoes in Latin literature. This of course is true. Fragments of indigenous and spontaneous mythology survive; Germanic, in Anglo-Saxon, Old Norse, and Old High German, or Celtic (to some undefined extent) in the French romances. Popular literature, such as the Ballads, may throw up more or less disguised fragments of this at quite late periods. But we must insist that these things loom much larger in the popular picture of the Middle Ages than they did in the reality. By the time we reach the High Middle Age all the old Germanic literature has been forgotten and the languages in which it was written are unknown. And as for the Ballad and the Romance, it is important to realize that both these attractive products are the reverse of typical. It is easy to be deceived here, because it was the Ballad and the Romance which first excited modern interest in the Middle Ages; Medieval studies began there. The reason is simple. These forms appealed to the Romanticism of the eighteenth and nineteenth centuries. Even now many of us were first lured to Medieval studies by this romantic attraction. Even now the 'man in the street' thinks of the Middle Ages, if at all, in terms of the romances; popular iconography—a joke in *Punch*, an advertisement —wishing to suggest the medieval, depicts a knight in armour riding through desolate country, adding castles, dragons, and distressed damsels *quantum suff*. But the paradox is that the note is one which the real Middle Ages struck only in a minority of Ballads and Romances and hardly at all in any other form. That boundlessness, indefiniteness, suggestiveness are not the common or characteristic medieval mood. The real temper of those ages was not romantic. The Arthurian stories represent, perhaps, a truancy or escape from habitual concerns.

Characteristically, medieval man was not a dreamer nor a spiritual adventurer; he was an organizer, a codifier, a man of system. His ideal could be not unfairly summed up in the old housewifely maxim 'A place for everything, and everything in its (right) place'. Three things are typical of him. First, that small minority of his cathedrals in which the design of the architect was actually achieved (usually, of course, it was overtaken by the next wave of architectural fashion long before it was finished). I am thinking of a thing like Salisbury. Secondly, the *Summa* of Thomas Aquinas. And thirdly, the *Divine Comedy* of Dante. In all these alike we see the tranquil, indefatigable, exultant energy of a passionately logical mind ordering a huge mass of heterogeneous details into unity. They desire unity and proportion, all the classical virtues, just as keenly as the Greeks did. But they have a greater and more varied collection of things to fit in. And they delight to do it. Hence the *Comedy* which is, I suppose, the supreme achievement: crowded and varied as a railway station on a bank holiday, but patterned and schematized as a battalion on a ceremonial parade.

You see how this arises naturally from their situation? I described them as literate people who had lost most of their books. And what survived was, to some extent, a chance collection. It contained ancient Hebrew, classical Greek, classical Roman, decadent Roman and early Christian elements. It had reached them by various routes. All Plato had disappeared except part of the *Timaeus* in a Latin version: one of the greatest, but also one of the least typical, of the dialogues. Aristotle's logic was at first missing, but you had a

Latin translation of a very late Greek introduction to it. Astronomy and medicine, and (later) Aristotle, came in Latin translations of Arabic translations of the Greek. That is the typical descent of learning: from Athens to Hellenistic Alexandria, from Alexandria to Baghdad, from Baghdad, *via* Sicily, to the university of Paris, and thence all over Europe.... A scratch collection, a corpus that frequently contradicted itself. But here we touch on a real credulity in the medieval mind. Faced with this self-contradictory corpus, they hardly ever decided that one of the authorities was simply right and the others wrong; never that all were wrong. To be sure, in the last resort it was taken for granted that the Christian writers must be right as against the Pagans. But it was hardly ever allowed to come to the last resort. It was apparently difficult to believe that anything in the books—so costly, fetched from so far, so old, often so lovely to the eye and hand, was just plumb wrong. No; if Seneca and St Paul disagreed with one another, and both with Cicero, and all these with Boethius, there must be some explanation which would harmonize them. What was not true literally might be true in some other sense; what was false *simpliciter* might be true *secundum quid*. And so on, through every possible subtlety and ramification. It is out of this that the medieval picture of the universe is evolved: a chance collection of materials, an inability to say 'Bosh', a temper systematic to the point of morbidity, great mental powers, un-wearied patience, and a robust delight in their work. All these factors led them to produce the greatest, most complex, specimen of syncretism or harmonization which, perhaps, the world has ever known. They tidied up the universe. To that tidy universe, and above all to its effect on the imagination, I now turn.

I assume that everyone knows, more or less, its material layout: a motionless Earth at the centre, transparent spheres revolving round it, of which the lowest, slowest, nearest and smallest carries the Moon, and thence upwards in the order Mercury, Venus, the Sun, Mars, Jupiter, Saturn; beyond these, all the stars in one sphere; beyond that, a sphere which carries no light but merely imparts movement to those below it; beyond that, the Empyrean, the boundary of the *mundus*, the beginning of the infinite true 'Heaven'.

No one, as far as I know, has exaggerated the emotional and

imaginative difference between such a universe and that which we now believe ourselves to inhabit; but a great many people have misconceived the nature of the difference. The cardinal error (ubiquitous in earlier modern writers, and still clung to by some who should know better today) may be expressed in the following words. 'The Earth, both by her supposed size and by her central position, had, for medieval thinkers, an importance to which we now know that she is by no means entitled.' Hence, of course, the probable conclusion that their theology—here, once more, pre-logical thinking might be suspected—was the offspring of their cosmology. The truth seems to me the reverse. Their theology might be thought to imply an Earth which counted for a good deal in the universe and was central in dignity as well as in space; the odd thing is that their cosmology does not, in any obvious sense, encourage this view.

First, as regards size. That the Earth is, by any cosmic scale, insignificant, is a truth that was forced on every intelligent man as soon as serious astronomical observations began to be made. I have already said that Aristotle thought the region above the Moon more divine than the airy, watery, and earthy realm below it. He also thought it incomparably large. As he says in the *Metaphysics*, 'The perceptible world around us'—that is, the realm of growth, decay and weather—'is, so to speak, a nothing if considered as part of the whole.'* Later in Ptolemy's compendium, which transmitted Greek astronomy to the Middle Ages, a more precise statement is made; the Earth, we are told, must, for astronomical purposes, be regarded as having no magnitude at all, as a point. This was accepted by the Middle Ages. It was not merely accepted by scholars; it was reechoed by moralists and poets again and again. To judge from the texts, medieval man thought about the insignificance of Earth more persistently, if anything, than his modern descendants. We even find quite popular texts hammering the lesson home by those methods which the scientific popularizer uses today. We are told how long it would take you to get to the sphere of the fixed stars if you travelled so many miles a day. The figure brings the distance out at something near 118 million miles.

Now of course this is a small distance compared with those of which modern astronomers talk. But we are here considering not the accuracy of the figure but its imaginative and emotional impact. From that point of view I maintain that the difference between a million, a hundred millions, and a million millions, is wholly negligible. All these figures can be used, manipulated, with equal ease by anyone who can do simple arithmetic; none of them can at all be imagined in the sense of 'visualized', and those who have most imagination know this best.

From that point of view, then, the medieval model of the universe is on a par with the Newtonian (I do not say, with the modern, for I want to defer the consideration of it). Either will allow you to lose yourself in unimaginable distances, to sink and say with Leopardi *il naufragar m'è dolce in questo mare,** and to see the Earth as a speck of dust—if, of course, that is the sort of thing you want to do. And now comes the point I really want to make. I have not said that the difference between the medieval and, say, the Newtonian picture was less than our grandfathers supposed. It was quite as great. But it was not the kind of difference we have been taught to expect.

What it really was I can, here and now, only suggest. The thing really needs to be learned not from a lecture but (you are scientists) by an experiment; an experiment on one's imagination. It is a simple one. Go out on any starry night and walk alone for half an hour, resolutely assuming that the pre-Copernican astronomy is true. Look up at the sky with that assumption in your mind. The real difference between living in that universe and living in ours will then, I predict, begin to dawn on you.

You will be looking at a world unimaginably large but quite definitely finite. At no speed possible to man, in no lifetime possible to man, could you ever reach its frontier, but the frontier is there; hard, clear, sudden as a national frontier. And secondly, because the Earth is an absolute centre, and Earthwards from any part of this immense universe is downwards, you will find that you are looking at the planets and stars in terms not merely of 'distance' but of that very special kind of distance which we call 'height'. They are not only a long way from the Earth but a long way above it. I need hardly point out that height is a very much livelier notion than distance; it has, the moment it is imagined, commerce with our nerves, with all our racial and infantile terrors, with our pleasures as mountaineers, our love of wide prospects, and a whole vast network of ethical and social metaphors which we could not shake off even if we tried. Now these two factors taken together—enormous but finite size, and distances which, however vast, remain unambiguously vertical, and indeed vertiginous—at once present you with something which differs from the Newtonian picture rather as a great building differs from a great jungle. You can lose yourself in infinity; there is indeed nothing much else you can do with it. It arouses questions, it prompts to a certain kind of wonder and reverie, usually a sombre kind, so that Wordsworth can speak of 'melancholy space and doleful time' or Carlyle can call the starry sky 'a sad sight'. But it answers no questions; necessarily shapeless and trackless, patient of no absolute order or direction, it leads, after a little, to boredom or despair or (often) to the haunting conviction that it must be an illusion. Earth and Man are, if you like, dwarfed by it, but not much more dwarfed than the Solar System, or the Galaxy, or anything else. One cannot be, in any very important sense, small where size has ceased to have a meaning. The old universe was wholly different in its effect. It was an answer, not a question. It offered not a field for musing but a single overwhelming object; an object which at once abashes and exalts the mind. For in it there is a final standard of size. The Primum Mobile is really large because it is the largest corporeal thing there is. We are really small because our whole Earth is a speck compared with the Primum Mobile.

I have been speaking so far only of dimensions. But the effect of the old model becomes even more interesting when we consider order. It is not merely very large, it is a whole of finely graded parts. Everything descends from the circumference with a steady diminution of size, speed, power and dignity. This ninefold division is harmoniously crossed by a threefold division. All above the Empyrean is in a special, immaterial, sense 'Heaven', full of the Divine Substance. From the Empyrean down to the Moon is the realm of aether—that strange halfmatter in which so many different ages have believed, on what seems to a layman very inadequate evidence—changeless, necessary, not subject to Fortune. From the Moon down to the Earth is the realm of air (for they thought the air extended to the Moon's orbit), which is also the realm of luck, change, birth, death, and contingence.

You see why I compared it to a building—though indeed any great, complex work of art—*Paradise Lost* or Euclid's *Elements* or Spinoza's *Ethics* or Beethoven's Ninth Symphony—would have done almost as well. It is a structure, a finished work, a unity articulated through a great and harmonious plurality. It evokes not mere wonder but admiration. It provides food for thought and satisfaction for our aesthetic nature. I think everyone will see what I mean if I say that in passing from the Newtonian to the Ptolemaic cosmos one passes from the romantic to the classical. Milton could describe the Moon as looking

> Like one that had bin led astray
> Through the Heav'ns wide pathles way.*

That hits off admirably the feeling many generations now have had when they look at the night sky: I do not think any ancient or medieval man would have felt so. That particular charm, the charm of the pathless, was one that the old universe lacked; it had a severer, a more robust attraction and appealed to a more formal imagination.

After the dimensions and the order, we must consider the dynamics. I have already said that movement earthward from any part of the whole was conceived as movement downward. In that sense they understood what we would call gravitation. Thus one philosopher says that if you could bore a hole through the Earth and drop a stone down, the stone would come to rest at the centre. And in the *Comedy*, Dante and Virgil come to the centre where they find Lucifer embedded and have to climb down his shaggy sides in order to continue their journey to the Antipodes; but Dante finds to his surprise that after they have passed his waist they have to climb *up* to his feet. For they have of course passed the centre of gravitation. But they never talk of gravitation. Their way of describing it is to say that every natural object has a native or 'proper' place and is always 'trying' or 'desiring' to get there. When unimpeded, flame moves upwards and solid bodies move downwards because they want to go, you may call it, 'home'. Is this animism? Did they really think that all matter was sentient? Apparently not. They will distinguish animate and inanimate as clearly as we do; will say that stones, for example, have only being; vegetables being and life; animals, being, life and sense; man, being, life, sense and reason. The truth is that their language about inanimate bodies was the same kind of language that the modern man uses—I mean, the modern 'plain' man, not the modern scientist or philosopher. When a modern says that the stone fell 'in obedience to the law of gravitation', he does not really think there is literally a law or literal obedience; that the stone, on being released, whips out a little book of statutes, finds the chapter and paragraph relevant to its predicament, and decides it had better be a law-abiding stone and 'come quiet'. Nor did the medieval man believe that the stone really felt homesick, or felt at all. Both ways of putting it are analogical; neither speaker would usually know any way of expressing the facts except by an analogy.

But of course it makes a great difference to the tone of your mind which analogy you adopt—whether you fill your universe with phantom police-courts and traffic regulations, or with phantom longings and endeavours. The second alternative, which the Middle Ages adopted, is connected with another and more far-reaching doctrine which is not merely analogical. We are now approaching the junction between their cosmology and their theology. The theology involved is, however, not that of the Bible, the Fathers, or the Councils, but that of Aristotle. Of course they thought it consistent with Christianity; whether they were right in so thinking is not my concern.

The infinite, according to Aristotle, is not actual. No infinite object exists; no infinite process occurs. Hence we cannot explain the movement of one body by the movement of another and so on forever. No such infinite series could, he thought, exist. All the movements of the universe must therefore, in the last resort, result from a compulsive force exercised by something immovable. He thought that such an Unmoved Mover could move other things only by being their end or object or (if you like) target—what he calls their 'Final Cause'—not as one billiard ball moves another, but as food moves the hungry man, as the mistress moves her lover, as truth moves the philosophical inquirer. He calls this Unmoved Mover either 'God' or 'Mind'. It moves the Primum Mobile (which of course sets all the inferior bodies in motion) by love.* But notice that this does not mean what a Christian would naturally mean by the word. There is no question here of a beneficent Being loving the world He has created and descending to redeem it. God, in Aristotle, moves the world by being loved, not by loving; by being the supremely desirable object. This of course implies not only consciousness but high rationality on the part of that which is moved. Accordingly we find (not now by analogy, but in strictest fact) that in every sphere there is a rational creature called an Intelligence which is compelled to move, and therefore to keep his sphere moving, by his incessant desire for God. It was disputed whether the Intelligence is 'in' the sphere as the soul is in the body (in which case the sphere must be envisaged as an eternal and exalted animal) or as a man is in a ship (in which case the corporeal sphere is a kind of instrument). On the whole the second view won. A modern may ask why a love for God should lead to perpetual rotation. I think, because this love or appetite for God is a desire to participate as much as possible in His nature; i.e. to imitate it. And the nearest approach to His eternal immobility, the second best, is eternal regular movement in the most perfect figure, which, for any Greek, is the circle. Hence the universe is kept going by the continual effort of its most excellent parts (each a little slower and feebler than the one above it) to conform their behaviour to a model of which they always fall short. That of course is the real meaning of Dante's (often misunderstood) line about 'the love that moves the sun and the other stars'. Even so, love is perhaps too ethical a word; 'appetite' would be better. In this scheme God is the quarry, the Intelligences the huntsmen; God is the mistress, all things else the suitors; God the candle, and the universe the moth.

2

In my last lecture I suggested the experiment of a starlit walk taken with the assumption that Ptolemaic astronomy is true. In order to bring that old model into fuller activity, I now want to recall an experience which, I suppose, everyone has had; that of coming out from some indoor function of pomp and importance, an opera or a debate or a feast, and suddenly looking up at the cold stars above the housetops. What seemed so big while we were inside is all at once dwarfed. The sky is like an ironic comment on this and on all other human concerns. If we remember our Pascal, we may even murmur 'The silence of those eternal spaces frightens me'. After that, we may rally and hit back and say, still using Pascal, that though we are small and transitory as dew-drops, still we are dew-drops that can think,* which is (we presume) more than can be said for the galaxies. Let us now try to understand why neither of these reactions— neither the initial deflation nor the come-back—was at all likely to occur to a man of the Middle Ages.

He did not think that the spaces he looked up at were silent, or dark or empty. Far from being silent, they were perpetually filled with sweet, immeasurable sound. The vast hollow spheres, turning each at its proper interval inside its superior, gave out a blended harmony. There were various explanations of the fact that we do not hear it. One of the oldest and most pleasing was based on the travellers' tale that those who lived near the great cataract on the Nile were unconscious of its noise. Because they had always heard it, they never heard it. The same would obviously hold true in an even higher degree of the music of the spheres. This is the only sound which has never for one split second ceased in any part of the universe; with this positive we have no negative to contrast. Presumably if (*per impossibile*) it ever did stop, then with terror and dismay, with a dislocation of our whole auditory life, we should feel that the bottom had dropped out of our lives. But it never does. The music which is too familiar to be heard enfolds us day and night and in all ages.

Nor were those high regions dark. The darkness in which the stars (for us) are set is merely the darkness of the long, conical shadow cast by the Earth when the sun is below our feet. They knew, from their theory of lunar eclipses, that the apex of this dark cone must fall well above the moon. Beyond that apex the higher heavens are bathed in perpetual sunshine. In a sense, no doubt, we should say the same. But then we are aware (as they, I think, were not) of the part played by the air in diffusing sunlight and producing that bubble of luminosity which we call day; we have even, in stratospheric ascents, gone high enough to see the blue curtain grow thin at the zenith so that blue turns to black and the night of space almost shows through. They knew that, up yonder, one was above the air, in whatever they meant by aether; they did not know that one would see the sun flaming in a black pit. They thought on the contrary that they would be floating (for Milton is here a medieval) in

> those happie climes that lye
> Where day never shuts his eye,
> Up in the broad fields of the skye.*

And these spaces, bright and resonant, were also inhabited. We have already peopled them with the Intelligences who either animate or guide the spheres. Distinct from these, but of course equally immortal and superhuman, are the angels. Their natural habitat is between the Empyrean and the Moon and their number is probably enormous. Unlike the aerial daemons who live between Moon and Earth, they have no bodies—such, at least, was the view that finally prevailed—but are naked minds. We, like them, are rational, but there is a great difference. We have an immediate and intuitive grasp only of axioms and have to seek all other knowledge by the laborious process of discursive thinking. They are wholly intuitive; concepts are as palpable to them as apples or pennies are to us. In fact, their reason is to ours as noon to dusk. Clearly when you look up at a sky peopled by such creatures as these, it is just no good asserting 'I am a dew-drop that thinks'. The very necessity of 'thinking' (as we ordinarily understand the word) is the measure of our inferiority.

Understand that the vast majority of these bodiless minds have no concern at all with us. We touch only the lowest fringe of angelic life. For angelic life also is graded; the word *angel* is, rather unfortunately, used both for the whole lot and also for the lowest rank—just as we use *sailors* sometimes in contrast to ships' officers, but sometimes in a sense that covers all who enable the ship to sail. They are ordered in nine classes which are arranged in three groups of three classes each. The top hierarchy, which consists of the creatures classified as Seraphim, Cherubim and Thrones, looks exclusively God-wards, absorbed in contemplation of the Divine essence, and unconcerned with the created universe. The next hierarchy (Dominations, Virtues, and Powers) has some responsibility for the general order of nature. The lowest hierarchy deals with human affairs;

Principalities with the destiny of nations, Archangels and Angels, in varying ways, with those of individuals. You will notice that even at such a unique crisis as the Annunciation the Mother of Christ was visited only by an Archangel, a member of the lowest class but one. That gets the perspective right. It is this conception, as well as the poet's own genius, which gives to Dante's angels a sublimity and masculinity never captured by later art. It is the loss of this conception which finally vulgarizes the angels into those consumptive girls with wings that figure in so much Victorian stained glass. The full degradation of the Cherub—the fat baby who has played that rôle ever since Raphael—will perhaps be clearest if we remember that the word probably comes from the same root as *gryphon*. Even for Chaucer a cherub was a creature of fire: not at all 'cuddly'.

But I must crowd the sky a little more. Medieval man looked up at a sky not only melodious, sunlit, and splendidly inhabited, but also incessantly active; he looked at agents to which he, and the whole earth, were patients. Besides the Intelligences and the angelic hierarchies there are the planets themselves. Each of them is doing things to us at every moment. First, on the physical side, the beams of each planet (which penetrate through the Earth's crust) find the appropriate soil and turn it into the appropriate metal; Saturn thus producing lead, Mars iron, the Moon silver, and so forth. The Moon's connexion with silver, and the Sun's with gold, may be real survivals (at many removes) of pre-logical, pictorial, thinking. Venus is, perhaps, a maker of copper because she was, centuries earlier, Kupris, the lady of Cyprus, and that accursed island produced copper in ancient times. Why Saturn made lead, or Jove tin, I do not know.

But of course, as everyone has heard, the planets had a more than physical effect. They influenced the course of events and they influenced human psychology. Born under Saturn, you were disposed to melancholy; born under Venus, to amorousness. At this point, clearly, there is a rich survival of classical Paganism into medieval culture. And of course the names of the planets, and their representations in art, are those of the ancient planetary gods. As far as my reading goes, no one appears to have been at all worried about it. There was, indeed, a quarrel between the theologians and the astrologers, but not exactly about that. So far as I know, no theologian denied the general theory of planetary influences. The important question, theologically, was whether the planets compelled or merely disposed men to action. If they compelled, then of course there was an end of human freedom and responsibility. If they merely disposed, then planetary influence, like heredity or health or education, was merely part of the concrete situation handed over to the individual to do the best he could with. The theologians were in fact, as so often, fighting against determinism. Nor were they fighting against a phantom: in renaissance times, if not before them, astrological determinism was very widely accepted. It seemed (odd as this sounds to us) to have the support of age-old experience and common sense, and the theological resistance seemed idealistic wishful thinking. In the Middle Ages men's minds no doubt wavered. The ordinary, moderate, respectable view was summed up in the maxim *sapiens dominabitur astris*; a wise man, assisted by Grace, could get over a bad horoscope just as he could get over a naturally bad temper.

That, as I have said, was the important question on the theoretical level. On the practical level orthodox people, while admitting planetary influence, strongly disapproved of 'judicial astrology', the lucrative practice of foretelling the future. They did not need to deny that some astrological predictions of human behaviour might be correct. Planetary influence could not remove free will but it could alter the states of mind and imagination which free will has to deal with. Any man can master this psychological raw material and thus refute the prediction; but few men do and therefore the predictions will succeed as regards the majority. Just in the same way and for similar reasons a modern theologian might say that Marxian predictions based on economic determinism or Freudian predictions based on psychological determinism will usually be true, and true about mass-behaviour, but not necessarily about a given individual.

I stress the parallel between astrology and more modern forms of determinism in order to bring out a point which, though I have made it elsewhere, is too important to be passed over. We must never allow ourselves to think of astrology as something that belonged to the romantic or dreaming or quasi-mystical side of the mind; above all, we must not connect it with magic. Astrology was a hard-headed, stern, anti-idealistic affair; the creed of men who wanted a universe which admitted no incalculables. Magic sought power over nature; astrology proclaimed nature's power over man. Hence the magician is the ancestor of the modern practising or 'applied' scientist, the inventor; the astrologer, of the nineteenth-century philosophical materialist. Neither figure, by the way, is specially typical of the Middle Ages.* Both flourished as much, if not more, in the ancient and in the renaissance world.

I have already said that the medieval man thought he was looking up at a luminous universe through the dark shadow of the Earth. He was also looking up at the region of aether through the region of air. The air was the medium through which all the influences from above reached him. The whole air could become healthy or un-healthy as the result of certain conjunctions in the upper sky. Hence a medieval doctor could explain widespread illness by saying 'It's due to this influence'. If he were talking Italian he would no doubt say *questa influenza*, and that word has stuck. I mention the air, however, not merely to bring in that curiosity but for two other reasons.

First: the air is below the Moon. That is, as you have heard, it is excluded from the region of necessity and regularity. In the air, as on the Earth, you have contingence and the irregular; in the air you have the aerial daemons who can, like men, do either good or evil. Here we come to an important difference between medieval and modern man. The ordinary modern (I do not mean the modern scientist) would regard regularity—or, if you like, monotony—as a symptom of inferiority. The fact that the heavenly bodies always behave in the same way, while men do this and that and change their minds, would be for him presumptive evidence that the former are irrational and inanimate and that we, we 'dew-drops' that think, are to that extent their betters. For the same reason, if he believed in the aerial daemons and the planetary Intelligences, he would probably prefer the daemons. The Middle Ages inherited from the Greeks a very different view. Aristotle in the *Metaphysics* remarks that in a household (he is of course assuming a household with slaves) the free members are precisely those who have least chance to live 'at random'. The slaves can do that; for the free people 'everything is mapped out'. It is a surprising picture but, I have no doubt, a true one; all ancient literature goes to show that a house‑slave is, of all servants, the least like a robot. But I quote it here for a different reason. Though Aristotle does not make it perfectly clear, scholars are agreed that he is intending to compare the heavenly bodies with the free people and the slaves with us. For the heavenly bodies 'everything is mapped out'; our liberty to live 'at random' marks our inferior status. We, like slaves, have or take 'spare time' and in it 'potter about', chatting, making love, playing games, cracking nuts or 'just sitting'; they, like Aristotle himself, have their strict programme.

Secondly, the mediation of celestial influences through the air illustrates a principle that runs through the whole universe. Last time I compared that universe to a great building: I should now like to compare it to a fugue—the orderly and varied reiteration of the same 'subject'. When Donne says

> On man heavens influence workes not so,
> But that it first imprints the ayre,*

he is making one statement of that subject. You have here, you see, a triad in the form: Agent (the planets), Medium (the air), Patient (man, and, in general, Earth). It is a triad which still has its appeal; I suppose that aether, at no very distant period, was accepted because we wanted a medium or go‑between. But it appealed very much more strongly in the Middle Ages. The Triad is repeated on every level.

First, among the angels themselves. The Middle Ages learned all about their triadic organization from a Latin version of a (probably sixth‑century) Greek theologian whom we know as Pseudo‑Dionysius. The method by which he dovetails his triadic angelology into his Old Testament, where (by our standards) nothing like it is to be found, is a charming example of the process I mentioned before—the great medieval labour of harmonization and syncretism.* He points out that in Isaiah vi the angels are crying out 'Holy, Holy, Holy' not (as we might expect) to God but to one another. Why? Obviously because each angel is handing on his knowledge of

the Divine Sanctity to the angel next below him. The only excep'
tion is the Seraphim. They alone of all creatures apprehend God
immediately. But as soon as you reach the Cherubim you have a
triad; God as agent, Seraphim as medium, Cherubim as patient.
Then below that, Seraphim as agent, Cherubim as medium,
Thrones as patient. And then the same triad within the second
hierarchy and the third; and of course between the first, second, and
third hierarchies as wholes. It is a continual devolution as if God,
who in a sense does all things, will yet do nothing immediately which
can possibly be done through the mediation of His creatures. And
as if even this were not enough, we are then told that within each
individual angel, of whatever class, the triad occurs again; each has
primary faculties which act through the medium of secondary
faculties on tertiary faculties. Thus you get not only triad above triad
but triad within triad till the mind is dizzy with them.

All this, within the angelic world itself. But the moment one
steps outside that world one finds that it itself, collectively, is part of a
vaster triad. For God governs the world through the angels; the
whole angelic population, without prejudice to its complex internal
triads, is the medium between God as agent and Nature (or Man) as
patient. Just so on Earth a King governs the commons through the
barons. But this of course was not, for the medieval mind, a mere
analogy. It was the real earthly and social reproduction of the triad.
I say 'social' to distinguish it from 'individual'; for within the
individual man, as within the individual angel, the triad is repeated.

It is indeed repeated twice, once on the ethical and once on the
psychological level. Ethically (and here, at many removes, they
were following Plato) the triad is Reason, Emotion, and Appetite.
Reason, seated in the head, governs the Appetites, seated in the
abdomen or beneath it, by the aid of the more fully human and
civilized emotions which were located in the thorax; such things as
shame, honour, pity, self'respect, affection. This ethical triad was
accepted for millennia. The effort now sometimes made to lead a
civilized life on reason alone, rejecting the emotions, the attempt of
the monarchic head to rule the plebeian belly without the aid of that
aristocracy in the thorax, would have seemed to Plato a rash venture;
like what motorists call 'driving on your brakes'. It is hard on the

brakes and leads to skids. On the psychological level the individual triad depends on the doctrine of the triple soul. But the word *anima* had a larger and less exclusively religious range of meaning than *soul*; 'life' would sometimes be a better translation. There is vegetable soul, common to all plants, which gives only life; sensitive soul, which gives life and sensation; and rational soul, by which we think. Man of course has all three: when things are going right inside him, his rational governs his vegetable through his sensitive.

A thirteenth-century author, Alanus, works out the theological, the social, and the individual triads in terms of castle (or citadel), city, and the lands beyond the city walls. These are literally given, of course, in the social one; a king in his citadel, the barons in the city, the peasants in the fields outside. In the individual the head is the citadel, where the empress Sapience keeps her court. In the City of the Breast lives the high baronage of Magnanimity. Outside, in the abdomen, or still more outside, in the genitals, live the common appetites. But it is the theological triad that most concerns us at the moment. The castle of God is the Empyrean, the region beyond the outermost sphere. In the city, in the vast ethereal spaces, dwell the cosmic nobility, the nine orders of angels. Down here on Earth there is a place permitted to us 'as to aliens', he says, 'outside the wall'.[1]

Outside the wall—that is the point. Go back for a moment to the experience I mentioned at the beginning; that of looking up at the stars as you come out from an opera or a feast. The full contrast between the medieval experience and ours is only now apparent. For whatever else we feel, we certainly feel that we are looking *out*; out of somewhere warm and lighted into dark, cold, indifferent desolation, out of a house on to the dark waste of the sea. But the medieval man felt he was looking *in*. Here is the outside. The Moon's orbit is the city wall. Night opens the gates for a moment and we catch a glimpse of the high pomps which are going on inside; staring as animals stare at the fires of the encampment they cannot enter, as rustics stare at a city, as suburbia stares at Mayfair.

I have spoken advisedly of 'high pomps'. My account so far has perhaps made this complex, densely peopled cosmos a little too

---

[1] *De Planctu Naturae*, P.L. CCX, *Prosa* III, col. 444 A, B.

severe, made the operations of the spheres and the angels sound, as we should say, 'a little too like work'. I could correct that more easily if I had slides. I am thinking in particular of one picture which represents the Intelligence of the Primum Mobile itself. It is of course wholly symbolical; they knew perfectly well that such a creature—it had no body—could not be literally depicted at all. But the symbol chosen is delightfully significant. It is a picture of a girl dancing and playing a tambourine; a picture of gaiety, almost of frolic. And why not? These spheres are moved by love, by intel‑lectual desire, never sated because they can never completely assimi‑late themselves to their object, and never frustrated because they continually do so to the fullest extent which their nature admits or requires. Their existence is thus one of delight. The motions of the universe are to be conceived not as those of a machine or even an army, but rather as a dance, a festival, a symphony, a ritual, a carnival, or all these in one. They are the unimpeded movement of the most perfect impulse towards the most perfect Object.

A modern mind will of course say that the men of that age fashioned heaven in the likeness of Earth and, because they liked high pomps, the Mass, coronations, pageants, tournaments, carols, at‑tributed such activities *par excellence* to the translunary world. But remember that they thought it was the other way round. They thought that the ecclesiastical hierarchy and the social hierarchy on Earth were dim reproductions of the celestial hierarchies. The pageantry and ceremony which they indulged in to the utmost of their powers were their attempt to imitate the *modus operandi* of the universe; to live, in that sense, 'according to nature'. That is why so much medieval art and literature is concerned simply with asserting the nature of things. They liked to tell, and to be told again and again, about the universe I have been describing. Any poet in any poem is liable to start describing the angels, the spheres, the in‑fluences, the metals, and a hundred other things I have not had time for—gems, beasts, the Zodiac, the Seven Virtues, the Seven Sins, the Nine Worthies, the nature of winds, the divisions of the soul, herbs, flowers, what not. They wrote it, they sang it, painted it and carved it. Sometimes a whole poem or a whole building seems almost nothing but verbalized or petrified cosmology. In all this I have never found one trace of the savage idea that by representing the things on Earth you somehow helped them to happen in the universe. Their minds were not like that. It was rather the spontaneous desire of us 'aliens outside the city wall' to participate as far as we can in the glory of the life of the city; like the Mothers' Union doing in the village hall the same play that was done in London—a legitimate, absurd attempt, and very good fun for all concerned.

Two points which may have caused some discomfort remain. Is it, imaginatively and emotionally, tolerable to have the Earth spatially central and, at the same time, in some other sense, a furlong outside the wall? And is it quite satisfactory to have an infinite space outside the highest heaven? It is, if we take their thought at its highest level. On that level it involves something of which no model could be drawn on a blackboard, nor even easily made in three dimensions.

Aristotle had said 'Whatever is outside the highest Heaven is of such a sort that it needs no place, nor does time affect it'.* It is typically Aristotelian in its dry caution, typically pagan in its reverent timidity. Taken over by Christians, this of course turns into something much more positive and resounding. As one author says, all that heaven is *Deo plenum*, full of God. Or, as Dante says, it is *luce intellettual piena d'amore* (*Paradiso*, XXX, 40). In other words there isn't exactly any space beyond the cosmos. The Empyrean is the boundary of space, not in the absurd sense which would force us to put more space outside it but in the sense that it is the point at which the spatial mode of thought breaks down. To reach the end of space is to reach the end of spatiality.

Dante makes this vivid to us by an astonishing *tour de force*. He cannot of course make the spaceless imaginable in the strict sense. What he does is to show us space turning inside out; that teaches us pretty effectively that spatial thinking, as we ordinarily know it, has broken down. First, to prepare us, he gives us this remarkable image. The Primum Mobile is described as the 'vase' in which time has its roots —'look elsewhere for its leaves' (*Paradiso*, XXVII, 118-20). Time, of course, in the old philosophy, was generated by the movement of the Primum Mobile. But consider the image—a gigantic tree growing downwards through those 118 million miles, its roots in the stars, its leaves being the days and minutes we live through on Earth. I had almost said 'the leaves of its *topmost* branches', for one cannot help thinking of them as topmost: what is down for us must be up for the tree, its sap must be coming up, its roots must be its lowest point. Thus he begins to turn the universe inside out. Then, later, in the Empyrean itself, he is shown a point of light round which nine lights are circling, the nearest to the centre moving at the highest speed and the furthest out at the lowest. Of the centre Beatrice says 'Heaven and all nature hangs upon that point' (*Paradiso*, XXVIII, 41–2); it is what Aristotle says in so many words of the Unmoved Mover. The point is an exposition of God; the nine (so to call them) planets are the nine angelic hierarchies and you see that this is our universe inside out. In our visible world the circumference, the Primum Mobile, moves quickest and is nearest to God; the Moon moves slowest and is nearest what we call the Centre—i.e. the Earth. But the true nature of the universe is exactly the opposite. In the visible and spatial order Earth is centre; in the dynamic, invisible order the Empyrean is centre, and we are indeed 'outside the city wall' at the end of all things. And the centre of that Centre, the centre of Earth, is the edge, the very point at which all being and reality finally peter out. For in there (as we call it), out there (as we ought to call it) is Hell—the last outpost, the rim, the place where being is nearest to not-being, where positive unbeing (so to call it) asymptotically approaches that zero it can never quite reach.

Such was the medieval cosmos. It had of course one serious drawback. It wasn't—or a good deal of it wasn't—true. I have rather been inviting you to consider it as a work of art; perhaps, after all, the greatest work of art the Middle Ages produced. Of course it was not a mere fantasy. It was intended to cover, and up to a point did cover, the facts as they knew them. And perhaps in calling it untrue, we should all now mean something other than our grandfathers meant. They would have taken the Newtonian account as simply true and the medieval as simply wrong. It would be for them like the difference between a good map and a bad one. I suppose most people would now admit that no picture of the universe we can form is 'true' in quite the sense our grandfathers hoped. We would rather speak of 'models'. And since all are only models, we should be prepared to find in each something of the nature of the artist as well as something of the object. From that point of view, too, a study of the various models has its interest. I think the medieval and Newtonian models—the one so ordered, so sublime, and so festive, the other so trackless, so incapable of form—reflect the older, more formal and intellectual world and the later enthusiastic, romantic world pretty well. What our own models—if you continue to allow us models at all—will reflect, posterity may judge.

4

DANTE'S SIMILES

There is some good poetry in the world, such as that of the Anglo-Saxons, which uses no similes. And there is some poetry, such as that of popular song, which uses about the same amount of simile as ordinary conversation: a woman is as fair as a flower, or a dancer as light as a leaf on a lime-tree. The simile, as a fully-fledged poetic device, falls generally into three classes. The class with which all of us are most familiar, the simile of Tennyson, Arnold, Wordsworth, Milton and Spenser, derives through Virgil from Homer. The second class is that of the unhappily named 'metaphysical' simile. The third class may be called the Dantesque simile, for in this, as in some other matters, 'the phoenix Dante is a vast species alone'. Indeed, Dante's position in the history of simile is an important one. The 'metaphysical' kind may be in some degree indebted to him: and he, in his turn, had read Virgil, if not Homer, and was quite familiar with the Homeric type of simile and sometimes used it. But standing outside the renaissance tradition of imitation, he made this type merely a starting-point for a development of his own. He thus gives us a specimen of what might, but for the Renaissance, have become the traditional usage of high European poetry, but what is, in fact, almost confined to himself.

The Homeric type must, I suppose, descend from a primeval conversational usage of simile. Someone must once have seen, and said, that a warrior went at the enemy like a lion and slaughtered them like sheep, his purpose being simply to convey the triumphant energy of the assault, to make clear his meaning and not to adorn it. In the actual Homeric poems we find similes of this sort. When we are told that Athene directs the arrow away from Menelaus as far as a mother drives away a fly from a sleeping child (*Iliad*, IV, 130), the whole simile taking a line and a half, I do not think this is said for the sake of bringing in a charming picture, for the picture is not elaborated, but simply to make clear the change of direction in the arrow's flight. The simile is really doing what all similes pretend to do—illustrating. And perhaps the same is true of the comparison between Ajax and the donkey in *Iliad*, XI, 558: a comparison ridiculous and bathetic in the extreme if it is taken as decoration, but illustrating to a nicety the situation it describes. But we find elsewhere that Homer has already allowed himself a liberty with similes much like the Roman senator's liberty of speaking beyond the question. Thus the foot-soldiers follow the two Ajantes not merely like a cloud, but like a cloud which a shepherd sees, from a high ridge, coming across a sea on a strong wind, black as pitch, and it makes him shudder and he sets about getting the sheep into a sheltered place (*Iliad*, IV, 275). The cares of the shepherd have nothing whatever to do with the Locrian contingent in Agamemnon's army. This is the 'long-tailed' simile, ancestor of all the similes in our modern poets down to Bridges. I question whether the *vignettes* of early Greek life which it so often admits into Homeric poetry are introduced on any very conscious principle of emotional echo or emotional contrast to the business in hand. It sounds much more as if a poet were interested in the *vignette* for its own sake. I say 'interested' rather than 'charmed', because the matter contained in these Homeric similes is not often very obviously poetical, and must have been even less so to contem-poraries. They are a product of that inexhaustible appetite for things as they are, which fills the Homeric poems so delightfully full of good, detailed butchering, cooking, carpentry, seamanship, laundry-work, house-building, and wood-cutting, and which makes it so hard for Homer to tear himself away from the shield of Achilles because, in the shield, everything he has ever seen and heard can be described. His unjaded zest for all that goes on in the world reminds one of an intelligent small dog's determination to find out what everything smells like and tastes like and whether it is edible; and it bears no small part in producing what Kinglake excellently calls the 'strong, vertical light of Homer's poetry'.*

But whatever Homer's motives in making long-tailed similes may have been, he left ready to Virgil's hand a licence which could be used for the most subtle poetic purposes. It must be allowed that the doctrine of imitation for imitation's sake weighed upon Virgil; unless my memory deceives me, there are some dull wolves and lions in his battle-pieces, mere 'property' animals who turn up there only because they had turned up in Homer. But Virgil at his best uses his similes, as he uses all the rest of the Homeric patrimony, for purposes both new and good. The Homeric Ajax had resembled the Homeric donkey in one respect only: in emotional value they were totally discrepant. But Virgil's Neptune quelling the waves resembles his grave citizen quelling a riot through and through: the picture in the simile is a kind of echo to the picture in the main story, playing out in diverse material the same theme of turbulence and authority, so that Neptune and the citizen each lend dignity to the other and between them the poetry rises to a quality which is quite un-Homeric (*Aeneid*, I, 148). But in other places the function of the simile is precisely the opposite. When Vulcan in the eighth book is compared to the poor sempstress the only point of contact between them is that they are both early risers. In that respect the simile is on all fours with Homer's Ajax and the donkey. But the difference is that whereas in Homer the unlikeness of Ajax to the donkey is made no use of—is just an irrelevant fact in spite of which the simile works—in Virgil the very unlikeness between Vulcan and a poor woman gives the simile its whole value. The pathos and homeliness of the sad, domestic scene are, first of all, a relief and refreshment at this point of the story, and then, when we return from it, by contrast it throws up the mythological figures into vaster proportion. But there is no need to make a complete list of the Virgilian uses of simile. Clearly, when it has reached this stage, the original purpose of illustration has become a mere excuse, though an excuse still necessary to lull the logical faculty to sleep, and the real purpose of simile is to turn epic poetry from a solo to an orchestra in which any theme the poet chooses may be brought to bear on the reader at any moment and for any number of purposes.

Now the later exploitation of this orchestral technique is to be found in Milton, but not in Dante. Why Dante did not develop it in the Miltonic direction is a large question. Partly, I think, he was in some ways a literal-minded man who perhaps never quite got over the notion that an illustration ought to illustrate; and partly, as we shall see, he had other things to do which were at least as good.

Dante's similes may be divided very roughly into four classes, of which the first is purely Virgilian or Homeric and the fourth purely

Dantesque. I put the Virgilian type first partly because it is natural to deal with it first, since we are approaching Dante from Virgil, but also because it is most frequent in the earlier parts of the Comedy. Examples of this class will recur easily to everyone's mind—the comparison of souls to leaves in *Inferno*, III, 112, of the damned lovers to cranes in V, 40, of the prodigal and avaricious to waves dashing against waves in VII, 22, or of the storks in *Paradiso*, XIX, 91. These are all good, straight similes built on the ancient principle; some state or action in the main story is compared to a state or action that can be observed in external nature, whether animate or inanimate. It will be noticed that most of them are, by Virgilian standards, pretty short. One of them, indeed, is longer than its Virgilian model—that of the souls and dead leaves, which Virgil disposed of in a line and a half:

> Quam multa in silvis autumni frigore primo
> Lapsa cadunt folia.   (*Aeneid*, VI, 309)

But it is not longer because Dante is adding logically irrelevant detail in the true ancient manner. He elaborates not to make the picture of the autumn woods more beautiful or interesting in itself, but to make the fall of the leaves, one by one, more accurately illustrative of the souls, dropping down, one after another, into Charon's boat. The result is that where Virgil gives us a dim, but potent, suggestion of the perennial melancholy inherent in autumn and in death, Dante gives us a sharp picture of a particular scene. That is why this simile, though almost certainly Virgilian in origin, really brings us to the borderline between the first and the second of my two classes.

The second class has been familiar to everyone since Macaulay's famous digression on Dante in his essay on Milton. Dante's similes, says Macaulay, 'are the illustrations of a traveller. Unlike those of other poets, and especially of Milton, they are introduced in a plain, business-like manner; not for the sake of any beauty in the objects from which they are drawn...but simply in order to make the meaning of the writer as clear to the reader as it is to himself'.* If this is intended to describe Dante as a whole, it misses a good many important truths, as Macaulay was apt to do: but it hits one nail admirably on the head. And let me digress here for a moment to emphasize his recognition of Dante's similes as the 'illustrations of a traveller'. Much of the strength of the *Comedy* comes from the fact that it is performing a complex function which has since been split up and distributed among several different kinds of book. It is, first, a book of travel into regions which the audience could not reach but in whose existence they had a literal belief, and is thus strictly comparable to Jules Verne's or H. G. Wells's voyages to the Moon. It is, secondly, a poetic expression of the current philosophy of the age, and so comparable to *The Essay on Man* or *The Testament of Beauty*. It is, thirdly, a religious allegory like Bunyan, and fourthly a history of the poet like *The Prelude*—not to mention its political and historical aspects which would set it side by side with the memoirs of some retired statesman. In this complexity of function it does not, of course, stand alone. All old works of art show the same contrast to modern works, and the history of all arts tells the same miserable story of progressive specialization and impoverishment. Thus Tasso is, in some sort, the Milton or Wordsworth of his age—the great serious poet: but he is mediating all his serious poetry through pastoral and chivalrous stories of the kind then generally enjoyed and so writing epic poetry and popular fiction at the same time, and we should get a modern parallel only if we had Ezra Pound and Lord Tweedsmuir rolled into one. In the same way, the great Italian painters are not only the Cézannes and Picassos of their day: they are also the popular illustrators whose work would now appear in Christmas magazines, the people who show you what some famous story really looked like: and, thirdly, they are the great decorators who can make a rich man's dining room look as he wants it to look. So, once more, an opera by Mozart is the ancestor both of the modern serious opera and of the revue. The separation of the low-brow from the high-brow in its present sharpness is a comparatively recent thing: and with the loss of the old unified function all curb on the eccentricity of real artists and the vulgarity of mere entertainers has vanished.

I hope this digression has not seemed too long. It is relevant to our subject because that second kind of Dantesque simile, which Macaulay has characterized, is probably a direct outcome of Dante's determination to satisfy a simple, popular taste which he himself shared to the full—a taste for vivid realism in the description of places none of us has seen but which are believed in, not only as a modern

Christian may believe in Heaven or a modern philosopher in the Absolute, but also, at the same time, as a modern scientist believes in the other side of the moon. The complete subservience of many Dantesque images to this purpose is even startling. When, in the *Inferno*, IX, 76, the souls scattering before the angel—by the way, surely the best angel ever made by a poet—are compared to frogs, we might suspect, since these souls are damned, some emotional con-nexion between them and the slimy and ugly creatures to which they are compared. In fact, however, the connexion is purely pictorial, as we shall see if we think of those blessed, or almost blessed, souls in *Purgatorio*, XXVI, 135 who dart back from the sur-face to the depth of the flame like fish. The poet is anxious simply to set the thing before our eyes, and is, of course, brilliantly successful. Sometimes, in his determination to make us see, he piles simile on simile. The almost transparent spirits whom he saw in the moon (*Paradiso*, III, 10) are said to be just as visible (no more) as the image of one's own face seen in a clear stream so shallow that the bottom, as well as the reflexion, is visible: and to make it clearer, he tells us that this image in the stream is as hard to see as a white pearl against a white forehead: and then, as if even that were not enough, he tells us that he mistook the spirits for reflexions and turned round expecting to find the reality behind him. This is an admirable instance of a kind of vividness which we still sometimes meet in popular prose fiction, but not often in modern poetry. It produces the maximum of illusion, and it will grip a mind to which the irrelevant liveliness of the Homeric simile or the dim suggestion of the Virgilian would mean nothing. A simple example occurs when the bleeding and speaking tree in *Inferno*, XIII, 40 is compared to a green branch in the fire hissing and spluttering. The Virgilian passage on the same subject in the third *Aeneid* is remote and mythological—an echo of old unhappy far-off things. Virgil has hardly asked himself what it would be like, in its immediate impact on the senses, if it happened here and now at the bottom of a man's own garden.

This intense realism naturally leads Dante into what is, perhaps, his favourite type of simile, of which I make my third class. It is rather remarkable that Homer and Virgil hardly ever compare an emotion with an emotion. They compare one material thing or action with another material thing or action—warrior with wolf or words with snowflakes. Or again, they compare an emotion with some external object, the invisible with the visible: a man's mind may bubble like a cauldron. But hardly ever do they say 'Achilles or Aeneas felt at this juncture as you or I, reader, might feel in this or that situation in ordinary life'. If I remember rightly there is only one place in Homer where the content of a simile is psychological, and there, oddly enough, the thing which is compared to the psychological action is not itself psychological but is a movement in space; I am referring to the passage in *Iliad*, XV where Hera, darting from Ida to Olympus, is likened to the thought of a much travelled man darting hither and thither, among the places he remembers (*Iliad*, XV, 78)—and I confess that to my ear this beautiful passage always sounds strangely unlike Homer. Now it might be predicted that a man who was trying to do what Dante is trying to do, would find frequent occasion for the psychological simile: and in fact, one of the chief memories we bear away from a first reading of Dante is the wealth of passages beginning *come colui* in which he tries to make us realize something indirectly by telling us that the feeling it excited was like some feeling we know. Two such similes occur in the first sixty lines of the poem. The poet looks back on his night in the terrible wood as a shipwrecked man looks back on the sea; and a few moments later he is driven back by the beast, feeling like a man who sees his hopes of a great gain suddenly disappointed. These are elementary examples. More notable is the preoccupied expression of the angel in *Inferno*, IX, 101–3, where we get the psychological and the pictorial simile combined, for he looked as a man looks when he is intent on something more important than the people before his eyes. Perhaps the best of all, in its combination of intense realism, deep appropriateness and satiric edge, is that in *Paradiso*, XXXI, 31–40, where Dante, in sight of the celestial rose, a newcomer from Florence to truth and justice, compares his almost stupid wonder to that of the Goths in Rome. But with this we are already on the verge of the fourth class. It will be seen that this simile is on the surface just a very good psychological simile; a man, at such a moment, would, we suppose, feel like that. But there is a deeper significance because the

Goths, like the Florentines, are wicked, or, more generally, because the world of time and sin is to Heaven what the barbaric world was to Rome: not simply that to Dante, at that moment, a possible analogy flashes on the mind as it might flash on the mind of a modern poet, but for two reasons rooted in his whole system of thought; first, because Heaven is essentially the City, as he had learned from the Apocalypse and from St Augustine, and secondly because, for him, the earthly city Rome, which in St Augustine had been almost exclusively the antitype, was predominantly the ectype, the earthly μίμησις, of the heavenly city.

I have been willing thus to glide into the fourth, and most Dantesque, of my classes without an attempt at definition because this fourth type is so difficult to define. The principle is that the things compared are not yoked together by a momentary poetic analogy, like Vulcan and the old woman—an analogy which dis appears the moment you step out of that particular poetic context— but by a profound philosophical analogy or even identity. *Like*, in these similes, is always tending to turn into *same*.

In *Purgatorio*, xv, 64–75 Dante re-states Aristotle's distinction be tween goods that are, and goods that are not, objects of competition. He uses the image of light which gives more of itself in proportion as the body it falls on is more highly polished, with the consequence that the greater the number of such bodies the more light there is for all. There are two things to notice about this simile. In the first place, though it is excellent poetry, it is the sort of simile that could equally well occur in philosophical prose. In the second place, the use of light as a symbol for what is here symbolized is almost a part of nature, not of art, for nothing else will do and it is almost dictated, as Dr Edwyn Bevan has shown,* by the shape of the human mind. God is, or is like, light, not for the purposes of this bit of poetry but for every devotional, philosophical, and theological purpose imaginable within a Christian, or indeed a monotheistic, frame of reference.

In *Purgatorio*, xxv, 22 the relation between the disembodied spirit and the phantasmal or aerial body (which is all the body it has till the resurrection) is expounded by the successive similes of Meleager wasting away as the brand wasted and a mirror image moving in accord with the reality. We should be quite deceived if we thought

Meleager was introduced here for the same emotional purposes as Milton's Proserpine and Orpheus. He is there for the sake of precision. The disembodied soul is not an animal and therefore does not animate its aerial vehicle as we now animate our terrestrial bodies. The relation between them is one of response or correspondence, like that of a mirror image to a real object, or (as Dante says later) of shadow to body: and of such relation the occult sympathies pre-supposed in such witchcrafts as that suffered by Meleager are a very good example. Perhaps this is not, strictly speaking, a simile. Meleager and the brand are not simply *like* the souls and their aerial bodies: they are another *instance* of the same law.

It will be easily seen in what sense Dante's similes are 'meta-physical'. The connexion between the two members is real, onto-logical, intelligible, and the material need not be in itself beautiful or may be even grotesque—as when Time is represented as a tree growing downwards with its roots in a vase which is the Primum Mobile (*Paradiso*, XXVII, 118). And this certainly connects them, in one way, with what literary critics call 'Metaphysical' conceits, meaning the conceits used by Donne and his followers. But there are only two points of contact—first, the difficult and (at first sight) unpoetical nature of the material, and, secondly, the intellectual rather than emotional connexion between this material and the thing compared with it. The spirit in which they are used is not the same in Donne and in Dante. In Donne, the connexion, though intellectual as in Dante, is as momentary, as incapable of life beyond the immediate context, as the connexions in Homer or Virgil. It may be true that Donne cannot court a mistress without bringing in scholastic philo-sophy, law, chemistry, and cosmography. But he has no interest in these things except as toys and does not care in the least what place they have, if any, in the real universe—if, indeed, there is a real universe outside the present emotion. The longer you look at Donne's comparison of the lovers to the compasses, the less alike they will seem, and the more certain you will become that the innumerable differences between them are a more interesting and fruitful field for thought than the single analogy. But in the greatest Dantesque similes, the longer you look the greater the likeness becomes and the more fruitful in thoughts that are interesting as long as you live. This, of course, is no disparagement to Donne: a witty love song, whether salacious or saturnine, is not meant to be chewed over like the great *Comedy* which made its author lean. If I seem to be breaking a butterfly upon a wheel, it is only because I want to avoid a mis⁄ understanding which would hinder our reading both of the great and of the little poet.

For I think it is true that the merit of Dante's metaphysical similes at their greatest is best disengaged in criticism by this contrast between them and the similes of Donne. We speak of a man stirring up a hornet's nest. If there were any corresponding and opposite proverb to describe the stirring of beneficent creatures into delightful and profitable energy by a single act, I should use it here. If bees were associated only with honey and not with stings, I should say that Dante every now and then wakes up a whole beehive, by giving us some image which seems to focus all the rays of his universe at a single point or touching some wire which sets the whole system vibrating in unison. A specimen of this we have already seen in the simile of the Goths of Rome. Another is the complex simile in the first canto of the *Paradiso*, 46–54. Beatrice gazes on the sun. Dante, who was gazing at Beatrice, imitates her and also gazes at the sun. The process whereby Beatrice's gaze produces Dante's is compared to the process of reflexion by which one beam begets a second. And this second beam is in its turn compared to a pilgrim desirous of return. Now here we have, in the first place, the ordinary point of contact, as it might be in Virgil or Homer—namely that the causal relation between Beatrice's action and Dante's was the same as that between a ray of light and a reflexion. But secondly the very thing which Beatrice was doing and Dante was doing after her is itself an instance of response to light, so that the relation between Dante and Beatrice, taken together, and the sun, resembles the same thing which the relation between Dante and Beatrice resembles. And thirdly, inside the simile, the reflected beam is a pilgrim desiring to return home and doing so, which is just what Dante and Beatrice are desiring and doing at the moment. So that Dante and Beatrice are *literaliter* to the sun (and *allegorice* to God) what all reflected beams are to the original source of light and what Dante is *literaliter* to Beatrice and the human understanding *allegorice* to

Wisdom and the whole universe (including beams of light and sources of light) is to the Unmoved Mover. The whole of Christian-Aristotelian theology is thus brought together. Every idea presented to the mind, as in a figure, repeats the subject in a slightly different way, and suggests further and further applications of it. It reverberates from that one imagined moment over all space and time, and further. This is a fairly easy example to treat because it is detachable. Elsewhere the force of the image depends on a context not much less than the whole *Comedy*. Thus, the passage already quoted about Time as a downward growing tree whose roots are in the Primum Mobile is effective by itself, especially to readers who remember Plato's conceit of man's root being in his head. It is much more effective, however, to those who remember the trees in *Purgatorio*, XXII, 133–5 and XXXII, 40–3, both of which had the peculiarity that they were fan-shaped, the branches becoming longer the higher you went. Of course the Time-tree would have looked like that if you didn't know which way it was growing. And all these images are, again, to be taken in connexion with the great vision of *Paradiso*, XXVIII, 55–7 where the universe is turned inside out and the circumference is found to be the centre. But the greatest of all is, fortunately, detachable. I mean the simile which operates the *salita* in *Paradiso*, XVIII, 58. Dante sees Beatrice's beauty increase: he knows from this phenomenon that they have risen to yet another of the spheres—just as (for he is thinking of Aristotle) a man knows that he has increased in virtue when he finds increased pleasure in virtuous acts. But Dante is not content simply to say that he knows they have risen higher: he says they have risen to a *larger* sphere. Notice first the admirable realism of this merely on the Wellsian level, leaving us to imagine the increased vertical distance (the radius) from the increased horizontal spaciousness (the circumference). And notice how this silence about the direct ascent, which gains our credence for the literal adventure, is implicitly excused or explained by the reminder that it is also like that in moral progress. And then notice that this is more than simile, that these material and spatial spheres are really, in Dante's view, and not only poetically, correspondent to progressive degrees of grace and virtue and how exactly the ascent accomplished while looking at Beatrice and recognized only by what is seen in her corresponds to the moral advance accomplished while intent on something outside a man's self; and then think of the increased size of the sphere and how well that symbolizes the new spaciousness of life when a good *habitus* has been acquired. The poetry of such a passage is almost inexhaustible.

One thing will have been noticed in all these examples, and has already been alluded to. They are all the kind of similes which a philosopher could use in prose, and some of them may come from Dante's philosophic sources. If we want to find parallels to them in verse we must go to Lucretius rather than Virgil. Their presence in Dante is to be connected with what I have already said about the multiple function he performs. They are there, in the first place perhaps, because he is writing as the *vulgarisateur* of the best thought of his time—acting as a medieval Jeans or Eddington no less than a medieval Wells, Wordsworth, Milton and Hopkins.

There is, therefore, a sense in which they are less poetical than the similes of Virgil. Virgil's similes are always poetical in the negative or exclusive sense that they could not exist outside poetry. Vulcan and the old woman are united by a thread which would be simply ridiculous in prose. For that reason a man's reaction to Virgil or Milton is in some ways a better test of his poetical aptitude than his reaction to Dante. There is so much besides poetry in Dante that anyone but a fool can enjoy him in some way or other, whereas a poem like *Lycidas* is merely poetry and therefore utterly detestable to the rather large class of critics who have a secret dislike of poetry but get along pretty well by dealing with poets, politics, private lives, and 'delineation of character'. But we must not think that because Virgil is more poetical in the negative sense, he is therefore more poetical *simpliciter*. That is what I call the fallacy of maximum differentiation. A thing is most itself, in the sense of being most recognizable, when it is most unlike everything else: but this does not mean that it is then in its best state. If you want to find out whether whisky is a spirit, you may take some neat whisky and apply a lighted match to it: but if you want a drink you may prefer to mix it with soda water. I do not think the best poetry is that which contains the fewest elements proper to prose. I think the greatest prose and poetry are least unlike each other, and that Dante has proved it. When he is most poetical he says most precisely what he really means in the prose sense of the verb to *mean*.

This has many curious results. It means, among other things, that he is the most translatable of the poets—not, probably, that he entrusts less wealth than others to the music of the words and the *nuance* of the phrase but that he entrusts more than others to the 'plain sense'. It is hard for a translator to ruin the great passages in Dante as every translation ruins Virgil. And it has a still more important and baffling consequence, which I find it hard to express save by a paradox. I think Dante's poetry, on the whole, the greatest of all the poetry I have read: yet when it is at its highest pitch of excellence, I hardly feel that Dante has very much to do. There is a curious feeling that the great poem is writing itself, or at most, that the tiny figure of the poet is merely giving the gentlest guiding touch, here and there, to energies which, for the most part, spontaneously group themselves and perform the delicate evolutions which make up the *Comedy*. When the ascent from one sphere to the next is compared to progress in virtue, the last thing I am inclined to do is to exclaim 'How did he think of that?'; given the metaphysics (which are not his own) and the physics (which are Ptolemy's) and the scheme of an ascent to Heaven (which is from Cicero, Martianus Capella, and Alanus), it seems almost as if this simile must occur, and that the inexhaustible potency of such a passage demanded nothing more from the poet than that he should not meddle nor spoil it, that he should let it take its course and then write down what had happened as well as he could. The very nature of his universe seems to fill his key words— words such as *love, light, up, down, high, low, sun, star* and *earth*—with such a wealth of significance that their mere mention, at those points where the literal narrative requires them, becomes solid poetry 'more gold than gold' without more ado. And so, by a long way round, we come back to Homer. For in his world too, a world very different from Dante's, the mere direct description of what happened: how they launched a ship or went to bed—seems also to turn into poetry, of its own accord. I do not mean for a moment that Homer and Dante are not great poets: rather I draw the conclusion that the highest reach of the whole poetic art turns out to be a kind of abdica⁄ tion, and is attained when the whole image of the world the poet sees has entered so deeply into his mind that henceforth he has only to get himself out of the way, to let the seas roll and the mountains shake their leaves or the light shine and the spheres revolve, and all this will *be* poetry, not things you write poetry about. Dare I confess that after Dante even Shakespeare seems to me a little factitious? It almost sounds as if he were 'just making it up'. But one cannot feel that about Dante even when one has stopped reading him. For whereas Lear's suggestion about smiting flat the thick rotundity of the earth has no existence outside the play, the great passages in Dante have a reality which our prosaic mind, as well as our poetic, can bite upon. They don't fade as you come awake. They can stand daylight. We are made to dream while keeping awake at the same time. Orpheus can look back and take as long a stare as he pleases: this Eurydice will not vanish.

5

IMAGERY IN THE LAST ELEVEN
CANTOS OF DANTE'S 'COMEDY'

This study will doubly lack the charm of novelty: for the method is
not my own and the subject is closely akin to one that I have treated
before in the presence of this society. My previous study was on
Dante's similes. My present theme is narrower in so far as I confine
myself to the last eleven cantos, but wider because it is not limited to
similes. I use the word Imagery to cover Metaphor, even those
metaphors which lurk in a single word and of which neither poet
nor reader need always be explicitly conscious, and even some which
may be suspected of being, in the philological sense, nearly 'dead'.
That is, we include every appeal to the imagined exercise of the five
senses, always excepting those images which are directly represented
as parts of Dante's story and which would appear on the screen if
anyone (which God forbid) made a film of it. Thus *roratelo alquanto*,
'bedew him a little', in XXIV, 8 is a specimen of the Imagery we shall
be studying: but the Empyrean itself, or Beatrice herself, is not. The
method is that which Dr Caroline Spurgeon has applied to Shake‑
speare.* The aim is to surprise the imagination of the poet in its more
secret workings, to disengage that incessant orchestration which
accompanies his drama and which, though it may escape notice
while our attention is fixed on the stage, probably contributes in the
highest degree to the total effect.

From such an examination one might hope to gain in knowledge
of two distinct but very closely connected subjects. On the one hand,
one might hope to learn many things about Dante, and perhaps
some which he did not know himself. We should discover to what
ideas his mind most habitually recurred, his likes and dislikes, his
semi‑conscious associations. Our results would be psychological.
On the other hand, we might hope to learn what these images,
however they came into Dante's mind, do to the mind of the reader

while he reads the poem and how they contribute to its effect. This second knowledge would be aesthetic: we should be learning how poetry operates. In her work on Shakespeare Dr Spurgeon was primarily interested in Shakespeare's psychology. In this paper I am primarily interested in Dante's poetry.

Even if my interests did not lead me away from the psychological to the aesthetic, my ignorance would. One of the most important distinctions for the psychological student would be that between imagery new-minted by the poet and imagery that is traditional. When a man uses traditional imagery he reveals little (I do not say nothing) of his idiosyncrasy. That the *Paradiso* speaks of the Church as the Bride (*sposa*) does not tell us much about Dante. Thus, to take a less obvious instance, in xxiv, 102 we read of miracles as works

a che natura
Non scaldò ferro mai, nè battè incude.

Nature's smithy will appear less important for the psychological student when he remembers that it had appeared in Alanus. But it will not be depreciated for the aesthetic student. Wherever the image came from, it has arrived in our minds, and acts upon us. I do not say that from this second point of view the distinction between traditional and novel loses all importance, and in what follows I shall point out (as far as my knowledge allows me) the traditional images. The more traditional they are, the less they affect us: but if we are sensitive readers their effect will never sink to zero. I shall of course often fail to recognize what is traditional. That error, which would be fatal in a psychological study, will, I trust, be merely an impoverish-ment in mine.

But inevitably in trying to distinguish my approach from Dr Spur-geon's I seem to claim a neater distinction between them than really exists. How the psychological and the aesthetic, not to mention the traditional and the novel, are actually blended can be seen from an example. In xxv, 38 Dante is half way through a *viva voce* examina-tion by three Apostles, when one of them, St James, addresses to him some words of encouragement. As a result

io levai gli occhi ai monti,
Che gl'incurvaron pria col troppo pondo.

There is here a double act of the imagination. First the Apostles are compared to mountains (probably with aid from a traditional allegorization of the psalm that Dante quotes). Then the majesty of the mountains (or of the Apostles, for they are momentarily one) which weighs upon the soul is equated with an actual weight which bends the bearer double. In most minds the aesthetic and the psychological conclusions will follow simultaneously. He makes us go through that imaginative transference whereby a mountain mass seems to crush us with its weight, and at the same moment we perceive that he was a man who looked at mountains in that way. Nor do I think that any reader of the *Comedy* will fail to ask 'Where, in an earlier canto, did we meet the image of intolerable weight?', and then to remember the Proud doubled beneath their loads on the first terrace of Purgatory: and how Dante continued to feel that weight in memory after he had left the first terrace (*Purgatorio*, XIII, 136 *et seq.*) and how he tells us that this was the punishment he feared for himself. That is, he judged Pride to be his besetting sin and therefore attached to its punishment sensations to which his imagination was very alive. But with that, we are fully embarked on psychology. For our study it is enough to notice how immensely venerable the Apostles have become first by the mountain image and then by the image of weight which, as it were, grows from it. No direct praise of their wisdom or sanctity could have made us respect them half so much.

Before beginning my analysis I should perhaps raise one problem. Some of the images which I shall mention are offered to us by a single word and that word comes at the end of a line: in other words the rhyme requires it. How far does that reduce its significance? It is true that Italian is a language rich in rhymes and Italian poets are less likely than English to be driven to an otherwise unsuitable word for the sake of its sound. It is also true that facility in rhyming, far from requiring the genius of Dante, is something which mere practice must infallibly bestow on anyone whatever who has made as many rhyming verses as Dante had done before he wrote the *Paradiso*. There is nothing mysterious about this. There are a certain number of rhyming words in the language as there are a certain number of books in a room: habituation will teach a man quickly to lay his hand on any rhyme as it will enable him to lay his hand on any book in his own library. On the other hand, the number of rhyming words in a language cannot be increased at will, except by comic coinages: and therefore, at a given moment the best poet may be as out of pocket as the worst. The word at the end of one line may be too good to give up, and yet there may be few rhymes to it. It may be worth keeping even at the cost of a slightly strained rhyme lower down. A place where some will suspect this is XXVII, 83–4

> il lito
> Nel qual si fece Europa dolce carco.

I myself do not think *carco* creaks: I leave it to the society. But clearly, the psychologist who was following out the significance in Dante's sensibility of that idea of weight which we have just touched on, would have to decide whether the periphrasis in *fece carco* came in because Dante thought of Europa's ride in terms of weight, or solely for the sake of rhyme, or for both reasons. For the aesthetic analyst the problem is different. What matters to him is not whether a given rhyme was in fact forced or not but whether it seems to the reader to be forced and therefore tends to be unconsciously discounted. For if so, it contributes less to the effect of the poem upon our minds.

The smallest class is images of Smell. Of these I find only two certain instances. I have excluded *inebriate dagli odori* at XXX, 67 because I am not sure whether it is imagery at all in our sense. The flowers are to be imagined as having real scent. Even if it were admitted we should still have only three, and one of them (*odor di lode*, XXX, 126) highly traditional. One might have expected that a poem about Heaven would be full of aromatic imagery. In fact it is there only by implication. There are flowers: and the angels, if I may use the expression, buzz like bees over the eternal Rose in canto XXXI. That makes us supply the olfactory images for ourselves. And what the reader is made to do for himself has a particular importance in literature. Hence the cynical dictum that *chaste* is the most erotically suggestive of all adjectives is not so wide of the mark, and *cool* evokes the idea of summer.

The Sea, in its own right, furnishes only two images. I say 'in its own right' because it is used in XXXI, 73–5

> Da quella region, che più su tuona,
> Occhio mortale alcun tanto non dista,
> Qualunque in mare più giù s'abbandona

but only as a measure of distance, and is again implied in the image of Fortune turning the ship (XXVII, 145). In neither of these does it seem to be used for its own marine quality. In the two instances where it is so used it symbolizes evil: the *mar dell'amor torto* (XXVI, 62) and the *onde* of *cupidigia* (XXVII, 121). Even when we remember the *mar sì crudele* of *Purgatorio*, I, 3, it would be foolish to conclude that Dante habitually thought of the sea with dislike. The beautiful seascapes with which the *Purgatorio* opens would sufficiently prove the contrary. In the eleven cantos which I am studying it happens to appear only as something one has to be pulled out of and is in both places associated with the verb *trarre*. The core of the image is rescue from drowning, and this is no doubt a potent imagination for all humanity. It would not appear in a poem written by a fish.

Another class which contains only two items is that of images drawn from the Student's life, and they will occur at once to everyone's mind: the bachelor preparing for his disputation in XXIV, 46, and the forward pupil in XXV, 64. Both arise so directly out of the narrative that, however humorously and affectionately touched, they hardly amount to imagery in the sense that here concerns us.

Of images that might roughly be said to involve Landscape there are only three—the mountains to which the three Apostles are compared in a passage already mentioned, the sunlight coming through a rift in the clouds on to a flower-bed (XXIII, 79), and the elaborate simile of the cliff mirrored in water at XXX, 109. I must warn you that at this point my classification might be disputed. Garden images in general I have put under another heading because their emphasis is on the garden as such, the place of growth, the gardener's work, not on what might be called 'the view'. The flower-bed of XXIII, 79 comes here because in it the emphasis is on the thing seen, the thing that would interest a painter. So defined, landscapes are rare in our eleven cantos; nor does this surprise me. It is perhaps a characteristic of the Middle Ages rather than of Dante. Medieval poets are interested in trees, flowers, beasts, birds, and rivers: not often, I think, in landscape. When they are, they are usually of Germanic stock.

Four images I have classified as Psychological; by which I mean that in them Dante compares the state of mind which his celestial experiences arouse in him with some state of mind commonly known in our daily life. Three of these four are connected with sleep. In XXIII, 49 Dante compares himself to a man vainly trying to remember a dream; in XXVI, 70, to a man wakened by sudden light, and in XXXIII, 58–60, more interestingly, to one waking from a dream and retaining the emotion it has created but not the dream itself,

> Qual è colui che somniando vede,
> Chè dopo il sogno la passione impressa
> Rimane, e l'altro alla mente non riede,

lines which strikingly anticipate Wordsworth's

> the soul
> Remembering how she felt, but what she felt
> Remembering not.   (*Prelude*, II, 315–17)

Nor of course is the resemblance accidental, for each poet is trying to describe what each thought ineffable.

The five images taken from Childhood show a remarkable uniformity. There is no reference, as we might have expected, to the innocence, the beauty, or the gaiety of children. Four out of the five present the same thing—the infant at the breast: one of these four, the fractious child turning away; three, the child feeding.

We now come to three classes each of which musters seven items. One of them calls, I think, for no comment—the class which I have headed Mythical and Historical, and which a medieval poet would, in English, have called simply 'Historical'. The most striking of them are that in which Dante compares his *stupor* at the sight of the Heavenly City with the *stupor* felt by the Goths on entering Rome, and the unforgettable statement which follows the Beatific Vision,

> Un punto solo m'è maggior letargo,
> Che venticinque secoli alla impresa,
> Che fe' Nettuno ammirar l'ombra d'Argo.
>
> (XXXIII, 94–6)

Notice here the art. Mere numbers—*venticinque secoli*—do nothing in poetry. Even words like *immeasurable* do little. But the Argo puts us at once in the dawn of time, in the old untravelled world when the shadow of a ship was a wonder, and thence causes us to view the whole distance which separates it from the moment of Dante's vision. The others in this class are, I think, such as we should expect to find in any medieval poet.

The second of the seven-membered classes is that of Erotic or Hymeneal imagery. I was at first surprised by the shortness of this list, and if we discount the traditional images in it—*sposa* in XXVII, 40, XXXI, 3, XXXII, 128, and *nozze* in XXX, 135—it reduces itself to three. Each of these is contained in a single word (*donnea* once, and *innamora* twice) and none of them is emphatic. It would seem that the close interconnexion of human with divine love which is the main explicit subject of all Dante's poetry did not twine itself so closely about the stem of his imagination as we might suppose: the proportion between eroticism in the foreground and eroticism in the background is in fact the opposite of what the Freudians would teach us to anticipate. But one must always remember that Dante's thought makes no fusion, much less confusion, of the two loves in the end. The whole ten cantos are climbing to that moment at which the human beloved

> sorrise, e riguardommi;
> Poi si tornò all'eterna fontana. (XXXI, 92–3)

We have still to consider a third class which contains seven images of Weight. If seven seemed a small number of erotic images, seven seems a large number of ponderosities in a poem where we are steadily moving away from the Earth to the rim of the universe. And none of them can strictly be called traditional, though one may be a 'dead' metaphor—the *punti lievi e gravi* of XXIV, 37. The others all suggest weight in more or less painful aspects. His subject itself is

> il ponderoso tema (XXIII, 64)

and weighs on his *òmero mortal*: the mountainous Apostles, as we have seen, bow him with their imagined weight: because of his *mortal pondo* he must, having seen Heaven, return to Earth (XXVII, 64); he is reminded in the Ninth Sphere how, at the Centre, he had seen Satan *da tutti i pesi del mondo costretto* (XXIX, 57): Christ is described as

> Carcar si volle della nostra salma. (XXXII, 114)

I have always felt that no poet—least of all, any poet whose theme is so unearthly as Dante's—has such an admirable solidity. Something of this may be due to these images of downward pressure. Perhaps we believe in his *salita* because we are not in such a world of irresponsible levitation as Shelley dreams of, but in a rigid Ptolemaic universe where all bodies draw to the centre, and only blessed souls and fire move upwards. For in poetry, if not necessarily in theology, Patmore may be right when he says

> Spirit is heavy Nature's wing
> And is not truly anything
> Without the weight.*

We now come to four classes which contain nine images each. Two of these, the Astronomical and the Military, are quite ordinary and deserve no mention in a study on the small scale I intend. But the other two are very curious and unexpected and closely connected with each other. I call the first Clothes and Attire. Now in a poem about Heaven we might expect to hear a good deal about white robes and golden crowns: but that turns out not to be the sort of thing that Dante is thinking of. We have one image of a crown, a garland (XXXII, 70), but the point is the fitness of the particular crown to the colour of the wearer's hair: allegorically, the fitness of each redeemed soul not only to Beatitude in general but to her unique Beatitude. Just before that, at line 57, we have a ring: but the point is that the ring exactly fits the finger. Adaptation, enclosure, fitting in, is the basic idea. The remaining images are based on a different, but related, idea. The whole cosmos is clothed in the Empyrean as in a *real manto* (XXIII, 112). Light travels into the eye *di gonna in gonna* (XXVI, 72), from gown to gown, through petticoat after petticoat. When St Peter circles round Beatrice, singing, his song is such that no verbal shading is adequate *a cotai pieghe*: the music has become the folds of a drapery (XXIV, 26). Adam calls God

> il sommo bene,
> Onde vien la letizia che mi fascia.   (XXVI, 134-5)

The joy wraps him up like a blanket or a bandage. In canto XXX, 50 Dante at the river of light finds himself *fasciato* in the *velo* of its refulgence. It is all, to me, quite unexpected. His mind (and therefore ours while we read) is apparently very sensitive to the experience of putting on, being enfolded, swathed, enveloped.

Closely connected with wrapping up is the idea of tying up, and therefore, inevitably, of untying: and these compose my next, for which I cannot find a better name than Cord images or images of Binding. In XXIV, 30 the prayer of Beatrice 'unties' St Peter from his sphere. The Blessed Virgin is prayed to 'untie' the cloud of mortality from Dante in XXXIII, 31. *Dislegare* is used in both passages. In XXXI, 90 Dante prays that his soul *piacente a te, dal corpo si disnodi*. In XXVI, 49 he is asked what other cords (*altre corde*) besides the intrinsic goodness of the Divine Essence draw him to God. In XXVIII, 11 he speaks of the fair eyes whence Love made the cord to take him. In the same canto (58) Beatrice speaks of the nature of the Hierarchies as a knot (*nodo*) which Dante cannot untie. In the next (XXIX, 36) the union of potentiality and actuality is *tal vime, che giammai non si divima*. In XXXII, 50 a hard problem is a *legame*. Finally, the supreme vision is expressed in the words *La forma universal di questo nodo* (XXXIII, 91). The world of Dante's imagination, like that of Ptolemaic science, is a world of knots, cords, envelopes.

Next come images of Travel and images which may be called Physiological in so far as they refer to parts or operations of the human or animal body. Each category yields eleven examples. The images of travel are not very remarkable. Two of them present the writing of the poem as a journey: it is no voyage for a light craft in XXIII, 67, and in XXIV, 25 the pen has to take a jump like a traveller on a bad road. The Incarnation appears as *il buon cammino* in XXIII, 75: and again in the same canto (105) the Holy Womb is the inn or lodging (*albergo*) of the Saviour. Elsewhere, the travel images illustrate spiritual or intellectual progress. Of the physiological images, some are unremarkable, like the *pelle bianca* and *pelle nera* in XXVII, 136, or the sin of Adam as a wound (*piaga*) in XXXII, 4. Laughter, metaphorically used, comes three times. The strangest and most interesting of all in this class is

Con quanti denti questo amor ti morde.   (XXVI, 51)

We have already seen Love as an affair of cords that draw. It is now something that bites. And there is no question here of erotic love: it is love for the Unmoved Mover that has teeth. Nothing, perhaps,

shows so clearly the difference between Dante's mind and that
of most of the men I know. It is true that *corde* and *morde* rhyme
with one another: but on the lowest view of his metrical skill,
one at least must have been chosen for its own sake—unless we
are to suppose, madly, that both are makeshifts put in to rhyme with
concorde.

We now come to a curiously large class (it numbers twelve) of
what I call images of Emission. The name is unsatisfactory, but I
trust I can make myself understood. They all concern letting out, or
keeping in, opening, or shutting: both psychologically and aestheti-
cally they are in close connexion with the wrappings up and tyings
and untyings which are enumerated under clothes and cords: and
they may also have a subconscious connexion with the physiological.
When Dante speaks, he describes himself as releasing the waters of
his *interno fonte* (XXIV, 57). Later in that canto (100) a proof
uncloses (*dischiude*) the truth. Doves open (*pande*) their love to one
another (XXV, 20). The young pupil is anxious that his knowledge
'unconceal itself' (*si disasconda*, XXV, 66). Images of distillation
occur at XXV, 71 and XXXIII, 62. Hope is a fountain. God is the
Eternal Fountain. In creation He 'opens Himself' (XXIX, 18).
These images form a sort of link between the tyings and untyings
and certain images of rain which we shall meet later.

Equal in number to the Emission images are the images from
Eating and Drinking. Two of them are traditional; or three if *pasciute
di vento* (XXIX, 107) is, as I suppose, proverbial. It is, I think,
characteristic that what is generally compared to food is the satisfaction of spiritual or intellectual desire: if indeed we can, in Dante,
distinguish the two. His joy at beholding the triumph of Christ in
XXIII, 43 is *quelle dape.* He is *pieno* with the drops that distil from an
Epistle of St James (XXV, 77). His curiosity about the River of
Light in XXX, 74 is *tanta sete.*

The last of the smaller classes, with sixteen members, is the
Zoological. Nine out of the sixteen are connected with birds, usually
by the mere suggestion of wings and feathers which symbolize
spiritual movement. Of the beast images the most remarkable is the
homely one of the *animal coperto* in XXVI, 97—presumably a pig in a
cart or a duck in a basket on the way to market.

And now there is a sudden jump in the size of our lists. We come to the Meteorological and Social, each with twenty-four items. My meteorological class consists of images taken from the lower sky and thus distinguished from the Astronomical. Two facts emerge at once. Of the six passages in which the general appearance of the sky is suggested, four deal with early morning (the *dolce stagione* of *Inferno*) and one with either morning or evening. I suspect that this is not peculiar to the eleven cantos we are studying: my memory of the whole *Commedia* is full of sunrises and the early *tremolar della marina*. But balancing these we find a high percentage of images drawn from dew or rain. The rains which will at once occur to the mind of any who has read Dante will probably be either the rain which fell upon the gluttonous or the fiery rain under which Brunetto Latini walked. But in the *Paradiso* the characteristic associations of rain are good ones: *La larga ploia Dello Spirito Santo* (XXIV, 91–2): the drops from the Epistle of St James of which Dante is so full that he can now shed them upon others (XXV, 77): the *virtù* which the Divine Mind *piove*, rains down upon the spheres (XXVII, 111): the *piover* of *allegrezza* which pours over Mary in XXXII, 88. There is, indeed, only one exception: the incessant rain which destroys the budding promise of human will in XXVII, 125. I believe these images of good rain to be very important. The descent of the fructifying rain from heaven to earth is in a sense the symbol of the Ptolemaic universe in which power is always transmitted downwards. In a larger sense it symbolizes any Agape religion, any system in which man (and nature) is the patient, and Grace the agent. And more obviously it has its hymeneal associations as the visible act of the ἱερὸς γάμος of sky and soil: associations made explicit by Spenser when

> angry *Jove* an hideous storme of raine
> Did poure into his Lemans lap.*

Under the heading of Social images I have included some which might rather be called Ecclesiastical or even Religious. The common bond is that they all concern either institutions or things seen in places where human beings are together. Thus the pilgrim in XXXI, 103 who gazes at the Veronica is for me a social image, because Dante is not thinking how he or we should feel in his place, but observing the stranger's behaviour as if he had seen him in a crowd. The pilgrim has come 'perhaps from Croazia' to see 'our Veronica'. The social images, thus defined, have one very remarkable charac' teristic. We know that Dante was an exile and an embittered politician: we might expect to find his social images full of satire. In reality they are without exception either happy and favourable or (more rarely) neutral. If these were our only evidence we should infer that we were reading the work of a man at complete harmony with his fellows. Many of them are concerned, as Charles Williams would have delighted to note, with the idea of the City or the Empire. Saints in bliss become Barons or *patrici*: God is the *imperadore*, Heaven His *basilica* or *aula*, sometimes a *convento* or *consistorio*, or a *città*. The poem is told that now it must dance (XXIII, 62). The blessed dance like a damsel who rises and enters the ball to do honour to a bride (XXV, 103). Beatrice, speaking of Papal corruption, works like a *donna onesta* who has heard of another's fault. There are images from a masquerade (XXX, 91) and a charming picture of a master embracing a servant who has brought good news (XXIV, 148). There is a chessboard, a salutation, a bride *tacita ed immota*, and a temple. The images in themselves call for no comment: what strikes us is their frequency and cheerfulness. We have all read books which place philanthropic and optimistic sentiments in the foreground, but betray, as it were in odd corners, how few people the author likes. In Dante the tension is reversed. Terrible denunciations are hurled at persons and abuses; but at the roots of his mind we discover an easy and unemphasized enjoyment of 'towered cities' and the 'busy hum of men'. He is not an oddity or a misfit; hence springs some at least of the security and exhilaration with which we read his severe and in some ways appalling poem.

The images of Light and Heat number twenty-five, of which we may discount seven as traditional. They are mostly references to the 'fire' of love, so common in the poets that we do not strongly notice them. Another subsection in this class consists of what may be called variations on the scriptural theme that God is light. These, no doubt, could also be called traditional; but they are so close to the internal narrative, so frequent, and often so strongly imagined, that I think they affect us as if they were new. They are also inevitable in

any monotheistic system, and especially in that of medieval Christendom. Thus when we read of the supreme *Essenza*

> Che ciascun ben che fuor di lei si trova
> Altro non è ch'un lume di suo raggio   (XXVI, 32–3)

we not only understand the doctrine but see the picture. The same
is true, if I may judge by my own experience, of the many images
from reflected light: as of the

> verace speglio
> Che fa di sè pareglio all'altre cose,
> E nulla face lui di sè pareglio—   (XXVI, 106–8)

which makes equally good sense and good poetry whichever
reading we adopt: in XXIX, 25 (*E come in vetro* etc.) the emphasis is
on the speed of reflexion: in line 144 of the same canto, on the
multiplicity of mirrors and, in contrast, the unity of the light which
they all reflect. But I will not enumerate further, for the importance
and relevance of these images, though great, is very obvious and will
have escaped no reader of Dante.

What concerns us more is to notice that side by side with these
twenty-five images of heat and light we have also twenty-five that
may be called Horticultural or Agricultural. The poetry of the
Paradiso is as full of roots and leaves and growth as it is of lights—
and far fuller of both than of jewels or crowns. It is worth noticing
that very few of these images are merely images of visible beauty.
Dante looks at vegetation with the eyes of a gardener more often than
with those of a tourist: he is interested in becoming, in process. The
nearest we get to the merely visual is in XXIII, 70 where the assembly
of the blessed is a fair garden; but then it is a garden 'blossoming
under the rays of Christ'—one feels that light drawing up those
flowers. The Blessed Virgin is compared to roses and lilies: but lilies
whose smell drew the Saviour on His *buon cammino* (*ibid.* 75).
Leaves are not mentioned for their greenness. Once they illustrate
serial progression when St Peter draws Dante *di ramo in ramo* to the
ultime fronde—that is, takes him systematically through the subject of
Faith (XXIV, 115). Elsewhere the saints come like leaves in the
garden of the Eternal Gardener (XXVI, 64): or, with a faint suggestion of Homer, human customs succeed one another like leaves

(XXVI, 136). Ripeness occurs thrice. Dante has to grow ripe for enduring the rays of the three great Apostles (XXV, 36): Adam, the man who had never been a child, is as *Pomo che maturo solo prodotto fosti* (XXVI, 91): it is explained in canto XXX that the river and the topazes that plunge into it and the laughter of the fields are only *ombriferi prefazii* of the truth—not that Dante is looking at unripe (*acerbe*) or preliminary things but that his vision is still immature. The whole life of the plant, seed, root, flower, and fruit comes in. Verbs like *seminare, inflorare, germogliare, germinare* provide an earthy ground-bass to the poetry of the higher heavens. The blessed are the

> frutto
> Ricolto del girar di queste spere. (XXIII, 20–1)

Toser is surely wrong in his comment that Dante here refers to the activity of stellar and planetary influence in producing the characters and lives of men. Wholesale astrology was simply the current medieval and renaissance form of determinism: only a modified astrology was possible to a Christian poet, and Dante in *Purgatorio*, XVI had put into the mouth of Marco Lombardo the orthodox view that 'constellation' leaves room for free will and that if not *sapiens* yet certainly *sanctus dominabitur astris*—

> A maggior forza ed a miglior natura
> Liberi soggiacete, e quella cria
> La mente in voi, che il ciel non ha in sua cura.
> (*Purgatorio*, XVI, 79–81)

To describe the saints in glory as the 'fruit' of 'constellation' would be to attribute to the lower 'nature', the created universe, that which is the gift of the *miglior natura* or Grace, and which even the unfallen Adam could not have achieved in his mere nature. In what sense, then, can the heavenly harvest be attributed to the spheres? I think Dante is here regarding them primarily as the embodiments of Time, and indeed almost identifying them with Time itself, having read in Chalcidius's version of the *Timaeus* (38 B), *tempus vero caelo aequaevum est ut una orta una dissolvantur*. The gathering of the Church Triumphant in Heaven is the final cause of the whole historical process and may thus be called the fruit of Time, or of the Spheres. If so, this image is closely linked with another which I have reserved to the last because it seems to me to combine the grotesque and the sublime more triumphantly than any other poetical image I have met. At the end of canto XXVII (118) the Ninth Sphere is compared to a flower pot and Dante bidden to observe

> come il tempo tenga in cotal testo
> Le sue radici e negli altri le fronde.

I must confess that all the Miltonic sublimities seem to me heavy and superficial things compared with this astonishing vision which reveals our race crawling among the topmost (or, if you will, the lowest) leaves of the great time-tree that grows head-downward from the Ninth Heaven. Not even from that crystalline soil but from a vase.

Only one category now remains, and it, with its nine and twenty images, has an easy lead. It would be interesting to know how many have guessed it. My title for it is 'Technical': it is imagery drawn from the arts, crafts, manufactures, and skilled occupations of men: from painting, musical instruments, seals and sealing-wax, clocks, thread, money in a purse, hammer and anvil, rowing, riddling with a sieve, archery at the butts, the cares of the artist, the jeweller, the geometrician and the astronomer observing an eclipse, and finally (on the very eve of the ineffable vision) a prudent reminder that a good tailor cuts his coat according to his cloth. So closely does Dante observe on the poetical level the rule given for the spiritual life in the *Imitation—summum non stat sine infimo* (II, x, 4).

Apart from its other defects, this little analysis suffers from dealing with only eleven cantos. I have no idea how my statistics would be altered if I had time to extend them to the whole *Comedy*. Yet even from these cantos something seems to emerge. Images whose only claim is their beauty are conspicuously rare. What would seem at first sight to be the prosaic is neither wooed nor avoided. What runs through many of my lists is the suggestion of a curious intensity of sensibility in directions where modern sensibility is, I believe, much weaker: the intensity which compares the gratification of curiosity to an infant sucking at the breast, which can feel *fasciato*, muffled or wrapped up, in joy, or in light, which feels love pulling with ropes or biting with teeth, which can see spiritual or even local transitions

as knots tied or untied. It is this strain which makes me uncertain of
the growing belief that if a Dante speaks of a professedly allegorical
lady in terms of violent passion we may conclude that she was not
wholly allegorical. That would be so with most of us: with Dante,
perhaps less. That is one aspect of his imagery: the curiousness, the
almost sensuous intensity about things not sensuous. But side by
side with that, we find other characteristics: Dante in the garden, and
Dante in the streets, his feeling for the silent growing life, and his
cheerful, spontaneous interest in the state and courtesies, the trades
and skills, of men. It is, perhaps, this continual reference both to
the quiet, moistened earth and to the resonant pavements, workshops,
and floors, which support and make convincing his invention of a
heaven which, in the obvious sense, makes very few concessions to
the natural man.

6

DANTE'S STATIUS

The stranger who joined Virgil and Dante on the fifth *cornice* of Purgatory presently revealed himself to be Statius.[1] He told them that Virgil had been his master in poetry,[2] that his besetting sin had been prodigality,[3] that his thoughts had been first turned to Christianity by Eclogue IV (5–7)[4] and that he had been baptized before he wrote the *Thebaid*.[5] All this may have been regarded by Dante as a *bella menzogna*. If Statius was to appear at that point he would have to have been baptized; and since Dante wanted us to like him there was good reason for attributing to him the most amiable of the vices. On the other hand Statius was a poet very well known in Dante's time. He was not a mere name, a *Simonide* or *Agatone*,[6] whom one could make what one pleased of. Dante would probably have expected his more learned readers to compare the character he gave of Statius with that which they might infer from their own copies of the *Thebaid*. It is therefore reasonable to suppose either that he found in the poem elements which convinced him that Statius was not far from the Christian faith, or else that he thought it could be so interpreted with plausibility enough for his purpose.

Besides a hidden Christianity Dante attributes to Statius an intense gratitude to Virgil, and the sin of prodigality. The first, he has certainly got out of the text. The discipleship of Statius to his great predecessor is obvious, and his humble reverence is expressed in the concluding lines of his poem.[7] The prodigality is harder to explain. I have sometimes entertained the fancy—it is little more—that the origin might be Juvenal, VII, 82–7. Statius is there presented as one whose poem, when recited, *fregit subsellia* (I suppose this means 'brought the house down'), but who still doesn't know where his next meal is to come from (*esurit*). Juvenal's point, I take it, is that epic poetry, like virtue, *laudatur et alget*: fortune does not

---

[1] *Purg.* XXI, 91. [2] *Ibid.* 94 *seq.* [3] *Ibid.* XXII, 34 *seq.*
[4] *Ibid.* 64 *seq.* [5] *Ibid.* 88 *seq.* [6] *Ibid.* 107.
[7] *Theb.* XII, 816 *seq.*

follow fame. It is just conceivable that some medieval commentator, missing that point, and assuming that largesse and patronage would result from the successful recitation, drew the conclusion that, if Statius hungered still, he must have been a foolish spender.

This, however, is the merest conjecture. I believe we are on surer ground when we examine the poem as a whole for traits which might have seemed to Dante Christian or closely sub-Christian. We must remember of course that he would have read both Lucan and Statius more seriously than most do now. The fatal words 'silver' and 'rhetoric' have done harm and modern ears are deaf. Perhaps Dante was here wiser than we. I think Lucan, Statius and the tragedies of Seneca are to be taken as if they really had something to say. I think the horrors they relate are a vehicle whereby to express their sincere reaction to the terrible period in which they lived. No honest man's comment on that age could be made in plain terms. History and satire could safely deal only with those criminals who were already dead or disgraced; and even then, the satire had little commerce with laughter; it was tragic satire (*satira sumente cothurnum*).[1] But the enormities of history and myth provided a medium through which men could still express their horror, amazement and despair. At all events, whether this was how it came about or not, I think the *Thebaid* itself will explain why Dante put Statius in Purgatory and left Virgil in Limbo. The lesser poem does in fact contain more that a Christian can accept and less that he need reject.

That he was steeped in the text of the *Thebaid* is obvious. Ugolino gnaws for ever the head of Ruggieri[2] as Tydeus for ever gnaws that of Melanippus.[3] The two-headed flame in which Ulysses and Diomede are tormented[4] reminds Dante of the *diviso vertice flammae* on the pyre of Eteocles and Polynices.[5] Every major character in the poem of Statius finds a mention in the *Comedy*: Amphiaraus, Antigone, Argia, Capaneus, Deipyle, Eriphyle, Hypsipyle, Ismene, Jocasta, Manto, Oedipus, Teiresias and Tydeus. In the *Convivio*[6] three examples are taken from *Stazio, lo dolce poeta*. A re-examination of the *Thebaid* may show what Dante thought he found, or even what he really found, in it.

[1] Juvenal, VI, 634. [2] *Inf.* XXXII, 127 *seq.* [3] *Theb.* XI, 87.
[4] *Inf.* XXVI, 52 *seq.* [5] *Theb.* XII, 431. [6] IV, XXV.

He would have found, first of all, something that would, in his day, have appeared modern, but not too modern, an image with which he was familiar: the great figure of *Natura*. Something that might almost be called an accident—the loss of Plato's other works and the partial survival of the *Timaeus* (*interprete Chalcidio*)—had concentrated attention on the cosmogonic elements in Plato. Nature, not made much of in the *Timaeus* itself, had been personified on a large scale by Bernardus Silvestris and after him by Alanus ab Insulis; thence to pass, with much enrichment, into the work of Jean de Meung. Dante did not know Lucretius. Of the ancients Statius would have given him the fullest anticipations of this medieval *Natura*. He would have found her there as *princeps* and *creatrix*.[1] He would have found her again as *princeps*, appealed to almost against the heathen gods—*heu princeps Natura! Ubi numina?*[2]— and acclaimed as *ducem* in what is almost the Pagan equivalent of a Crusade.[3] This of course is not explicitly Christian: if we press *creatrix* it is anti-Christian. But it is nearer the medieval picture of the world than most of Virgil.

What would have mattered more, I think, would have been the Statian conception of man. There are, to be sure, ethical emphases in Statius to which he would hardly have responded. After opening his poem with some pitiful flattery of Domitian (the detested *corvée* to which all poets were then subject) Statius reimburses himself by praising defiance of kings,[4] vividly painting the degradation which boundless power works in its possessor,[5] and rendering courtiers contemptible.[6] This was not much in Dante's line perhaps. But he would also have found in Statius's Stoic doctrine of human brother-hood something he must accept—

> Mitto genus, clarosque patres: hominum, inclite Theseu,
> Sanguis erant, homines. (XII, 555–6)

And still more, in the darker traits of Statius's anthropology, he would have found perhaps the only ancient authority he knew which seemed to endorse the doctrine of the Fall. For Statius the human race are so evil that it would be better if Earth had never been

---

[1] *Theb.* XI, 466.   [2] *Ibid.* XII, 561.   [3] *Ibid.* 645.
[4] *Ibid.* III, 99 *seq.*   [5] *Ibid.* XI, 665–9, 755.   [6] *Ibid.* 686.

re-peopled after the deluge—*Quam bene post Pyrrham tellus pontusque vacabant.*[1] In Hades the accursed souls far outnumber the *pii.*[2] The very bent or nature of man is inexhaustibly evil—*nec exsaturabile Diris ingenium mortale.*[3] We are as miserable as we are wicked, for care follows sin;[4] and as silly as we are miserable—if you told us there were two suns in the sky we should not only believe you but believe we had seen them ourselves.[5] One notable instance of our continual folly and sin is the art of divination. On this Statius and Dante are fully agreed:

> unde iste per orbem
> Primus venturi miseris animantibus aeger
> Crevit amor?...
>
> ...quid crastina volveret aetas
> Scire nefas homini. Nos pravum et flebile vulgus
> Scrutari penitus superos: hinc pallor et irae,
> Hinc scelus insidiaeque et nulla modestia voti.[6]

Accordingly the typical sinners in this kind whom we meet in *Inferno*, xx include Amphiaraus,[7] Teiresias,[8] and Manto,[9] all from the *Thebaid.*

The over-all picture of humanity in Statius is indeed darker than that we get from the *Comedy*, but they are logically consistent. Exceptional mercies might raise a Trajan or a Rhipeus to heaven,[10] or Cato to an official position on the staff of Purgatory;[11] and the Divine purpose might work through the imperial history of Rome. But in general the Pagan world was for Dante a world of the damned; almost the first thing we are told about Hell is that we shall there meet the *antichi spiriti.*[12] Statius would seem to him to have understood better than Virgil the world both had lived in.

Dante would also have found in the *Thebaid* a recognition that humanity, bad in itself, is further assisted in evil by diabolical agents. Preternatural help is never sought in vain by those who seek it for bad purposes. Such help, like the 'murdering ministers' who tend on Lady Macbeth's thoughts, comes almost before it is asked—

[1] *Ibid.* 469. [2] *Ibid.* IV, 484. [3] *Ibid.* I, 214–15.
[4] *Ibid.* III, 4. [5] *Ibid.* VII, 114. [6] *Ibid.* III, 551–65.
[7] *Ibid.* 460–98. [8] *Ibid.* IV, 406 *seq.* [9] *Ibid.* 463, 518.
[10] *Par.* XX, 45, 68. [11] *Purg.* I. [12] *Inf.* I, 116.

Stygiaeque... ante preces venere deae.[1] Curses are always granted: *justo magis exaudita.*[2] Those rulers whom the dead will meet below regard them with impartial malice, and the king of ghosts is hostile to ghosts as such—*nil hominum miserans, iratusque omnibus umbris.*[3] All this is by no means peculiar to Statius among the ancients, but it is in him, perhaps, unusually stressed. It would of course fit in with Dante's picture of the universe.

But even more significant than the fiends of Statius are his gods. There are inconsistencies in his treatment of them to which I shall have to return; but more often than not his poem might well have seemed to be the work of one who already knew that the Olympians were really devils. In an important passage they can be lumped together with the human criminals: *immitesque deos regemque cruentum.*[4] Hypsipyle, I am sure with the poet's sympathy, calls them *sontes.*[5] A few lines later, in his own person, he says ironically *Ecce fides superum.*[6] Jupiter, in a passage unintentionally comic, refers to the *reticenda deorum crimina.*[7] As part of the scenery of Hades, Styx flows by bearing witness to the perjuries of the gods.[8] At the very climax of the poem *Pietas*, that 'rebel passion', protests that she was born *saevis animantum ac saepe deorum obstaturam animis.*[9] But perhaps the most striking instance is the scene between Coroebus and Apollo in Book I. Apollo has seduced the daughter of Crotopus. The girl bears a child which she successfully hides till it is unfortunately killed by dogs. Her grief betrays the secret to her father who kills her in a fit of parental virtue. Apollo at this stage (*sero memor thalami*, as Statius justifiably observes)[10] interests himself to the extent of producing a monster which goes about the country killing babies until it is itself killed by Coroebus. Apollo retorts with a pestilence which will not cease unless the culprit gives himself up. Coroebus at once visits the god in his temple. 'I'm not here as a suppliant', he says. '*Pietas* and *conscia virtus* are my incentives. I did kill your monster. Are brutes like that so dear to you gods? Is the death of men a *jactura vilior*? Very well. Don't let all Argos suffer. Kill me.' Apollo was completely overawed. *Reverentia* seized him. He was

---

[1] *Theb.* V, 156–7.   [2] *Ibid.* XI, 616.   [3] *Ibid.* VIII, 23.
[4] *Ibid.* XII, 184.   [5] *Ibid.* V, 610.   [6] *Ibid.* 650.
[7] *Ibid.* I, 230–1.   [8] *Ibid.* VIII, 30.   [9] *Ibid.* XI, 465–6.   [10] *Ibid.* I, 596.

stupefactus[1] ('stupidly good' for a moment like that later Devil in Milton), and

tristemque viro submissus honorem

Largitur vitae.   (I, 663–4)

Coroebus leaves the temple *exoratus*, not having appeased the god but having been himself appeased, having accepted, from his superior position, the submissive god's tender of *tristis vita*. Of course, if Apollo were to be a devil in the strict Christian definition he would not have felt *reverentia* (though he might have been *stupefactus*). But the unambiguous inferiority of Olympian to mortal has been proclaimed.

Over against these diabolic, or nearly diabolic, gods stand the great ethical personifications, *Virtus*,[2] *Pietas*[3] and *Clementia*.[4] If the first two are the more active, the third is given the most eloquent praise. The passage is one in which Dante might well be pardoned if he found Christian feeling.

I have already warned the reader that the theology (so to call it) of Statius is not fully consistent; but its very inconsistencies bring it, or seem to bring it, closer to Christianity. The great exception among his Olympians is, as we should expect, Jupiter. This Jupiter, if I mistake not, comes far closer than that of the *Aeneid* to the god of strict monotheism, the transcendent Creator. It would not, of course, have shocked or surprised Dante if Statius should speak of the true God under the Pagan name. He does so himself;[5] he for poetic adornment, why not Statius because he dared not speak plainly? For this Jove is clearly the Creator of the universe, *sator astrorum*.[6] A *grave et immutabile pondus* belongs to his words and the Fates follow his voice[7] (though elsewhere, I must admit, he himself says *immoto deducimur orbe Fatorum*).[8] Though the vindicator of the moral order, he is also a god who delights to show mercy—

Nam cui tanta quies irarum aut sanguinis usus
Parcior humani? Videt axis et ista per aevom
Mecum aeterna domus, quotiens jam torta reponam
Fulmina, quam rarus terris hic imperet ignis.   (VII, 199–202)

---

[1] *Ibid.* 643–65.   [2] *Ibid.* x, 632 *seq.*   [3] *Ibid.* XI, 457 *seq.*
[4] *Ibid.* XII, 481 *seq.*   [5] *Purg.* VI, 118.   [6] *Theb.* III, 218.
[7] *Ibid.* I, 212–13.   [8] *Ibid.* VII, 197–8.

99

Perhaps the most monotheistic touch of all (it almost reminds one of Hebrews vi. 13) is his oath; he swears not only, in the traditional manner, by Styx but by *arcem hanc aeternam mentis sacraria nostrae*.[1]

It would also (and justly) have impressed Dante that the soul of a good man can be wafted to the throne of this Jupiter at the moment of death. The apotheosis of certain heroes in Pagan story is, no doubt, familiar, but it is a rather different conception. The apotheosis of Hercules in Ovid is due not only to his great deeds but to his divine origin; there are in fact two natures in Hercules,

> Nec nisi materna Vulcanum parte potentem
> Sentiet: aeternum est a me quod traxit et expers
> Atque immune necis.[2]

As the burning goes on, Hercules looks less and less like Alcmena and more and more like Jove.[3] He is not so much deified after death as saved from death by his semi-deity—*parte sui meliore viget*—and snatched to heaven in a celestial chariot. The Christian parallels[4] here would be Incarnation (as regards his nature) and Assumption (as regards his destiny). The death of Menoeceus is represented in terms far closer to Christian hope. It is in fact strangely like *Morz est Rollant, Deus en ad l'anme es cels*.[5] As his body reached the ground, *spiritus olim ante Jovem*,[6] his soul already, long since, stood before the throne.

In one passage (possibly more) by another inconsistency 'The gods' are clearly referred to as good powers. This inconsistency is unimportant, for the god really concerned is not an Olympian but the personification *Virtus*. The passage is, however, of great interest for it brings us as near as anything I know in Pagan poetry to something like a doctrine of Grace. Menoeceus is just about to incur certain death for the sake of Thebes. What is the impulse which drives and enables men to do such deeds? Already in the *Aeneid* a character had raised this question, suggested two alternative answers and refused to decide between them:

> Dine hunc ardorem mentibus addunt,
> Euryale, an sua cuique deus fit dira cupido?[7]

---

[1] *Theb.* III, 246.   [2] *Metam.* IX, 251–3.   [3] *Ibid.* 265–6.
[4] Of course very imperfect.   [5] *Chanson de Roland*, 2397.
[6] *Theb.* X, 781–2.   [7] *Aen.* IX, 184–5.

That is typically Pagan in its doubt whether the *cupido* is not *dira*, its fundamental, though reverent, suspicion. (Hope itself is usually a dangerous thing before St Paul, and ἐλπίς in ancient writers would often be best translated 'wishful thinking'.) Statius knew his *Aeneid* very well indeed. He must have known exactly what he was doing when, speaking in his own person about Menoeceus, he answered precisely this question with no shadow of doubt—

> neque enim haec absentibus umquam
> Mens homini transmissa deis.   (x, 629–30)

The human race is bad, yet examples of high virtue occur. When they do, some superhuman influence has always been at work. *Haec mens*—this 'frame', as our ancestors called it—is never merely human and natural.

Finally, Dante would have found in the *Thebaid* an attitude to the sexual life which he would not easily have found in any other ancient text. He had alluded in the *Convivio*[1] to the extreme bashful‑ness of Argia and Deipyle, of course with approval.[2] That passage does not go beyond the traditional Pagan picture of maidenly behaviour. But the extreme embarrassment with which Ismene relates her dream in Book VIII, the assurance that she would never think about that sort of thing even if there weren't a war on, is a little remarkable,[3] and the degree of *pudor* which she displays to her unhappy lover on his deathbed is, not unjustly, described by the poet himself as *saevus*.[4] Stranger still, to me, are the following. Or Argia and Deipyle, just before their wedding, we are told

> tacite subit ille supremus
> Virginitatis amor, primaeque modestia *culpae*
> Confundit vultus.   (II, 232–4)

Is the act, then, even within marriage, a *culpa*? Not many lines later we learn how Argive brides, with certain ceremonies,

> Virgineas libare comas primosque solebant
> *Excusare* toros.   (II, 255–6)

Did marriage, then, need to be excused? It may be that the resemblance between Statius and some medieval moralists at this point is a mere accident. He may be thinking of some purely ritual

---

[1] *Conv.* IV, xxv.   [2] *Theb.* I, 536 *seq.*   [3] *Ibid.* VIII, 626 *seq.*   [4] *Ibid.* 645.

obligation to Diana and Pallas, and *culpa* and *excusatio* may carry no meaning which we should recognize as ethical. But Dante would inevitably have read his words in a different spirit. Statius would seem to him to have written as a medieval moral theologian of the more rigorous type.

It seems to me therefore that Dante had very good grounds for feigning (if he feigned) and no contemptible grounds for believing (if he believed) that Statius had known the truth: or, at the very least, that his ignorance, if presented with the truth, would have been by no means invincible. Even the modern reader (if he does not put down everything in Statius to 'rhetoric') will find in him impressive evidence of the degree to which a Roman of his age, helped by Stoicism, could anticipate some elements of Christianity. It was not perverse of Dante to save Statius and damn Virgil; especially as it never led him to forget for a moment that Virgil is far the greater poet, and even, as Statius was not, a prophet. He was the lantern-bearer,[1] but it was Statius who profited by the lantern's light.

[1] *Purg.* XXII, 67–9.

7

THE 'MORTE DARTHUR'

It was on 23 July 1934 that Mr W. F. Oakeshott made in the library of Winchester College the most startling literary discovery of the century—a manuscript of Malory's Arthurian romances roughly contemporary with Caxton's print and independent of it. By so doing he secured something not unlike immortality for his name and also reduced the study of Malory to a state of suspense for thirteen years. During that period nothing could be said about the *Morte Darthur* without a reservation; no one knew what the Winchester manuscript, when once it was published, might refute or confirm. Professor Vinaver's three-volume *Works of Sir Thomas Malory* (the title, as we shall see, is significant) ends this uneasy interim and puts all previous work on this subject out of date. It has been worth waiting for. It is a very great work and a work which hardly any other man in England was qualified to perform.[1]

It is not, of course, to be expected that all Professor Vinaver's views will finally win the acceptance of scholars. At the very threshold some will dispute the argument on which his chronology of Malory's literary career is based. All turns on an 'analogy' which Professor Vinaver pronounces 'obvious' between Arthur's fight with the giant at St Michael's Mount and Sir Marhaute's fight with a giant Taulard. (The passages are Caxton, v, 5 and iv, 25; Vinaver, p. 128 and p. 175.) Yet the analogy will escape some. Even if we allow that Arthur's giant sat between fir-trees and Taulard under a 'tre of hooly', it does not seem to be very strong; but if, as the whole account of Arthur's combat suggests, the 'two fyrys' were not fir-trees at all but fires, it may be thought to amount to very little. But there will be long debate between specialists before this and many like questions are decided. In the meantime, however, not only

---

[1] *The Works of Sir Thomas Malory*, edited by Eugene Vinaver, in three volumes (Oxford: Clarendon Press, 1947).

specialists but a far larger circle of those who have known and loved Caxton's text from boyhood are anxious to learn how Malory emerges from this new crisis in his fame. How far must we revise our conception of the *Morte Darthur* and its author? For it is no specialist's book; it is Milton's book, Tennyson's book, Morris's book, a sacred and central possession of all who speak the English tongue.

The most embarrassing things which Professor Vinaver has to tell us (some of them had got abroad before the present edition) concern Malory himself; the most embarrassing, that is, for those who love the *Morte* and would wish to respect its author. To others, to those who love to see old altars defaced, Malory's life offers a rich banquet. Wordsworth's French daughter was a mere kickshaw in comparison. Malory appears to have been convicted of cattle-lifting, theft, extortion, sacrilegious robbery, attempted murder and rape. At first sight it is a thing not only to shock our sensibilities but to puzzle our intellects, and it is not surprising that some would cut the knot by assuming that this black record belongs not to our Malory but to another man of the same name. Professor Vinaver takes a different line. He tries to reconcile the book with the man by arguing that the book is less noble than has usually been supposed, and even that the idea of its 'nobility' is largely derived from Caxton's preface.

It all depends on what is meant by nobility. The predominant ethical tone of Malory's work is certainly not the bourgeois, still less the proletarian, morality of our own day. And, on its own showing, it is not the Christian rule of life; all the chief characters end as penitents. It is aristocratic. It does not forbid homicide provided it is done in clean battle. It does not demand chastity, though it highly honours lifelong fidelity to the chosen mistress. Though it admires mercy it allows private war and the vendetta. And it has no respect at all for property or for laws as such. It is distinguished from heroic morality by its insistence on humility. It can be very accurately called nobility if the noble is defined as the opposite of the vulgar. It does not condemn all whom we would now call 'criminals'; its displeasure is primarily for the cad. It is magnificently summed up in Sir Ector's final lament, which, so far as we know, is Malory's own invention: 'Thou was the mekest man and the jentyllest that ever ete in halle emonge ladyes and thou were the sternest knyght to thy mortal foe that ever put spere in the rest.' There is the real, and indispensable, contribution of chivalry to ethics.*

In this sense, then, there is really no question about the 'nobility' of the *Morte*. But how different such nobility may be from the virtues of the law-abiding citizen will appear if we imagine the life of Sir Tristram as it would be presented to us by King Mark's solicitors.

It is from the lawyers that we get Malory's life. In the courts of that age evidence was not very scientifically sifted, and accusers 'laid it on thick'. Every county was the scene of family feuds exploiting, and exploited by, the larger dynastic struggle. 'Crimes' and criminal proceedings alike were often primarily moves in private war. There is no need to suppose that Malory did all the things of which he was convicted: much less that those which he did do were necessarily crimes in his own eyes. Cattle-lifting has always been a gentlemanly vice. The 'robberies' and 'extortions' may have been acts of private war not only permitted but demanded by honour. 'Attempted murder' may have been knightly encounter. Rape need mean no more than abduction. When Launcelot saved Guinevere from the stake and carried her off to Joyous Gard the law would have called it rape. Malory may have had equally good reasons for removing from an orgulous and discourteous husband, a local King Mark, some gentlewoman whom he loved *par amors*. We may be sure that he did not succeed in living up to the level of his own Launcelot; but there is no reason for assuming him to be at all like a modern 'criminal'. The records tell us nothing more than we might expect such records to tell of a man on the locally unpopular side who attempted on the whole to live as a good knight should.

When we turn from the man to the book, the first thing Professor Vinaver has to tell us is that it was not in our sense a book at all. Malory really wrote eight separate romances. The apparent unity of the old text, like its division into books and chapters, is the work of Caxton, and criticisms of Malory's inconsistencies fall to the ground. Hence Professor Vinaver's title, *The Works of Sir Thomas Malory*.

In general the Winchester text does not differ very much from Caxton's, and neither is textually much purer than the other. Sometimes Winchester clears up difficulties in Caxton. At least once it has that smoothness which textual critics distrust where Caxton has the honest *difficilior lectio*. At I, 16 (Vinaver, p. 35) Winchester's 'And whoso that fledde all they sholde be slayne' is almost certainly a scribal evasion of the unknown difficulty which produced Caxton's 'And who so that fledde but did as they dyd shold be slayne'. Elsewhere a Caxton reading which is not 'better' in the textual sense is so much better imaginatively that we wish it to be correct. In I, 35 (Vinaver, p. 638) Caxton prints 'that they sorceresses wold sette alle the countrey in fyre with ladyes that were enchantresses', where Winchester for *in fyre* has merely *envyrone*.

To this general close similarity between the two texts there is one notable exception. In the Roman War (his 'Book v') Caxton quite frankly acts as an editor. He drastically abridges and he radically alters the style. At this point, as has long been known, Malory was following a work very different from his usual French sources; the English alliterative *Morte*. This alters both his temper and his style. The temper becomes more heroic (you might say, more barbaric) and the prose is filled with alliterative tags and inversions. Even in Caxton these elements had shown through in the description of Arthur's dream (v, 4), but now that we have both texts in full we see the magnitude of his alteration; and it is almost certainly for the better. Malory had failed to turn his verse original into true prose. This means that while in isolated quotation his phrases often have a pith and race which Caxton's want, yet the cumulative effect of his verse rhythms and tags becomes intolerable. Caxton found them discordant, just as he found the crude epic vitality of the matter discordant with the general tone of Malory's stories. He therefore ironed out the style and dispatched the whole affair as shortly as he could. It is indeed the most tasteless fiction in the whole Arthuriad. Caxton's judgement was sound. The artificial unity which he gave to the whole *corpus* almost justifies itself when we see him here working to produce unity in a much higher sense. Even his chapter-headings (now no more irrelevant to our delight than the glosses in *The Ancient Mariner*) we cannot spare. However warmly we welcome the Winchester text there must be no question of expelling Caxton from the tradition.

The Roman War, read in the Winchester text, raises a point about Malory's prose which is too little mentioned. Critics talk of his style as if he were in secure possession of it throughout. It is not so. As we have just seen, when his source is alliterative verse he reproduces its rhythm and much of its diction. Turn a few pages and you find something quite different—the gentle yet hardy prose for which he is so famed; but it is in fact the nearest English equivalent of the French prose he is following. Turn on to the end, where he is following the stanzaic English *Morte*, and again you will find inversion and verse rhythms (this time of a different sort) intruding. Turn to his own original excursion into non-narrative prose (Caxton, XVIII, 25; Vinaver, p. 1119) and you will find something different from any of these—a strange lack of progressiveness and an unusual percentage of romance words. This does not mean that Malory is not a fine artist; but his fineness is responsive, not creative. As he has lately read, so he writes. He is at the mercy of his originals.

This is true, in a certain sense, not only of his style but of his work as a whole. Professor Vinaver sees him as a realist because he cuts down the marvellous elements in the stories and adds prosaic details. But it is quite possible that he did so because he was a more serious romantic than his masters. It is the isolated marvel that tells. Multiplication of enchantments is no proof that the writer is himself enchanted; it rather suggests that they are to him mere stage properties. Every superfluous fay carries us farther away from the world of evocative wonder and nearer to that of Baron Munchausen. It is the same with homely details. The more devoutly romantic we are, the more we admit and demand them. It is the child, not the adult, who wants such details in a fairy-tale, because their absence hinders the serious suspension of disbelief which he wishes to make. All Malory's 'realistic' alterations may have been made in a spirit opposite to that which Professor Vinaver supposes. But even if they were not it makes curiously little difference. It would only mean that, wishing to rationalize, he has produced the contrary effect. He laboured in Professor Vinaver's view to thin the romantic forest and make the labyrinth less mysterious; and, for his pains, the impression made on posterity is that which Milton unerringly recalls of

> faery damsels met in forest wide
> By knights of Logres or of Lyonesse.*

By pruning the marvellous he has strengthened its growth. By homely details he has given his story that air of sober conviction in which it excels all other romantic narratives. If Guinevere had merely sought Launcelot 'through the world' (like Ceres) it would seem a pretty fancy; when Sir Ector says 'Hyt hath coste my lady the quene twenty thousand pounds the sekynge of you', who can disbelieve?

The effect is certain, Malory's motives conjectural. If he intended a different effect, then the genius of the story has been too strong for him; nay, if Professor Vinaver is right, has been strengthened by his very efforts to resist it.

There is a similar obscurity about Malory's attitude to the story of the Sangreal. In the most recent and one of the most vital re- handlings of the legend, in *Taliessin through Logres* and *The Region of the Summer Stars*, the Grail has been made central and the final tragedy is seen as the inevitable ruin of a society that had refused its high vocation.* And Williams certainly thought he was finding this in Malory's version. Professor Vinaver, on the contrary, insists that Malory took little interest in the Sangreal; and especially that he saw no connexion between it and the fall of the Round Table. The question will be long debated. The Winchester text certainly brings new support to the professor's view. In it the *Quest* and the *Morte* are separate works, divided by a third work. And yet, if Malory wanted us to forget the quest he has given us little help to do so. Since his 'works' all deal with the same characters, impressions made in one must affect us in the next. He has left Galahad the son of Launcelot. He has left, therefore, the divine irony whereby Launce- lot's begetting of that son was at once his sole offence against the courtly code and, on the heavenly plane, his sole *raison d'être*. He has left that piercing moment when, as Williams says, 'Joy remembered joylessness' and the spiritual bids its courteous, implacable farewell to the natural, 'My fayre lorde, salew me unto my lorde Sir Launce-lot, my fadir, and bydde hym remembir of this worlde unstable'.

When the quest is over and we return to the court, the first thing he shows us is Launcelot's attempt to break off his intrigue with the Queen, and her ruthless recapture of him. His motives were ad-mittedly mixed; partly to avoid the growing scandal in court, but partly because 'I was but late in the quest of the Sankgreall'—and then, dying away, as such a speech would at such a juncture, into embarrassed repetition, 'and therefore Madam I was but late in that queste'. On top of this Malory introduces, perhaps even invents, the exquisite episode of Sir Urry, where Launcelot at the very summit of earthly (and hardly earthly) glory 'wepte as he had bene a chylde that had bene betyn'. Why, unless he remembered a higher glory and 'pined his loss'? Finally, when all is ended and Launcelot comes to take his last leave of Guinevere, Malory again harks back to the Grail; 'God deffende but that I shulde forsake the worlde as ye have done. For in the queste of the Sankgreall I had that tyme forsakyn the vanytees of the worlde, had not youre love been' (Caxton had given *lord* for *love*, but Winchester confirms the conjectural emenda-tion which many readers had pencilled long since in the margin).

Once again Malory's intentions can only be guessed. And to guess them aright would be important if there were in fact any logical or emotional incompatibility between the religious interpre-tation and the human tragedy of blood feud and conflicting loyalties which, in Professor Vinaver's view, was all that Malory had in mind. But there is none. The human tragedy becomes all the more impres-sive if we see it against the background of the Grail, and the failure of the Quest becomes all the more impressive if it is felt thus rever-berating through all the human relationships of the Arthurian world. No one wants the Grail to overthrow the Round Table directly, by a *fiat* of spiritual magic. What we want is to see the Round Table *sibi relictus*, falling back from the peak that failed to reach heaven and so abandoned to those tendencies within it which must work its destruction. And that is what we are shown. All the touches which Malory has added—especially the love between Gareth and Launcelot—only make it more overwhelming, and of the final contrition it is surely too harsh to say with Professor Vinaver that Launcelot repents not of his sins against God but of having brought all whom he loved to earthly ruin. It is in such a tragic glass that most men, especially Englishmen, first see their sins with clarity.

Perhaps Malory did not mean it. Perhaps here also the genius of the story proved too strong for him. If so, it would be the crowning paradox, for it would have overcome him where he himself was at his strongest. In these last chapters, as Professor Vinaver shows, his originality is at its height and reveals itself in tragic dialogue which has hardly yet been praised as it deserves.

There is no reason to be surprised or dismayed if the pure Malory thus always evades us. We are not reading the work of an independent artist; we are reading what is almost such a 'traditional book' as Professor Gilbert Murray believed the *Iliad* to be. Whatever he does Malory's personal contribution to the total effect cannot be very great, though it may be very good. We should approach the book not as we approach Liverpool Cathedral, but as we approach Wells Cathedral. At Liverpool we see what a particular artist invented. At Wells we see something on which many generations laboured, which no man foresaw or intended as it now is, and which occupies a position half-way between the works of art and those of nature.

The *Morte* is like that. Professor Vinaver is the skilled guide; he will point you out here a Middle English crypt, there an Anglo-Norman chapel, a late French bit and bits that are almost pure Malory, and then Malory worked over by Caxton, and then Caxton simply. It is extraordinarily interesting. And fortunately a book, unlike a building, does not reduce us to the alternative of either leaving it alone or 'restoring'. The new *Works of Malory* is the restoration; but the cathedral, our old familiar Caxton, is also still there. We should all read the *Works*; but it would be an impoverishment if we did not return to the *Morte*. As for Malory, we shall never know him. He is hidden in the work; do not say 'his' work. Only once does he address us directly. He asks us to pray for his soul; with that our direct relation to him begins and ends.*

8

TASSO

The reputation of Tasso in England has never, I think, stood as high as that of Ariosto, and this may seem a little surprising. We might have supposed that a nation of Puritans and a nation which has been acknowledged by a foreign critic as supreme in the energy of its moral poetry would have preferred the edifying *Gerusalemme* to the licentious *Furioso*. Yet I think the explanation is fairly simple. Ariosto has been preferred because, we must reluctantly admit, he is by almost any standard the greater poet. Nor ought we to press too far the contrast between his ribaldry and the grave loftiness of Tasso. Tragic, and even religious, elements do co-exist in Ariosto with his licentiousness, his mockery, and his wonderful comic invention. That indeed is his greatness. He treats the formulae of chivalrous romance now as a burlesque, now seriously, and without discomfort enables, nay compels, us to conform to his mood. Within that particular convention *totam vitae imaginem expressit*. He had also the advantage of coming first. When a poet like Spenser turned to the *Jerusalem* his ideas of what a romantic epic ought to be had already been formed by the *Furioso*—I should add, by the *Innamorato* as well. When in *The Faerie Queene*, IV, iii, 45 Spenser writes

> Much more of price and of more gratious powre
> Is this, then that same water of Ardenne,
> The which Rinaldo drunck in happie howre,

he means Boiardo's Rinaldo, not Tasso's.

At the same time there have been very few periods in which English taste has not acknowledged Tasso as one of the great masters. In Abraham Fraunce's *Arcadian Rhetoric, or the precepts of rhetoric made plain by examples*, published in 1588, he is mentioned on the title-page as one of the sources from which these examples are to be drawn, along with Homer, Virgil, Sidney and Sallust—who is not the author of *Catiline* and *Jugurtha* but du Bartas. Gabriel Harvey praises him for his *civile ingenium et heroicus animus*:* Sir John

Harington refers to his 'excellent work'.* We do not in the Elizabethan period find him much praised for what he himself would
perhaps have regarded as his greatest achievement. I mean his
solution of the problem which occupies so much of his own critical
writings, the problem of combining the romantic variety which
popular taste demanded with the unity of action demanded by the
Humanists. Thus in the dedicatory letter prefixed to *The Faerie
Queene* Spenser seems quite unaware of the structural difference
between the *Furioso* and the *Gerusalemme*. The difference which he
stresses is of quite another order, based on the assumption that epic
poets teach virtue not (as le Bossu was later to think) by the general
tendency of their fable but by the exemplary character of their hero.
Hence comes a curious classification, distinguishing poets who teach
public and private virtue in the same hero, as Virgil did in Aeneas
and Ariosto in Orlando, and those who have a different hero for
each, as Homer had. Agamemnon in the *Iliad* showed public
virtue, Odysseus in the *Odyssey*, private. Tasso is a poet of this kind,
with Goffredo for political and Rinaldo for ethical virtue. All this
comes from a critical background very *naïf* compared with that of
the *Discorsi*.

In the seventeenth century the position is somewhat different. To
Milton Tasso is one of the great models of epic mentioned in *The
Reason of Church Government* along with Homer, Virgil, and the
book of Job: but he is also, in the *Tractate*, one of the great critics,
side by side with Castelvetro. There is no doubt that Milton fully
understood the critical problem of which Tasso's epic was the
practical solution: he himself was deeply concerned with it and had
pondered 'whether the rules of Aristotle are to be followed'. He
writes as a man of the Renaissance but one better informed than our
Elizabethans. In that respect, however, he was (as I suspect great
men often are) 'behind his age'. In this century trends of taste
hostile to Tasso were beginning to make themselves felt. In 1634
Sir William Alexander in his *Anacrisis* quotes with approval from
Sperone Speroni who 'thinking his exquisite work of Godfred to be
too full of rich conceits and more dainty than did become the
gravity of such a work, said that it was a heroic poem written in
madrigals'. That is the beginning of a line of attack which culminates

in Boileau's notorious denunciation. I say notorious because it seems no common insolence for a Frenchman, one of a nation that has produced no epic since the *chansons de geste*, to speak thus of a poem which man and boy can still read with unflagging interest for the story alone. One sees, of course, what such critics mean. What they are objecting to might be called by a modern the operatic quality in Tasso. The speech of Olindo at the stake in canto II—the one that begins *Altre fiamme, altri nodi amor promise*—is an example. But I doubt if this sort of criticism was the most serious threat launched against Tasso's popularity in the seventeenth century. Far more important, because it went down to deeper preferences and aversions, was the revolt against the supernatural and the marvellous, in that sense the counter-romanticism, which we see in Davenant, Hobbes and Rymer. (Notice in passing that in romantic England poetic rebellions are usually anti-romantic; in France it is the romantics who rebel.) Davenant thought that Tasso's errors—by which he means magicians and enchanted woods—were derived from the ancients and were 'excusable in them' but 'by being his admit no pardon'.* He means that the ancients, poor Pagans, knew no better than to believe in mythology whereas Tasso went in for marvels gratuitously. The same critical attitude can be seen working out to a very different result in Rymer, who says that Spenser 'though he had read Tasso suffered himself to be misled by Ariosto'. Here Tasso is the good boy and Ariosto the bad: partly, I suppose, because of Tasso's superior unity, but partly because Ariosto gives us even more of those marvels which Rymer disliked. As a result of Ariosto's influence *The Faerie Queene*, Rymer complains, 'is perfect fairy land' —using in reprobation the very words which a romantic might have used as the highest praise. At the same time he treats Tasso with respect and quotes *Gerusalemme*, II, 96 for comparison with the corresponding descriptions of nocturnal silence in Apollonius Rhodius and Virgil. He criticizes Tasso's stanza on the characteristically Rymerian ground that 'there seems to be some superfluity of Fish'.*

But even in the late seventeenth century opposite forces were present. Dryden never shared the anti-romantic bias of his age. He always admired and often tried to contribute to what he called the 'enthusiastic parts of poetry' and 'the fairy way of writing'.* Many of his worst miscarriages indeed result from his efforts to do what nature had disqualified him from doing: a thing worth notice for we are too apt to assume that what a writer likes and what he can do coincide. Nor was Dryden romantic only in the sense of loving marvels: he was also *romanesque*, he desired the grandiose and the heroic. Accordingly it is not surprising to find him defending his own Alma by the precedent of Homer's Achilles, Tasso's Rinaldo, and Calprenède's Artaban and even declaring that these were his models. The third is significant. The heroic prose romances are now unread, but they were once most intimately connected in men's minds with the romantic epics. Scaliger and Tasso himself both mention Heliodorus among epic writers and Sidney, with some reservation, treats *Amadis* as a heroic poem. The huge French successors of these romances continued to enjoy great popularity throughout the seventeenth century: prose like that and poetry like Tasso's must have given one another mutual support. There must have been —and Dryden partly reveals it to us—a continuous possibility of escape into such regions from the prison of 'good sense'.

Whether the taste ever quite died out I do not know; but if it did, the revival was not long in coming. The desire for the 'gothick' begins almost with the beginning of the eighteenth century and grows steadily. And the 'world of fine fabling' which a critic like Hurd denied is found in Spenser and Tasso. To a modern critic the differences between Tasso and real medieval poetry may seem very much more important than the similarities: is not the *Gerusalemme* rooted in the Counter-Reformation? But we must remember, firstly, how ignorant these early medievalists were of the true Middle Ages, and secondly how ill provided the Middle Ages are with the sort of poetry they wanted to read. They wanted chivalry, not scholastic philosophy; enchanters, not allegory. They wanted, quite simply, knights in armour, castles, and love stories. They wanted precisely the imaginary Middle Ages which Boiardo had created, Ariosto perfected, and Tasso delivered from their satiric elements. Hence the romantic young lady asking Waverley to help her over her translation of Tasso. Since then there has been a decline in his fame. The herald of this new decline was perhaps Vernon Lee. That gifted lady wrote under the spell of not the imagined Middle Ages but the imagined 'Renaissance'—the glorious, coloured, full-blooded, Pagan phantasmagoria of poisoning cardinals and Machiavellian Popes and wicked beauties which so enchanted our fathers. Tasso is not at all like that: Harvey had noted his *civile ingenium*. According to Vernon Lee we find in him 'the pallor of Autumn'.* At the moment, we live in the full tide of the most violent counter-romanticism that has ever been seen, and Tasso's English readers are few. We can only guess where he will be found when this tide also ebbs.

It would appear, then, that ever since he wrote, with some few eclipses—none of them complete—Tasso has been a major star in the poetical sky visible from this island. But when we come to look for traces of his influence on our own poetry, they are not so marked as we might perhaps have expected. Compared with the traces of Petrarch they are insignificant. It would even be difficult to point to any one book so continuously affected by Tasso as *The Water Babies* is by Rabelais, or Chaucer by Boccaccio. This does not mean that he has not been taken to our hearts: it may even mean the opposite. It is not the greatest authors who are most directly imitated, or, if they are, not for their true greatness. Petrarch in the shades might envy Tasso for having escaped the tasteless imitation which Elizabethan England lavished on himself: for what could give one less idea of the drugged yet golden melancholy, the rapt immobility of the *Rime* than the conceits which our sonneteers are always stealing from them and making frigid by the theft?

There is in Spenser one long passage very recognizably derived from the *Gerusalemme* and there are, of course, a number of sonnets. The sonnets hardly matter: this amatory Italianate vein in English poetry always sounds exactly the same whoever it is taken from. But the passage in *The Faerie Queene* is of some interest. Both poets are doing the same thing: they are describing the rescue of a young man from an enchanted garden, a garden of erotic enchantment in which he is held captive by a beautiful female figure. And both poets, by modern standards, lie open to the same charge: at any rate, at first sight. We are told that they both make the thing which was meant to be evil too beautiful: so beautiful that all the reader's sympathies go out to it, and it may be supposed that the poets' sympathies did the same. This would be a serious charge, if true: not on moral grounds, which are not my concern at the moment, but on artistic. There would be a fatal discrepancy between the profound and the super/ ficial meaning of the poetry. I do not myself believe that the charge is true. As regards Tasso I believe it proceeds from a misunder/ standing both of his mind and of his art, and first as regards his mind. Professor Tolkien, lecturing at St Andrews not many years ago, remarked how the idea of the beautiful but evil fay has disappeared from the modern imagination.* Perhaps in the world built by industrialism beauty has become so rare and evil so undisguisedly ugly that we can no longer believe ill of beauty. With the old poets it was not so. They believed that a thing might be perfectly beautiful, might be of a beauty to break the heart, and yet be evil. As for their art, it must be allowed that in one respect art has become more integrated since their times. The old poet, or painter, or musician does seem to have aimed simply at giving each part of his work the greatest beauty. The speeches of wicked characters were made as plausible as the poet could make them, the alluring temptations as alluring as he could make them. He did not feel it necessary to sow hints of falsity in the villain's speech. Perhaps this change is seen most clearly in the history of opera. A modern composer underlines his evil characters or places with discords. An old composer was content with making a courtesan's song soft and melting or a tyrant's song loud and declamatory; within that very general limit he then made each simply good of its kind. Thus Wagner gives Alberich ugly music to sing: but Mozart gives to the Queen of Night music as beautiful as he gives to Sarastro.

That would be my defence of Tasso. But the point is that no such defence is needed for the passages borrowed from Tasso in *The Faerie Queene*. Elsewhere I have already analysed them at some length and it would be tedious to repeat the details. I will here content myself with saying that though Spenser's Bower of Bliss is closely copied from Tasso's garden of Armida, everything in Spenser's Bower is deliberately contrasted with his garden of Adonis which comes about six cantos later: everything therefore has a significance in him which it had not in Tasso. Tasso, quite inno/

cently, and following a well established tradition, frequently uses the contrast of art and nature—

> E quel che il bello e il caro accresce all'opre
> L'arte che tutto fa, nulla si scopre.*

Spenser reproduces these passages for a different purpose. He emphasizes the art of the evil garden in order that, six cantos later, he may contrast it with the naturalness of the good one. In the one all is imitation, arrangement and sterility; in the other all is spontaneous and fertile. Thus Spenser's poem contains, as Tasso's does not, the answer to the evil garden on its own ground. In Tasso we have merely the conflict between sensuality and valour. In Spenser we have the answer to depraved and artful sensuality given by innocent and natural sensuousness. Armida is defeated only by virtue she could never understand: Acrasia is answered by something which does much better what she professed to do—beaten, as we say, on her home ground. This will be very surprising to those who expect to find Spenser differing from Tasso by his 'Puritanism' in the popular modern sense of the word. But in reality Puritanism and the Counter-Reformation, or even Puritanism and the Middle Ages, were on this point in positions almost opposite to those that moderns imagine for them. Asceticism is far more characteristic of Catholicism than of the Puritans. Celibacy and the praise of virginity are Catholic: the honour of the marriage bed is Puritan. Milton was being typically Puritan when he wrote, something too excessively, of the loves of Adam and Eve. *Comus* is his least Puritan poem.

Poetically the chief contrast between Spenser and Tasso at this point is one of complexity. Tasso does a very simple thing and does it extremely well. Spenser builds up a contrast which will be lost unless the reader can carry it in his head for six cantos—that is, for thousands of lines. I don't think that means that Spenser is more modern; I think it means that he is more medieval. For surely intricacy is a mark of the medieval mind: intricacy in scholastic philosophy, in Gothic architecture, in dress, in the rhyme schemes of poetry, and (what here concerns us most) the intricacy of allegory. It is not fanciful to see an analogy between the superior intricacy of Spenser's fable over Tasso's and the difference between his stanza and the *ottava rima*. Both are things of untiring beauty, but how different they are. The Italian stanza is all clear bell-like music; it carries you on with untroubled speed through the whole length of some of the longest poems in the world. The Spenserian is labyrinthine and meditative, turning back upon itself in the centre where the two rhymes meet and then pausing again, either for recapitulation or thundering defiance, or for a dying fall in the final alexandrine.

Professor Mario Praz has justly pointed out how Milton's abstinence from the particular, his *lunghezza de' membri e de' periodi*, and his verses entering *l'uno nell'altro*, conform to Tasso's precepts.* Yet it is extraordinary how little recognizable Tasso we find in Milton. The councils in Heaven and Hell, the descent of Gabriel and Michael, and other such 'machines' (as the old critics would have called them) are part of the Homeric and Virgilian tradition as Christianized by Vida amidst the tasteless absurdities of the *Christiad*. There is possibly a closer connexion in these two pictures:

> Quando dall'alto soglio il Padre Eterno,
> Ch'è nella parte più del Ciel sincera,
> E quanto è dalle stelle al basso inferno,
> Tanto è più in su della stellata spera,
> Gli occhi in giù volse, e in un sol punto, e in una
> Vista mirò ciò, ch'in se il mondo aduna—
>
> (*Gerusalemme Liberata*, I, vii, 3–8)

and

> Now had the Almighty Father from above,
> From the pure empyrean where he sits
> High throned above all highth, bent down his eye,
> His own works and their works at once to view.
>
> (*P.L.* III, 56–9)

But even here the similarity is not of the closest. Where Milton explicitly recalls the Italian epics it is usually Tasso's predecessors he thinks of. Thus at the very outset he challenges comparison with Ariosto by promising

> Things unattempted yet in prose or rhyme,*

a direct translation of

> Cosa non detta in prosa mai né in rima.*

And in the severest of all his poems he turns aside to remember, of all people, Boiardo:

> Such forces met not, nor so wide a camp
> When Agrican with all his Northern powers
> Beseig'd Albracca, as Romances tell,
> The City of Gallaphrone, from thence to win
> The fairest of her Sex, Angelica,
> His daughter, sought by many prowest Knights,
> Both Paynim and the peers of Charlemagne.

(P.R. III, 337–43)

How closely he had read the *Innamorato* may be seen from a passage in *Paradise Lost* where he reproduces a passage from it, I suppose unconsciously. Boiardo has said (II, xxx, 44–8)

> Da l'altra parte anchora i Saracini
> Facean tremar di stridi tutto il loco,
> Correndo l'un ver l'altro, son vicini,
> Scema il campo in mezzo a poco a poco;
> Fossa non v'è, nè fiume, che confini....

Part of this comes in *P.L.* VI at line 68

> On they move
> Indissolubly firm; nor obvious Hill
> Nor straitening Vale, nor Wood, nor Stream, divides
> Their perfect ranks.

The other part comes about thirty lines later in the form

> for now
> 'Twixt Host and Host but narrow space was left.

This is not conscious imitation: it is the involuntary reminiscence of a man steeped in another author. Yet who would have thought *a priori* that Milton delighted in the winning absurdities of Boiardo? It raises our opinion of both poets.

But it is time to draw to a close an inquiry which is already proving itself so negative. Of Tasso's minor works we find traces in English, but usually so much of a piece with the general Italian influence as to be hardly worth picking out. Of his great poem we find much praise and constant enjoyment and one translation which is very well worth reading on its own merits. Perhaps the truth is that what is best in the *Gerusalemme* is not very imitable. Its conceits, those conceits which led Speroni to call it an epic in madrigals, could be copied; we may be thankful they were not. But its virtues do not easily flow over into other men's work. No poem is more completely, and in a sense severely, the poem it set out to be and no other. And that, I suggest, is its abiding merit. A certain kind and degree of artificiality, a certain very skilful balance of unity and variety, a certain tone of disciplined ardour—these prevail from the first line to those wholly satisfactory last words *e scioglie il voto* which Tasso had in mind before he put pen to paper. Those words may be applied to the poet as well as to the hero. *Scioglie il voto*: he did what he meant, he made good his promise. The actions and the characters are far removed from reality as a modern critic understands it. But then they are all at exactly the same distance from it and thus all real in relation to one another—the shepherds who entertain Erminia being neither nearer to nor further from actual rusticity than the great deeds of Argante and Rinaldo are from actual war or Clorinda herself from the Countess in Froissart at the siege of Hennebont who 'had a glaive in her hand and was that day as good as a man'. In this perfect keeping, which enables us to accept Tasso's world as real while we are reading, lies the great charm of the poem; in that and in something better. I mean that quite unforced and quite sincere elevation of sentiment which makes us feel that Tasso is, in a very serious and even reverent sense of the word, the most *boyish* of the poets.

9

EDMUND SPENSER, 1552–99

1

Edmund Spenser, born in 1552, was (like most great English writers) a member of the middle class, the son of a Londoner. He was sent to the Merchant Taylors' School, where he learned, and doubtless suffered, under the famous Richard Mulcaster. There is some evidence that Mulcaster, even by the ferocious standards of that age, was a cruel teacher, but he was an interesting man whose views on education can still be studied in his *Positions* (1581) and *Elementary* (1582). Though long and very serious, they hardly go further than the theory of spelling, and if Mulcaster had completed a system of education on the same scale it would have been about as long as the Bible; a fact which might possibly have some bearing on the gigantic project (only a quarter of it was carried out) of *The Faerie Queene*. In 1569 Spenser entered Pembroke Hall at Cambridge. The most interesting thing about his university career is that he passed through it without becoming attached to either of the two intellectual movements by which Cambridge was then agitated.

We can hardly help calling them 'Puritanism' and 'humanism', but neither word meant the same as it does in modern America. By purity the Elizabethan Puritan meant not chastity but 'pure' theology and, still more, 'pure' church discipline. That is, he wanted an all-powerful Presbyterian Church, a church stronger than the state, set up in England, on the model of Calvin's church at Geneva. Knox in Scotland loudly demanded, and at least one English Puritan hinted, that this should be done by armed revolution. Calvin, the great successful doctrinaire who had actually set up the 'new order', was the man who had dazzled them all. We must picture these Puritans as the very opposite of those who bear that name today: as young, fierce, progressive intellectuals, very fashionable and up-to-date. They were not teetotallers; bishops, not beer, were their special aversion. And humanists in this context means simply 'classicists'—men very interested in Greek, but more interested in Latin, and far more interested in the 'correct' or 'classical' style of Latin than in what the Latin authors said. They wanted English drama to observe the (supposedly) Aristotelian 'unities', and some of them wanted English poets to abandon rhyme—a nasty, 'barbarous' or 'Gothic' affair—and use classical metres in English. There was no necessary enmity between Puritans and humanists. They were often the same people, and nearly always the same sort of people: the young men 'in the Movement', the impatient progressives demanding a 'clean sweep'. And they were united by a common (and usually ignorant) hatred for everything medieval: for scholastic philosophy, medieval Latin, romance, fairies, and chivalry.

There are some possible signs (but all ambiguous) in Spenser's *Shepheards Calendar* (1579) that he was once or twice nearly captured by the Puritans, but it certainly did not last long. What is more remarkable is that he never surrendered to humanism, though he clearly lived in a humanistic circle of the narrowest sort. His friend Gabriel Harvey—a very grotesque creature and, to judge from his surviving records, a textbook case of the Inferiority Complex— disapproved of the whole design of *The Faerie Queene*. He com-plained that in it 'Hobgoblin' was stealing the garland from 'Apollo': in other words, that medieval romance was winning the day against classicism. Another member of the circle, the rather fatuous young man who contributed a commentary to *The Shep-heards Calendar* over the signature E.K., could not let Spenser's references to fairies pass without adding 'To roote that rancke opinion of Elfes out of mens hearts, the truth is, that there be no such thinges'. Nothing is more impressive about Spenser than his reaction to these humanist friends. He did neither of the two things we should expect. He never quarrelled with them; and he never took the slightest notice of their advice. He remained a faithful friend to Harvey (who had few friends); and he devoted his whole poetical career to a revival, or prolongation, of those medieval motifs which humanism wished to abolish.

Spenser had taken his M.A. in 1576, and in 1578 had found temporary employment as secretary to the Bishop of Rochester. In

1579 he had been at Leicester House and enjoyed the very exciting experience of being noticed (and even used with some 'familiarity') by Philip Sidney himself. It must have seemed to the young poet that the world was opening to him. There was of course no question of living by his pen. In the 90's it was possible to live (precariously) by pamphleteering or (rather better) by writing and acting for the new companies of players, but this was hardly so in the 70's; nor would such a Bohemian and 'rake-helly' career have been at all to Spenser's mind. On the other hand, we must not picture him choosing a profession or looking for a business opening as a young man might do today. Literary distinction could still lead to employment in the service of one of those great nobles who carried on the work of government. Such a reward fell to Spenser when he became secretary to Lord Grey of Wilton in 1580. Doubtless, it was not the kind of post Spenser had hoped for. It meant 'foreign service', for Lord Grey had just been appointed Deputy of Ireland, and Spenser arrived in Dublin in August 1580. He thus became (for life, had he known it) an instrument of the English domination in a hostile and incompletely conquered country. He had already begun *The Faerie Queene*.

Conquest is an evil productive of almost every other evil both to those who commit and to those who suffer it, and we should look in vain for any fruitful or pleasant relations between Spenser and the Irish. Nothing of that sort was possible. They were to him merely 'natives', rebels, and Papists; he to them, a vile heretic and alien Sassenach. The plans which he propounded for their subjugation in his *View of the Present State of Ireland* (never printed in his lifetime, but written in 1596) are harsh and even cynical; and if some scholars have pleaded, not without success, that they are excusable, this of itself admits that they require excuse. But that, as we shall presently see, is not the whole story about Spenser's relations to Ireland.

In 1589, after receiving a visit from Raleigh, Spenser returned to England, bringing with him the manuscript of the first three Books of *The Faerie Queene*, which were published in the following year. They brought him fame, but not the post in England for which, no doubt, he had been hoping, and he returned to his house at Kilcolman in the county Cork. In 1594 he married Elizabeth Boyle: the sonnets (*Amoretti*) and the *Epithalamion*, both published in 1595, poetize his courtship and its conclusion. *Epithalamion* is his happiest poem. But happiness did not last long. There was another visit to England in 1595, and the second instalment of *The Faerie Queene* was printed in 1596. Then came his doom. In 1598 the Irish rose under the Earl of Tyrone, defeated the English near Armagh, and flung a force into Munster. What they would do when they reached Kilcolman, every reader of Irish history knows in advance. It was, after all, the old seat of the Desmonds: the heretic, foreigner, and upstart had usurped it long enough. It is said (by Ben Jonson) that Spenser's third child, a baby, died in the flames. By December Spenser had contrived to reach London, carrying dispatches about the late rising. He died, certainly in poverty, as some say actually of hunger, in January 1599.

2

Though Spenser seldom made poetry out of his own life in the direct fashion of Wordsworth's *Prelude*, the pattern of his biography and that of his poetical output are nevertheless interlocked in an interesting way. On the biographical side we have the long years of residence in Ireland punctuated by brief visits to England: that is, to civilization, safety, the court, patrons, and the hope of social success. On the poetical side, we have the single great work, certainly begun very early and perhaps begun even before the appearance of *The Shepheards Calendar*, obstinately adhered to in the teeth of criticism, worked at all his life and left unfinished; its composition punctuated, or interrupted, by the minor poems, all of them (except the *Epithalamion*) inferior to it. They usually came out just after a visit to England. It is not hard to guess what was happening. Whenever Spenser can reach England—whenever, in our language, he 'goes on leave'—he brings with him some more *Faerie Queene* to be published. That is what he cares about. But of course the publisher urges him to 'follow it up'. Spenser gets together a volume of odds and ends, some of them not very recent work. Thus we get the *Complaints* volume of 1591 and the *Colin Clouts Come Home Againe* volume of '95. However their contents were written, they were published, we feel, less by Spenser the poet than by Spenser the man; Spenser the man, seizing an opportunity of reminding the patrons and the public that he was still in existence. For of course a great work slowly growing, stanza by stanza, through a lifetime, is a thing that people easily overlook. It thus comes about that the many years in Ireland lie behind Spenser's greatest poetry, and the few years in England behind his minor poetry. It is hard to resist the conviction that his prolonged exile was a great gain to English literature. It removed him perforce from the rapid changes of fashion, the ephemeral hopes and fears, the petty intrigues, and the time-wasting attendance upon great persons, which would almost certainly have been the portion of a literary man hanging upon the fringes of the court: it forced him to sink deeper and deeper into the world he was creating. To that extent, we can call *The Faerie Queene* an Irish product.

We can perhaps say a little more. Spenser could not love the people, but, surprisingly, he loved the country. He chose an Irish hill, Arlo, for his assembly of gods (Book VII, the 'Mutability' cantos, vi and vii). He introduced a poetic catalogue of Irish rivers (Book IV, canto xi) into one of his most highly wrought passages. In prose (*View of the Present State*) he pronounced Ulster 'a most beautifull and sweete countrie as any is under heaven'. He delighted in Irish history and antiquities and hoped to write a book about them. What is even stranger (and helps to show his freedom from the narrowness of humanistic taste), he had listened to Irish poetry in translation and thought that it 'savored of sweete witt and good invencion'. Most interesting from this point of view is the poem *Colin Clouts Come Home Againe*, not published until 1595 but written to celebrate Colin Clout's (that is, Spenser's) return from his first English visit in 1590—his return to an Ireland which, as the title shows, has now become 'home'. It is a curiously broken-backed poem. It starts out with the view that we should expect. The visit to England has been wonderful because there Colin Clout saw the 'blessed eye' of 'that Angel' Queen Elizabeth, because her realm is all 'fruitful corne, faire trees, fresh herbage', because (unlike Ireland) it has no 'raging sword', no 'ravenous wolves' nor 'outlawes', and because the court is full of exquisite ladies and admirable poets. This, I say, is what we should expect: a compliment to the queen and the possible patrons and an appeal for an English job. But then Colin goes on in the latter part of the poem to paint a wholly different picture. His Anglo-Irish friends ask him why he ever returned from such a delightful country to 'this barren soil' of Ireland 'where cold and care and penury do dwell'. Colin replies: one glance at the 'enormities' of the English court convinced him that it would be a great mistake to 'abandon quiet home' for court life and far wiser 'back to his sheep to turne'. For now it appears that court is full of 'malice and strife', lying, backbiting, treachery, and dissimulation, no place 'for any gentle wit', and that the love which courtiers incessantly talk of is a lewd, faithless affair quite unlike the high mystery of love as 'we poore shepheards' know it. All this rings true. Spenser's visit to England had been a disappoint-ment. He was not made for the fashionable world. This contrast between the 'vain shows' of court and the simplicities of rustic life recurs increasingly in the later parts of *The Faerie Queene*. Shepherds, hermits, satyrs, even the Savage, become types to which he turns with love. It is difficult not to conclude that this represents his growing (though perhaps unadmitted) reconciliation to what had once been his place of exile but had now become home. He was coming to need that Irish life: the freedom, the informality, the old clothes, the hunting, farming, and fishing (he was proud of the super-excellent trout in his own river at Kilcolman). He may, as a poet, have needed the very country. There is a real affinity between his *Faerie Queene*, a poem of quests and wanderings and inextin-guishable desires, and Ireland itself—the soft, wet air, the loneliness, the muffled shapes of the hills, the heart-rending sunsets. It was of course a different Ireland from ours, an Ireland without potatoes, whitewashed cottages, or bottled stout: but it must already have been 'the land of longing'. *The Faerie Queene* should perhaps be regarded as the work of one who is turning into an Irishman. For Ireland shares with China the power of assimilating all her invaders. It is an old complaint that all who go there—Danes, Normans, English, Scotch, very Firbolgs—rapidly become 'more Irish than the Irish themselves'. With Spenser the process was perhaps beginning. It is true he hated the Irish and they him: but, as an Irishman myself, I take leave to doubt whether that is a very un-Irish trait. ('The Irish, sir,' said Dr Johnson, 'are an honest people. They never speak well of one another.')

3

When Spenser and Sidney began writing, English poetry was in a deplorable condition. Short histories of literature sometimes give the impression that the 'Revival of Learning' began from the first to exercise a quickening influence upon our literature. I find no evidence that this was so. Nearly all the good poetry of the sixteenth century is crowded into its last twenty years (except in Scotland, where it comes at the beginning of the century and is overwhelmingly medieval in character). In England, until Sidney and Spenser arose, the last poet of real importance had been Sir Thomas Wyatt, who died in 1542: and his poetry, at its best, owes at least as much to the Middle Ages as the Revival of Learning. Between Wyatt and Spenser there extends a period in which it looks as though English poetry were never going to rise again even half so high as it had already risen in the Middle Ages. The best product of this dull period had been the *Songs and Sonnets* (1557), usually called *Tottel's Miscellany* from the name of its publisher, which had contained, along with a very large body of wooden and clumsy verse, Wyatt's lyrics and some graceful (though rather tame) pieces by Surrey and others. Far worse and more characteristic was the huge *Mirror for Magistrates* which came out, repeatedly added to, at various dates from 1555 to 1587. In it the ghosts of various historical characters appeared to tell their stories or, as the *Mirror* calls them, their 'tragedies'. Apart from a good 'induction' by Thomas Sackville and one goodish 'tragedie' by John Dolman, the *Mirror* is about as bad as it could be. But it was fatally popular and thus important for its bad influence on later poets and as an index of the depths to which taste had sunk. In it, as in the work of Googe, Brooke, Turberville, or the truly appalling translators of Seneca, we see a total loss of that feeling for style which seems to have come so easily to most medieval poets. It is against this background that we can best understand the value, for their own age, of Spenser's minor works and most easily pardon the fact that even in his greatest poetry he was seldom safe from a relapse into the bad manner of his predecessors. He was not a man laying the coping stone on an edifice of good poetry already half-built; he was a man struggling by his own exertions out of a horrible swamp of dull verbiage, ruthlessly over-emphatic metre, and screaming rhetoric.

Thus *The Shepheards Calendar* is not, at this distance of time, a very attractive work. Even if we can re-acquire (and if we are to study English literature, we must try) a taste for the pastoral, we shall still find that Spenser's shepherds fall between two stools. They are not realistic enough to give us the pleasure we get from the rustics of Hardy or of *Huckleberry Finn*: yet they are far too realistic to waft us away into the purely poetic pastoral world of Drayton's *Muses Elizium* or Milton's *Lycidas*. This happened, I believe, because Spenser was hesitating between two incompatible models: the wholly idealized *Arcadia* of Sannazaro and the more realistic (but poetically negligible) *Eclogues* (1515 and 1521) of Alexander Barclay. But if we had come to the *Calendar*, as its first readers did, from verse like that of the *Mirror*, we should feel as if we were passing from winter to spring. We should read

> The simple ayre, the gentle warbling wynde,
> So calme, so coole, as no where else I fynde:
> The grassye ground with daintye Daysies dight,
> The Bramble bush, where Byrds of every kynde
> To the waters fall their tunes attemper right,
>
> (*Calendar*, 'June', 4–8)

and we should perceive that poetry, which for nearly forty years had been able only to shout or mumble, was now once more beginning to sing. There are moments in literary history at which to achieve a manner and a music is more important than to deliver any 'message', however profound or prophetic. The message can wait; it will have to wait forever unless the manner and music are found. It is idle to talk about a great ballet until people have, in the crudest and simplest sense, learned to dance, learned the steps. In the *Calendar* Spenser is learning—in its best passages has already learned—the steps.

Three poems which were not printed till they appeared in the *Complaints* of 1591 may have been written shortly after the *Calendar*. One of them is merely a translation from the difficult and very minor poem of Virgil's called the 'Culex', or 'Gnat', but the other two are interesting because they are so different from each other and from

The Faerie Queene, thus warning us not to suppose that a great poet can write only the sort of poetry which he chooses to write chiefly. *Muiopotmos* is about the adventures of a butterfly, a poem full of flowers and sunshine written with great enjoyment in a lighter and swifter stanza than the famous 'Spenserian'. In it, as nowhere else, we see Spenser at play. Many critics believe that it is a veiled account of some affair at court, but I do not think this is certain. The third poem is *Mother Hubberds Tale*, a satire, modelled not (as Spenser's humanist friends would doubtless have wished) on the formal satire of the Romans but on the great medieval beast fable *Reynard the Fox*. The Ape and the Fox go into partnership and play all manner of tricks on the other beasts, even stealing the Lion's crown and sceptre. The tale is, of course, full of allusions to contemporary politics which cannot be discussed here. In this poem we find none of the slow, stately pace which is characteristic of *The Faerie Queene*. Spenser writes in couplets, uses a homely style, and gets over the ground briskly.

Colin Clouts Come Home Againe has already been mentioned; the 'ambivalence' which makes it so interesting as a personal document spoils its unity of effect as a poem. *Daphnaida* (1591), an elegy on the death of a noble lady, is perhaps the worst poem Spenser ever wrote. It is modelled on Chaucer's *Book of the Duchess* but entirely loses the charm of its original by exaggeration and straining after effect. The Elizabethans, even at their best, seem to lack that effortless good taste —one might almost say, that good breeding—which we nearly always find in the work of the Middle Ages. The Renaissance did not make men, in all senses, more *civilized*.

In the years '95 and '96 Spenser published a body of poetry about love which perhaps marks the summit of his achievement outside *The Faerie Queene*. The sonnets, or *Amoretti* (1595), are not among our greatest sonnets. We shall not find in them the almost divine selflessness and evocative power of Shakespeare's sonnets nor the immediacy of Drayton's 'Since there's no help, come let us kiss and part'. Yet if we go to them for what they have to give, for grace and harmony, we can read them with enjoyment. But the *Epithalamion* which was added to them belongs to a different world, and indeed there is no poem in English at all like it. It traces the whole bridal day and night from the moment at which the bride is awaked to the moment at which the tired lovers fall asleep and the stars pour down good influences on the child they have engendered and on all their descendants yet to be. Into this buoyant poem Spenser has worked all the diverse associations of marriage, actual and poetic, Pagan and Christian: summer, landscape, neighbours, pageantry, religion, riotous eating and drinking, sensuality, moonlight—are all harmonized. The metre is a very long stanza with varying line lengths and a refrain, modelled, in fact, on the Italian *canzone* but filled with such festal pomp and jollity, such sustained exuberance of the whole man (spiritual, imaginative, and animal), that the effect is much closer to that of some great ode by Pindar than to any Italian poem. Those who have attempted to write poetry will know how very much easier it is to express sorrow than joy. That is what makes the *Epithalamion* matchless. Music has often reached that jocundity; poetry, seldom.

The *Foure Hymnes* (of Love and Beauty) which followed in 1596 are not on the same level. It would be hopeless, in the space at my disposal, to attempt to unravel their very learned and curious blend of scriptural, Platonic, and medieval ideas. They contain good poetry, but poetry hardly great enough for the arduous, and indeed overwhelming, themes that Spenser has chosen. The same year saw the publication of the *Prothalamion* in which Spenser, now writing on someone else's marriage, tries to repeat the splendours of his own marriage song: I think, with very imperfect success.

But it is high time that we turned to the life work by which Spenser's name really lives.

Like most of his contemporaries Spenser believed that English literature could never hold up its head in the world until it had produced a great epic, and that a poet ought to be a moral teacher; unlike some of his contemporaries, he also felt a strong impulse to continue and develop the medieval tradition of chivalrous romance. He did not in fact know very much medieval literature. Much of it was inaccessible in his time and, anyway, too hard for him in language: he makes little use of Malory; what he called 'Chaucer' included many un-Chaucerian works and was so textually corrupt that Spenser could not have read it metrically even if he had understood Middle English metre (which he did not). The English poem which probably influenced him most was the late, allegorical romance *The Pastime of Pleasure* by Stephen Hawes, who wrote in the reign of Henry VII. This lack of medieval scholarship in Spenser was, however, far from being such a disadvantage as we might suppose. In the first place it set him free to embody, almost unconsciously, those elements of the Middle Ages which were still alive all round him in tournament and heraldry, pageant and symbolical pictures, whereas accurate knowledge might have made him merely a pedant and an antiquarian. In the second place, he could find a great deal of the method and temper of medieval romance, already refashioned, already, as it were, predigested and made more available for his purpose, in three great Italian poems: the *Orlando Innamorato* of Boiardo, the *Orlando Furioso* of Ariosto, and the *Gerusalemme Liberata* of Tasso. The first two of these deal with the adventures of Charlemagne and his paladins at war with the Saracens, and admit large comic elements; they are sometimes laughing at the marvels and high-flown sentiments of romance, but then at other times seriously enjoying these very same things. It is not absolutely certain that, in their comic passages, Spenser always saw the joke. The third is about the capture of Jerusalem by Godfrey of Bouillon and his crusaders: it is as serious and religious a poem as Spenser's own. All three together constitute such a varied, vigorous, unflagging body of poetical storytelling as is hardly equalled anywhere in European literature. They are Spenser's chief models.

By turning to them he turned his back on the strict humanists, who would have wished him to write a pseudo-classical epic, closely modelled on Virgil, like Ronsard's *Franciade*. By making Arthur the hero, or at least the nominal hero, of his poem he nevertheless attempted to gratify the humanists' wish, and his own, that the great poem should be, in some sort, a national epic. But in order to fulfil the demand that the poet should be a moral teacher he decided that he would follow Hawes as well as the Italians. His poem was to be a romance of chivalry, but it was also to have a secondary meaning throughout: to be, as he said, 'a continued allegory'. He decided, further, to introduce a new metre. All the Italians had used what is called *ottava rima*, the stanza which rhymes *abababcc*, best known to English readers in Byron's *Don Juan* or Shelley's *Witch of Atlas*. It is a beautifully light, rapid medium, excellently adapted for describing a breathless chase on horseback or telling an amusing anecdote with a dash of impropriety in it. Spenser himself had used it very well in *Muiopotmos*. But for *The Faerie Queene* he invented his new nine-line stanza which has wholly different qualities. The more complex interlacing of the rhymes and, still more, the concluding alexandrine, which gives to each stanza the effect of a wave falling on a beach, combine to make it slower, weightier, more stately. Of all Spenser's innovations his stanza is perhaps the most important. It makes all his resemblances to the Italians merely superficial. It dictates the peculiar tone of *The Faerie Queene*. Milton, who knew and loved both Spenser and Spenser's models, described it as 'sage and solemn tunes'. A brooding solemnity—now deeply joyful, now sensuous, now melancholy, now loaded with dread—is characteristic of the poem at its best.

This brief account of the genesis of *The Faerie Queene* is needed in order to explain some features of it which may deter modern readers. The necessity is, of course, to be deplored; and it is of very recent growth. From the time of its publication down to about 1914 it was everyone's poem—the book in which many and many a boy first discovered that he liked poetry; a book which spoke at once, like Homer or Shakespeare or Dickens, to every reader's imagination. Spenser did not rank as a hard poet like Pindar, Donne, or Browning. How we have lost that approach I do not know. And unfortunately *The Faerie Queene* suffers even more than most great works from being approached through the medium of commentaries and 'literary history'. These all demand from us a sophisticated, self-conscious frame of mind. But then, when we have used all these aids, we discover that the poem itself demands exactly the opposite response. Its primary appeal is to the most naïve and innocent tastes: to that level of our consciousness which is divided only by the thinnest veil from the immemorial lights and glooms of the collective Unconscious itself. It demands of us a child's love of marvels and dread of bogies, a boy's thirst for adventures, a young man's passion for physical beauty. If you have lost or cannot re-arouse these attitudes, all the commentaries, all your scholarship about 'the Renaissance' or 'Platonism' or Elizabeth's Irish policy, will not avail. The poem is a great palace, but the door into it is so low that you must stoop to go in. No prig can be a Spenserian. It is of course much more than a fairy-tale, but unless we can enjoy it as a fairy-tale first of all, we shall not really care for it.

Those features in the poem which might deter a reader are: (1) its narrative technique; (2) its allegory; and (3) the texture of its language.

(1) The narrative technique, especially after the first two Books, consists in constantly shifting from one story and one set of characters to another, but with a 'dovetail' or liaison at the point where we change. Thus in Book III, canto i, we start out on a journey with Sir Guyon, Prince Arthur, and Prince Arthur's squire, Timias. Presently a strange knight appears riding towards them and tries a course of the lance with Guyon, who is unhorsed. Guyon's annoyance at this reverse is soothed down by the others, and the strange knight now joins the party. They are all proceeding quietly together when suddenly an unknown lady on a milk-white horse flashes past, obviously in flight. A moment later her pursuer, a forester, is seen galloping after her. Arthur, Guyon, and Timias give chase, but the strange knight does not. And Spenser, instead of telling us what happened to the lady and the forester and Arthur and Guyon and Timias, now proceeds to relate the further adventures of the strange knight, which are quite irrelevant to the story we began with. We have thus got rid of all the characters we started with (not to meet Arthur again till canto iv, or Timias till v) and, in effect, changed trains.

The uninstructed reader would get the impression that Spenser was merely rambling, drifting at the mercy of his own imagination, as a man does in a dream. But the reader who knows a little more would remember that he had met exactly the same technique in Malory; and that it is also the technique of Boiardo, Ariosto and Tasso. It is, I think, ultimately derived from Ovid's *Metamorphoses*, and may be called the 'interwoven' or 'polyphonic' narrative. Spenser is obeying a method as well established as the fugue. To what I have previously said about the naïve or childlike appeal of the stories he tells, we must now add the opposite truth that his method of disposing them is highly formal and sophisticated. (This contrast of naïve matter and sophisticated arrangement will seem less paradoxical if we remember how a composer can weave into a most learned symphonic whole the materials which he has derived from simple folk songs.) Now of course to explain that a certain method had a long history behind it does not, of itself, prove that it is a good one. Polyphonic narrative might be a vicious form, however many people had used it. But when we know that this technique domi-nated European fiction both in prose and verse from the thirteenth to the seventeenth century, that civilized audiences in so many different countries went on demanding it, and that Tasso's father (also a poet) lost all his popularity when he wrote a narrative poem without it, common sense will surely make us pause before we assume that it was simply wrong and that the technique of modern fiction is simply right. The old polyphonic story, after all, enjoyed a longer success than the modern novel has enjoyed yet. We do not know which will seem the more considerable literary phenomenon to a critic looking back from the year 2500. Such reflexions should induce us to give the old technique, at least, a fair trial. Perhaps, if we have patience, it will begin to charm us as it charmed our ancestors.

Obviously, it produces great variety. In a polyphonic narrative the weird, the voluptuous, the exciting, the melancholy scenes can succeed one another not where the exigencies of a single rigid 'plot' permit but wherever artistic fitness demands them. To that extent it is more like the technique of music than like that of modern litera-ture. Obviously, too, the interruption of one story by another, often at a critical moment, has something in common with the technique of the serial story: the adventures of Arthur in pursuit of the fugitive lady are left 'to be continued in our next'. If we reply that this kind of suspense is lost on us because our bad memories frustrate it and when we get back to Arthur we have forgotten all about him, then, since our ancestors made no such objection, it would seem that we differ from them by an inferiority, not by a superiority. And no doubt we do. Cheap paper, typewriters, notebooks, and indexes have impaired our memories just as automobiles have made some people almost incapable of walking. (One of the great uses of literary history is to keep on reminding us that while man is con-stantly acquiring new powers he is also constantly losing old ones.)

It behoves us therefore to be humble and do our best. The obstacle is not, in fact, insurmountable: growing familiarity with this kind of poetry will presently enable us to hold the different, and constantly suspended, stories in our heads, just as growing familiarity enables us to follow complex music. And even if we sometimes lose our way, I think we shall find, as we go on reading, that the polyphonic technique has a far more important effect than those two which I have already mentioned, although it is one very difficult to describe. It is an effect particularly suitable to a tale of strange adventures.

It adds to the poem what might be called depth, or thickness, or density. Because the (improbable) adventure which we are following is liable at any moment to be interrupted by some quite different (improbable) adventure, there steals upon us unawares the conviction that adventures of this sort are going on all round us, that in this vast forest (we are nearly always in a forest) this is the sort of thing that goes on all the time, that it was going on before we arrived and will continue after we have left. We lose the feeling that the stories we are shown were arbitrarily made up by the poet. On the contrary, we are sure there are plenty more which he has not time to show us. We are being given mere selections, specimens: instances of the normal life of that wooded, faerie world. The result of this is an astonishing sense of reality.

The young student should here be warned that the word 'lifelike' as applied to literature is ambiguous. It may mean 'like life as we know it in the real world'; in that sense the dullest character in a realistic novel may be 'lifelike'; i.e. he is very like some real people and as lifeless as they. On the other hand 'lifelike' may mean 'seeming to have a life of its own'; in that sense Captain Ahab, old Karamazov, Caliban, Br'er Rabbit, and the giant who says 'fee-fi-fo-fum' in *Jack the Giant-Killer*, are all lifelike. Whether we have met anything like them in the real world is irrelevant. Now Spenser's 'faerie lond' is very unlike life in the first sense, but the polyphonic technique makes it extremely lifelike in the second. It is lifelike by its consistency—all the adventures bear the stamp of the world that produced them, have the right flavour, make each other probable; in its apparent planlessness—they collide, and get mixed up with one another and drift apart, just as events would in a real world; in its infinity—we can, so obviously, never get to the end of them, there are so obviously more and more, round the next corner. That is why Keats in his sonnet 'To Spenser' speaks of one who loved *The Faerie Queene* as 'a forester deep in thy midmost trees'. There is forest, and more forest, wherever you look: you cannot see out of that world, just as you cannot see out of this.

(2) The allegory or 'inner meaning' of *The Faerie Queene* is generally regarded as twofold: a 'moral' or 'philosophical' allegory, and a 'historical' or 'political' allegory. The first is clear, certain, essential; the second obscure, often doubtful, and poetically of little importance. Spenser himself in his prefatory 'Letter' to Raleigh has told us that Gloriana, the Faerie Queene, means (in a certain sense) Queen Elizabeth; James I complained that Duessa was obviously Mary Queen of Scots; and there are places, in the worst parts of the worst Book (v), where the allegory about foreign affairs becomes unmistakable. Apart from these few equivalences, interpretation of the historical allegory is controversial and speculative. I myself (here differing from many scholars whom I respect) regard it with a good deal of scepticism. Some published fantasies of my own have had foisted on them (often by the kindliest critics) so many admirable allegorical meanings that I never dreamed of as to throw me into doubt whether it is possible for the wit of man to devise anything in which the wit of some other man cannot find, and plausibly find, an allegory. I do not believe that a consistent and detailed historical allegory (such as we find, say, in Dryden's *Absalom and Achitophel*) runs through *The Faerie Queene*. Particular scenes contain, in addition to their moral or philosophical meaning, a parallel to some contemporary event. Probably it does not last beyond the scene in which it occurs: when we meet the same characters in a different scene we need not expect them to have the same (or, necessarily, any) historical meaning. How lightly the whole thing should be taken may be judged from the way in which Spenser himself speaks of it. Gloriana at some points and for some purposes symbolizes Elizabeth, but Elizabeth is also at other points and for other purposes, Belphoebe. But in his 'generall intention' Gloriana is 'Glory'; that is her permanent and essential meaning in the poem. The many generations who have read and re-read *The Faerie Queene* with

delight paid very little attention to the historical allegory; the modern student, at his first reading, will be well advised to pay it none at all.

The moral or philosophical meaning is, on the other hand, essential; and fortunately in approaching this we have an advantage which the nineteenth century lacked. Our grandfathers might regard allegory as an arbitrary literary device, a 'figure' listed in the books on rhetoric. The work of Jung and Freud, and the practice of many modern poets and prose writers, has taught us an entirely different view. We now know that symbols are the natural speech of the soul, a language older and more universal than words. This truth, if not understood exactly as modern psychology would understand it, was accepted and acted upon by the ancient and medieval world, and had not yet been lost in Spenser's day. He came, in fact, just in time, just before the birth of that new outwardlooking, rationalizing spirit which was going to give us victory over the inanimate while cutting us off from the depths of our own nature. After Spenser allegory became, till quite modern times, merely a sort of literary toy, as it is in Addison's or Johnson's essays. Spenser was the last poet who could use the old language seriously and who had an audience that understood it.

They understood it because they had been brought up to it. We shall understand it best (though this may seem paradoxical) by not trying too hard to understand it. Many things—such as loving, going to sleep, or behaving unaffectedly—are done worst when we try hardest to do them. Allegory is not a puzzle. As each place or person is presented to us in *The Faerie Queene* we must not sit down to examine it detail by detail for clues to its meaning as if we were trying to work out a cipher. That is the very worst thing we can do. We must surrender ourselves with childlike attention to the mood of the story. The broad outlines of the allegory are quite unmistakable. Spenser himself tells us that the six knights who are the heroes of the six Books are six virtues; and each therefore fights against, or is endangered by, the vices particularly opposed to the virtue he represents.[1] Thus in Book 1 Holiness encounters the various ob

---

[1] Unity was to be secured by the overriding rôle of Arthur, who appears in every Book and helps minor champions out of difficulties. Unfortunately his own story remains unfinished in the fragment we have. On his quest for Gloriana, see below.

stacles to the religious life—error, heresy, pride, despair, and so forth; in Book II Temperance encounters anger, avarice, and lust; in V Justice encounters graft or bribery (Lady Munera), egalitaria
nism, and the giantess who represents the domination of women over men. At a first glance, indeed, the reader might complain not so much of obscurity as of copybook platitude.

But he would be mistaken. In the first place, what looks like a platitude when it is set out in the abstract may become a different sort of thing when it puts on flesh and blood in the story; according to the theory which Sidney set out in his *Defence of Poesie*, the poetic art existed for the precise purpose of thus turning dead truism into vital experience. Secondly, ideas have changed since the sixteenth century, and much of Spenser's thought is now not platitudinous but highly controversial. Not many readers of this book have been brought up to think either equality or feminism a form of injustice. On these points, therefore, *The Faerie Queene* can now do us one of the services for the sake of which (among other things) we read old literature. It can re<admit us to bygone modes of thought and enable us to imagine what they felt like, to see the world through our ancestors' eyes. After we have done that, our rejection of those modes of thought (if we still reject them) will have some value. There is a great difference between rejecting something you have known from the inside and rejecting something (as uneducated people tend to do) simply because it happens to be out of fashion in your own time. It is like the difference between a mature and travelled man's love for his own country and the cocksure conviction of an ignorant adolescent that his own village (which is the only one he knows) is the hub of the universe and does everything in the Only Right Way. For our own age, with all its accepted ideas, stands to the vast extent of historical time much as one village stands to the whole world.

And thirdly, Spenser's moral thought is not in itself so platitu<dinous as we might at first suppose.[1] Guyon, the knight of Book II who represents Temperance, comes to the Bower of Acrasia, ob<viously a place of sexual temptation. But then the female knight of

---

[1] It is, for example, worth considering why the ludicrous and disgusting figure of Malbecco (Jealousy) comes in the Book on Chastity. If Hellenore's wantonness sets a man in a rage, he must not assume that his rage results from a disinterested love of virtue.

Book III, Britomart, represents Chastity. Obviously she too must be brought through a place of sexual temptation; and so she is, in the House of Busirane. If we were writing an allegory instead of reading one, we should at once see that we were coming to a difficulty. What are we to do with these two places? How are we to prevent the second from being merely a repetition of the first? But in Spenser there is no resemblance between them and no trace (which would have been just as bad) of a faked or forced difference between them. The Bower of Acrasia is a luscious garden, genuinely luscious but in rather bad taste (they have metal ivy, painted to look like real, round a fountain); two naked girls are playing the fool in a bathing pond to attract Guyon's attention; Acrasia herself, in a beautiful 'creation' of transparent lingerie, lies on a bed of roses leaning over the last young man she has captured. This is all plain sailing: the simplest reader cannot fail to understand it. But the House of Busirane is a vast building, hard to get into and hard to get out of when you are in. Britomart is there for hours. One empty room leads endlessly into another empty room: all silent, all blazing with an almost sickly splendour of intricate decoration. It is only at midnight, in the last room of all, that a little iron door opens and out of it comes a strange procession, like a masque, of silent people who ignore Britomart, intent upon their own strange ceremonial. Behind that iron door the girl whom Britomart has come to rescue is being tortured.

As I have said before, we must not look for clues as if we were solving a puzzle. We must, if need be, re-read both passages and soak ourselves in their differing atmospheres; the obvious, provocative, even garish sensuality of Acrasia's Bower, which is the foe to 'temperance', to mere self-control and moderation, and the monotonous glitter, the claustrophobia, the costliness, loneliness, anguish of Busirane's House which is the foe to 'chastity' (Spenser makes quite clear that 'chastity' for him includes faithful love, married, or hoping to be married). To a man tempted by the Bower, one would say 'Pull yourself together', but to a man tempted by Busirane, one would say 'Can you not *come out*? Out into the free air and sunlight? Can you never break this lifelong obsession?' It will dawn on every reader in the end that the difference between Acrasia and

Busirane is that between Lust (appetite) and Love, bad love. Many moderns have been brought up to think that the difference between good and evil in sexual matters simply coincides with that between Love and Lust, that every *affaire* becomes 'good' just in so far as it concerns the heart and not merely the senses. If that is our view, then Spenser is here offering us not (as we feared) platitude but full paradox. For he thinks there may be Loves quite distinct from Lust, but evil, miserable, poisoning a whole life; illicit, secret loves that break up homes and lead to divorce courts, suicide pacts, and murders. They are expensive; the House of Busirane is ablaze with gold. They take a long time; the House of Busirane goes on and on. After fully comprehending Acrasia and Busirane (not as I have here given them in abstract but as they really live in the poem), the reader may of course still disagree with Spenser. He may think that the solemnity and grandeur of Busirane's House make it obviously superior to any establishment Acrasia could ever run. Or he may agree with Spenser and feel that he has learned something about human life which will stand him in very good stead. But whichever way he decides, his decision will be a more informed one than any he could have made without reading *The Faerie Queene*. Even that is not the whole story. A poet inventing with such energy as Spenser produces things that mean more than he knew or intended. The House of Busirane may become, to this or that reader, a symbol of (hence, partly a liberation from) some other psychic imprisonment which has nothing to do with love. This kind of poetry, if receptively read, has psychotherapeutic powers.

Another factor which saves Spenser's moral allegory from platitude is his method of hinting in each Book at what may be called 'the virtue behind the virtue', the inner shrine. Book VI is about Courtesy (which in those days meant much more than etiquette or good manners, and included what we should call 'chivalry') and is, of course, full of examples of courteous behaviour. But then in canto X we discover that our attempts at courtesy, however laudable and necessary, will never make us perfectly courteous men. We shall still be clumsy, unless the Graces come and dance with us, unless a beauty which no man can achieve by effort flows into our daily acts of its own will. So in Book IV we discover that Justice can never be perfect while it remains mere Justice: it must go into the temple of Isis and learn better things from 'clemence' or 'equity'. So in Book 1, all the Redcrosse Knight's struggles with Error and Pride will not make him holy until he has been in the House of Caelia. This may be cold comfort to most of us, but it is hardly a copybook platitude; and it might be true.

Three obstacles may prevent a receptive reading of Spenser's allegory. The first great obstacle for the reader of this volume is that he is being given only selections from it, not the poem itself. I have found it impossible to select in such a way that the pieces I included required no support from those I left out—if not support in respect of the 'plot' or sequence of events, yet support from contrasting or harmonizing moods. Far from wishing to conceal this defect, I wish to emphasize it as much as possible. In that way I may possibly convince a reader what selections are for. Except for some (poetically irrelevant) purpose such as passing an examination, the only use of selections is to deter those readers who will never appreciate the original, and thus to save them from wasting their time on it, and to send all the others on to the original as quickly as possible. The sooner you toss my selections impatiently aside and go out to buy a copy of *The Faerie Queene*, the better I shall have succeeded. If I lead anyone to imagine, twenty years hence, that he has really read the poem, when in fact he has read only these shreds and patches, I shall have done him (but not without his own assistance) a grave injury.

The second obstacle is this. The picture-language of allegory is ultimately derived, as I have said, from the unconscious. But by Spenser's time allegory (both literary and pictorial) had been practised so long that certain symbols had an agreed meaning which everyone could understand directly, without plunging into the depths. Many of these are lost on the modern reader who does not know the Bible, the classics, astrology, or the old emblem books. A simple example (still, we may hope, intelligible to many) would be the silver anchor which lay on Speranza's arm (1, x, 14). The text in Hebrews vi. 19 explains it. Similarly in 1, iv, 24 not all readers will now know why Lechery should be riding a goat: all Elizabethans knew that the goat was the sign of Lust. Again, Spenser's readers, comparing the Bower of Acrasia with the House of Busirane, would have noticed at the very outset a difference which I never mentioned (because I did not think it would help the modern student). Cupid is absent from the Bower and very much present in the House. Now in medieval allegory Cupid regularly meant Love (humanized, sentimental, refined, but not necessarily innocent); when they wanted to symbolize the mere sexual appetite they usually represented it by Cupid's mother, Venus.

Finally, an obstacle may arise from our own preconceptions. We may be so certain in advance what a word or an image ought to mean that we omit to notice what it really does mean in the poem. A ludicrous example would be if anyone took 'Temperance' (the subject of Book II) to mean 'not getting drunk', instead of control and moderation of all our passions, including our desire for wealth. A much more serious preconception occurs about the significance of beautiful, naked women in The Faerie Queene. A man may have a 'puritan obsession' (in the modern, not the Elizabethan sense of the word 'puritan') which leads him to assume that these will all be images of sin. Much more probably in our days he will have an anti-puritan obsession and assume that they are all to be welcomed as fruits of Spenser's 'renaissance' or 'Pagan' liberty. Both obsessions, if uncorrected, will lead to false reading. In the poem (as perhaps also in dreams and myths) this image may mean quite different things. And there is no need at all to be puzzled. If read without preconceptions the poem itself will make this perfectly clear. Everyone will see that the two young women in Acrasia's swimming pool are images of Sin; and that the Graces who dance round Colin Clout (VI, x) are nothing of the sort. They are the 'virtue behind the virtue' of Courtesy, what Burke called 'the unbought grace of life'.

(3) The general quality of The Faerie Queene is so highly poetic that it has earned Spenser the name of 'the poet's poet'. But if we examine the texture of the language line by line we may think that it is sometimes flat and very often little distinguished from that of prose. There are, no doubt, some stanzas which, even in isolation, anyone would acclaim as high poetry. But usually we shall look in vain for anything like the phrase-by-phrase deliciousness of Shakespeare's sonnets, the 'gigantic loftiness' of Milton's epic style, or the point and subtlety and pressure of Donne or the modern poets. The

truth is that Spenser belongs to an older school. In the earliest times theology, science, history, fiction, singing, instrumental music, and dancing were all a single activity. Traces of this can still be found in Greek poetry. Then the different arts which had once all been elements of *poesis* developed and became more different from one another, and drew apart (the enormous gains and losses of this process perhaps equal one another). Poetry became more and more unlike prose. It is now so unlike it that the number of those who can read it is hardly greater than the number of those who write it. Spenser is of course a long way from the ancient Greeks, but he belongs to an older school than Shakespeare. He is about midway between Shakespeare and Boiardo. Boiardo is first and foremost a storyteller, not a 'poet' in the more specialized modern sense. As far as language is concerned, his poetry might be improvised—the phrases could be made up as one goes along. Spenser's style is richer, more elaborated than that. But it still has in view an audience who have settled down to hear a long story and do not want to savour each line as a separate work of art. Much of *The Faerie Queene* will therefore seem thin or over-obvious if judged by modern standards. The 'thickness' or 'density' which I have claimed for it does not come from its language. It comes from its polyphonic narrative, from its different layers of meaning, and from the high degree in which Spenser's symbols embody not simply his own experience, nor that of his characters at a given moment, but the experience of ages. In one sense a passage of Spenser is childishly simple compared with a poem by Donne, but in another sense this is not so. Donne wrote from his vivid consciousness of his own situation at a particular moment. He knew what he was putting into his poem, and we cannot get out of it more than he knew he was putting in. But Spenser, with his conscious mind, knew only the least part of what he was doing, and we are never sure that we have got to the end of his significance. The water is very clear, but we cannot see to the bottom. That is one of the delights of the older kind of poetry: 'thoughts beyond their thoughts to those high bards were given'. I do not mean by this that we should prefer the older kind. Their difference is a reason for reading both. There is no one right or absolute kind of poetry.

Spenser wrote primarily as a (Protestant) Christian and secondarily as a Platonist. Both systems are united with one another and cut off from some—not all—modern thought by their conviction that Nature, the totality of phenomena in space and time, is not the only thing that exists: is, indeed, the least important thing. Christians and Platonists both believe in an 'other' world. They differ, at least in emphasis, when they describe the relations between that other world and Nature. For a Platonist the contrast is usually that between an original and a copy, between the real and the merely apparent, between the clear and the confused: for a Christian, between the eternal and the temporary, or the perfect and the partially spoiled. The essential attitude of Platonism is aspiration or longing: the human soul, imprisoned in the shadowy, unreal world of Nature, stretches out its hands and struggles towards the beauty and reality of that which lies (as Plato says) 'on the other side of existence'. Shelley's phrase 'the desire of the moth for the star' sums it up. In Christianity, however, the human soul is not the seeker but the sought: it is God who seeks, who descends from the other world to find and heal Man; the parable about the Good Shepherd looking for and finding the lost sheep sums it up. Whether in the long run there is any flat contradiction between the two pictures need not be discussed here. It is certainly possible to combine and interchange them for a considerable time without finding a contradiction, and this is what Spenser does. The Christian picture dominates the first two Books: divine grace, in the person of Una, is constantly helping St George out of his difficulties, and an angel is sent down to preserve Guyon. On the other hand the central story of the whole poem was to have been Platonic: I say 'was to have been' because Spenser did not live to finish it. In the fragment that we have, Prince Arthur is always seeking for 'Gloriana'. He knows almost nothing about her. When the beautiful Florimell flashes past him in the forest, he at once pursues her: she might be Gloriana (III, iv, 54). He has seen the real Gloriana only in a dream (I, ix, 13 ff.). This is a picture of the soul, as in Platonism, endlessly seeking that perfect beauty of which it has some dim premonition but which cannot be found—only shadows and blurred images of it—in the realm of Nature. This enables us to see what Spenser means when he says that Gloriana is 'Glory'. In his many-levelled poetry 'Glory' is the divine glory or splendour which the Christian soul will not only see but share in Heaven; it is the glory of that real and perfect world which the Platonist is seeking; it is also, in so far as Arthur is a knight-errant in a romance of chivalry, 'Glory' in the sense of fame or honour. To add that it is also in some sense and at some moments Queen Elizabeth seems to us a profane and silly anti-climax. But we are not to suppose that Elizabeth appeared to Spenser as she does to us or even as she did to contem-poraries who really knew her; and we must understand that her royal office had an importance for him which it could have for no modern. For monarchy, like everything else in this world, had its chief value in being the shadow or reflexion of something in that other and more real world. Every earthly court was an imitation, however imperfect, of the Divine Court. Its splendour and order had a poetic, religious, and metaphysical appeal which had nothing to do with snobbery—a ritual appeal. Spenser would have understood the ancient Chinese idea that the function of the Emperor was to reproduce on earth the 'Order of Heaven'. His view was consistent, as we have seen, with the clearest insight into the corruptions of actual court life.

10

ON READING
'THE FAERIE QUEENE'

Beyond all doubt it is best to have made one's first acquaintance with Spenser in a very large—and, preferably, illustrated—edition of *The Faerie Queene*, on a wet day, between the ages of twelve and sixteen; and if, even at that age, certain of the names aroused unidentified memories of some still earlier, some almost prehistoric, commerce with a selection of 'Stories from Spenser', heard before we could read, so much the better. But those who have had this good fortune are not likely to be reading the following extracts. They will never have lost touch with the poet. His great book will have accompanied them year by year and grown up with them as books do: to the youthful appreciation of mere wonder-tale they will have added a critically sensuous enjoyment of the melodious stanza, to both these a historical understanding of its significance in English poetry as a whole, and an ever-increasing perception of its wisdom. To them I need not speak; the problem is rather how to find substitutes for their slowly ripened habit of mind which may enable a mature reader to enter the Spenserian world for the first time: to do for him, in a few minutes, what they have done for themselves in many years.

It must be admitted that this is impossible, but on the following lines an effort may be made. Our imaginary child began with *The Faerie Queene*, and the mature reader must do the same. Passages from Spenser's other works appear, quite rightly, in the following pages, and it would certainly be a pity not to know the *Epithalamion*: but it must never be forgotten that he stands or falls by his great poetic romance, and if you do not like it and yet believe that you like Spenser you are probably deceiving yourself. Secondly, there is that large edition and that wet day. It is not, perhaps, absolutely necessary to have a large edition *in fact*; but it is imperative that you should think of *The Faerie Queene* as a book suitable for reading in a heavy volume, at a table—a book to which limp leather is insulting—a massy, antique story with a blackletter flavour about it—a book for devout, prolonged, and leisurely perusal. The illustrations (real or imagined) raise a problem. There are fantastic palaces and voluptuous nudes in Spenser which seem to ask for Tintoretto or Correggio or Claude: but there are also, and more abundantly, wicket-gates and ugly fiends and stiffly bearded elders which we would rather see in woodcuts—such violent, unforgettable little cuts as Wordsworth mentions in *The Excursion*. This double need for two quite different kinds of picture is characteristic. There is a renaissance element in *The Faerie Queene*—a gorgeous, luxurious, Italianate, and florid element: but this is not the basis of it. All this new growth sprouts out of an old, gnarled wood, and, as in very early spring, mists it over in places without concealing it. The cloth of gold is an occasional decoration: most of the coat is homespun. And it is best to begin with a taste for homespun, accepting the cloth of gold when it comes but by no means depending on it for your pleasure, or you will be disappointed—to keep your *Faerie Queene* on the same shelf with Bunyan and Malory and *The Seven Champions* and even with *Jack the Giant-Killer*, rather than with *Hero and Leander* or *Venus and Adonis*. For this is the paradox of Spenser's poem; it is not really medieval—no medieval romance is very like it—yet everyone who has really enjoyed it, from the Wartons down, has enjoyed it as the very consummation of the Middle Ages, the quintessence of 'the blackletter flavour'.

It came about in this way. Spenser's friends wanted him to be in the Movement, to be an extreme Puritan and a servile classicist, which were the two fashionable things at Cambridge in his day. Under their tutelage he produced the pretentious, and (to tell the truth) nearly worthless, *Shepheards Calendar*. But even in it he was straining at the tether, and his friend E.K. had to write pretty sharp cautionary notes on 'Ladies of the Lake' and 'friendly fairies', hinting that the poet had approached much too nearly to the medieval and the papistical—things as shocking to the fierce young intellectuals of that day as the bourgeois and the Victorian are to their descendants in our own. But Spenser, in his great work, went back to what he had always liked, and took all his renaissance accomplishments with him. What he had always liked was the Middle Ages as he imagined them to have been and as they survived in his time in the pageant, the morality play, and the metrical romance. They were real survivals, yet they smelled already a little archaic: they had already, for Spenser himself, a touch of the black-letter flavour. He thus became something between the last of the medieval poets and the first of the romantic medievalists; he was enabled to produce a tale more solemn, more redolent of the past, more venerable, than any real medieval romance—to deny, in his own person, the breach between the Middle Ages and the Renaissance and to hand on to succeeding generations a poetic symbol of the former whose charms have proved inexhaustible.

It will be remembered that we attributed to our ideal reader—along with the wet day, the large volume, and the unjaded appetite of boyhood—a haunting memory that he has met all these knights and ladies, all these monsters and enchanters, somewhere before. What corresponds to this in the experience of the mature reader is the consciousness of Spenser's moral allegory. Critics differ as regards the degree of attention which we must pay to it. It may not be necessary for all readers at all stages of the narrative to know exactly what the poet means, but it is emphatically necessary that they should surrender themselves to the sense of some dim significance in the background—that they should feel themselves to be moving in regions 'where more is meant than meets the ear'. Even if this feeling were only an illusion, it would be an essential part of the whole poetic illusion intended. The present writer, however, thinks that it is nothing of the sort: that Spenser's beautiful or alarming visions do truly embody, in forms as unsophisticated as those of our pantomime fairies and devils, though incomparably more potent, moral and psychological realities of the utmost simplicity and profundity. Certainly they are, at their best, as Mr Yeats says of the figures in Spenser's House of Busirane, 'so visionary, so full of ghostly midnight animation, that one is persuaded that they had some strange purpose and did truly appear in just that way'.

11

NEOPLATONISM IN THE POETRY OF SPENSER[1]

The thesis of this important book is that Spenser knew (and cared) much less about Neoplatonism and even about Plato than many of his critics believe, and that numerous interpretations of his work which their belief has led them to advance are chimerical.

Dr Ellrodt brings rare qualifications to his task. A very wide and careful reading of Spenserian criticism and of texts relevant to Spenser in many languages is almost the least of them. His deep insight into, and sympathy with, Spenser's cast of mind is less usual. Better still, he is refreshingly free from that deadly outlook (so incident to *Quellenforschung*) which treats a poet as a mere conduit pipe through which 'motifs' and 'influences' pass by some energy of their own. Spenser always remains for him a concrete human being writing a particular poem in which much will be begotten by the 'necessities of subject matter' (pp. 18–19). Best of all, he has that wide and balanced erudition which so many literary specialists lack today; he never sees evidence of Pantheism, Platonism, or Calvinism in *gnomae* which are really the commonplaces of all Western Christendom.

In his Introduction he lays a firm foundation by distinguishing three things. (1) The diffused and Christianized Platonism which descends to the Middle Ages through St Augustine, Boethius, Macrobius, Chalcidius, Pseudo-Dionysius and many others. (2) The 'seething mass' (p. 9) of theosophy which men like Ficino, Pico, and Abrabanel got, or thought they were getting, out of Zoroaster, Orphism, Plato, Plotinus, Porphyry, and the Hermetica. (3) A more courtly, erotic, and aesthetic Platonism such as we find in the *trattati d'amore*: not always to be very sharply distinguished

[1] Robert Ellrodt, *Neoplatonism in the Poetry of Spenser* (Genève: Librairie E. Droz, 1960).

from Petrarchism, which in its turn shades off imperceptibly into *dolce stil nuovo* and thence into *amour courtois*.

The author's contention is that while the first of these is often influential, and the third sometimes, on Spenser, the influence of the second (to which alone he gives the title *Neoplatonism*) can hardly be detected with certainty anywhere outside some sonnets in the *Amoretti* and the *Foure Hymnes*.

Dr Ellrodt then turns to chronology; and, believing all four hymns to be late, he necessarily believes that Spenser lied when he attributed the first two to 'the greener times of his youth'. The argument here is close and weighty and cannot be dealt with in the space at my disposal. But this is the less to be regretted since, as the author clearly sees, the dating he accepts is not really necessary to his main position. He, like us, could conceive a process opposite to that which he thinks more probable. Spenser might have begun with a short-lived enthusiasm for the Florentines and written the first two hymns with the accuracy of a neophite. The lack of demonstrably Neoplatonic echoes in the rest of his work would then represent, not (as in Dr Ellrodt's picture) a period when he was still ignorant of their system, but a period in which he learned to sit to it more and more loosely. The exigencies of romantic narrative and (perhaps still more) the experience of real love for a real woman might well have worn away all the sharp, and therefore recognizable, features, leaving only what he had fully digested and turned to his own use. For the digested is usually the unrecognizable. It is the contents of a man's stomach rather than the analysis of his blood, that show you what he has been eating.

But even in the *Hymnes* themselves Dr Ellrodt finds the strictly Neoplatonic elements to be less, and less important, than some suppose. He justly stresses the Ovidian, medieval, and Petrarchan strains in the first two. He points out that the myth of Poros and Penia (HL, 52-3) is dismissed in two lines with no hint of the metaphysical significance it had for Ficino (or even for Plato himself). Spenser's Venus (HL, 62-73) can only loosely be equated with the celestial Venus of the Neoplatonists; their characteristic theosophy of graded emanations is never mentioned. The account of Love's cosmic operations (HL, 78 *seq.*) needs no other source than

Timaeus interprete Chalcidio, 28–9; or if it did, Dr Ellrodt might consider Boethius's *De Cons.* II Metr. 8, or even Chaucer's *Troilus*, III, 1744–64. More important still, the 'eternitie' (HL, 104) sought by Spenser's lover has nothing to do with the fruition of intelligible Beauty, being (as in *Epithalamion*, 418 *seq.*) the eternal life in heaven of the children he hopes to beget. For the goal of the love which Spenser here celebrates is lawful, carnal fruition within marriage (HL, 280–93). By orthodox Neoplatonists fruition was either repudiated or coldly conceded. Even Abrabanel and Varchi, who approve it more warmly, feel obliged (as Donne felt) to defend it; Spenser, like a Shakespearian lover, takes it for granted. This, the unbridgeable gap between him and true Neoplatonism, makes any ascent of the Platonic ladder impossible in the *Hymnes*. In HB the contrast between the love of corporeal and that of archetypal beauty is replaced by a far homelier contrast between 'disloiall lust' and 'loiall love' (170, 176). The relation between the first and second pair of hymns, therefore, is not and cannot be one of progression; rather, as the author well says, the two pairs form a diptych. In the 'heavenly' hymns we do not go on through and beyond the love of woman; we make an absolutely fresh start from the ground floor with the beauties of nature. The earthly loves are not treated as the first step of an ascent now to be made. They are set aside as 'vaine' and 'follies' (HHL, 15, 12) in the light of something sheerly other than themselves. There is no attempt to say with Donne 'the admiring her my mind did whett to seek thee, God'; we are much closer to *si quis venit ad me et non odit...uxorem*. The attitude is similar to that which Dr Ellrodt sees in the ultimate rejection of Cleopolis for the New Jerusalem and of the knight's adventures for the hermit's cell (pp. 208–9). For the rest, we have Christianity poetized by a mere colouring of Neoplatonism. Where Spenser comes nearest to the Florentines he never clearly crosses the frontier. He will attribute fertility to the self-love of the First Fair; but for him this does not produce a mere emanation, it begets co-equal Deity (HHL, 29 *seq.*).

In most of this Dr Ellrodt seems to me clearly right. Other fortresses of Neoplatonic interpretation remain to be attacked.

The Mutability fragment he admits to be Platonic; but with the diffused and baptized Platonism of the Middle Ages, not with the 'Platonic Theology' of the Renaissance. Even its astronomy is medieval. The element of fire is not put out (vi, 7). Mutability never plays what would have been her ace of trumps—the *Nova* of 1572. The celestial irregularities which she boasts are such as had been observed for centuries. Ficino's Nature had been an emanation, lower than Mind, lower even than Soul, without volition or con‑sciousness. Spenser's Nature is a figure far more august. Her descent from the 'Christian naturalism' of the Middle Ages is unmistakable. Dr Ellrodt compares the veiling of her face with Jean de Meung's statement that its beauty *ne peut estre d'ome compris* (*Roman de la Rose*, 16248). Far from going beyond medieval Platonism, Spenser recedes from it. He sees the relation between the eternal and the mutable in more Christian and eschatological terms than Boethius. The temporal world for him is not, as it is in the *De Consolatione*, a perpetual and therefore (on its own level) unimprovable image of the eternal. Change works towards an End (both in the temporal and the teleological senses of that word) which, once achieved, will abolish change in the 'stedfast rest of all things' (viii, 2).

Here I agree with Dr Ellrodt in the main but differ from him on some details. I do not understand why he wishes to give to Jove, besides his planetary and Olympian character, that of one who symbolizes the Christian God (p. 68). It is very true that in Spenser, as in Milton and many others, Jove is often Jehovah *incognito*. But never, I suggest, less so than here. He is powerless to cope with Mutability's insurrection and did 'inly grudge' at her appeal, which he apparently could not disallow, to a higher court (vi, 35). He is as nothing before Nature. If his reply to Mutability (vi, 31–4) sounds like the speech of God, must not the speech (from the throne) of any lawful, just, wise, and beneficent sovereign do the same? The king of gods, the best of planets, the *fortuna major*, is—like Gloriana—*ex officio* a vicegerent and 'idole' of the Almighty. There is no need to identify Mutability's father Titan at all rigorously with Satan. It is enough that there should be an analogy; Titan is to Jove as Satan to God.

The parallel between Jean de Meung's lines and Spenser's reference to the veiled, because insupportable, countenance of Nature, does not seem so strong to me as to Dr Ellrodt. Jean de Meung uses *occupatio*, the familiar device of saying that something is too fine to be described or even comprehended. Spenser makes three quite different points: (*a*) that perhaps Nature is a hermaphrodite; (*b*) that perhaps her face is too terrible to see and 'like a Lion'; (*c*) that perhaps it is too radiant—not to describe, but to 'indure' (vii, 5–6). All this suggests to me a different, and deeper, level of ideas from anything in the passage from the *Roman*. Whatever the sources, we may note some affinities. Cusanus tells us (*Doct. Ignorantia*, I, 25) that Hermes attributed both sexes to God and that the ancients called God, among many other names, 'Nature'. In the previous chapter he has told us that in the infinite Unity there is no diversity and 'man does not differ from lion'. And we can find one possible reason for the veil in Macrobius: (*Philosophi*) *sciunt inimicam esse Naturae apertam nudamque expositionem sui...arcana voluit per fabulosa tractari* (*In Somn. Scip.* I, ii, 17).

The garden of Adonis is the most cryptic image in *The Faerie Queene* and I am not sure that Dr Ellrodt, or any of us, has solved its mystery. I agree with him that it was 'conceived for Amoret' (p. 26) and that Ovid, interpreted by Golding, was the germ—or one germ, for surely the *Cebetis Tabula* ought also to have been mentioned? And no doubt we all agree that the garden is the garden of genera⁄tion, therefore of sexual love. The 'weedes that bud and blossome there' (III, vi, 30) are in Dr Ellrodt's opinion Forms; not Platonic, archetypal Forms *ante rem* but the *rationes seminales* of St Augustine. Since not all these structural plans or schemata have yet been bio⁄logically actualized, this has the great advantage of explaining the 'uncouth formes which none yet ever knew' (35). They would be the Augustinian *creaturae nobis ignotae*. But two difficulties remain.

Why does Time 'mow the flowring herbes and goodly things' (39) of the garden? Certainly this makes havoc of Dr J. W. Bennett's claim that the garden is the timeless realm of (Platonic) Forms.* Dr Ellrodt's solution, if I have understood him, is that Time mows not the *rationes seminales* but the concrete and corporeal creatures in which—outside the garden, in our world—they are realized. This seems to me a valuable suggestion. As a corollary we might even maintain that it is we, not Spenser, who imagine Time plying his scythe within the garden itself. He destroys its products: but perhaps he destroys them after they have entered this world. Perhaps he 'flyes about' here, not there. Or is it conceivable that he mows and is their 'troubler' (41) because he brings the inexorable hour that sends them 'forth to live in mortall state' (32)? For their birth is of course the beginning of their death.

Stanza 33 is still harder. Dr Ellrodt holds it impossible that so Christian a poet as Spenser can really mean that rational, human souls undergo reincarnation. He suggests that the 'babes' (32) must be either 'seeds' of human bodies or the vegetable souls of men. As to the first, I do not understand in what sense he uses the word *seeds*. The second presupposes the existence of vegetable (human) soul in separation from the sensitive and rational. I admit that the poets sometimes talk as if there were not a three-storied soul, but three distinct souls, in man. But I think they speak tropically. A trope is not basis enough for such a passage as this. Above all, neither hypothesis explains the alternative presented in stanza 33. It there appears that these 'babes' have two possible destinies; *either* they will be 'clad with other hew' *or else* 'sent into the chaungefull world againe'. I fear there is only one system into which this really fits: the (originally Orphic) doctrine which underlies Plutarch's *De Facie*, and which, far later, an author so Christian in intention as Henry More set out uncompromisingly in his *Immortality of the Soul* (III, i, 16). According to this all human souls become aerial daemons after death. But at a later stage some pass on beyond the air, change their aerial for aetherial bodies ('are clad in other hew') and are henceforth immutable and blessed; others, rejected, sink back to earth and suffer reincarnation in terrestrial bodies ('are sent into the chaungefull world againe'). We need not hold that Spenser 'believed' this in the same sense that he believed his creed. He might well have said, like Johnson, that what scripture teaches on such matters is certain, and what 'philosophy' teaches is probable; at least, probable enough for poetry. This picture is not inconsistent with the Christian doctrine of ultimately unalterable salvation or perdition. It adds to it a doctrine, but not 'the Romish doctrine', of Purgatory. It is a permissible speculation. It is, as Plato's 'myths' were to Plato himself, a not unlikely tale.

This is not to say that Spenser's garden, like Plutarch's 'orchard', must be located between Earth and Moon. The truth is that it cannot be located at all. As a biological fact (sexual generation) it is terrestrial, for it is on earth that Venus as Form-giver concerns herself with reproduction and it is to earth that Venus as planet descends by her influence when she makes us amorous (29). As psychological fact, it is again terrestrial, for we experience the delights of love on earth; that is why Spenser knows the pleasures of the garden 'by tryall' (*ibid.*). But as cosmic or metaphysical fact, as the meeting place of Forms (in whatever sense) and matter, it has no position in space.

There remains the problem of Venus and Adonis themselves. Venus ought to be the Form-giver. She dwells only sometimes on earth. Her native region is 'the house of goodly formes and faire aspects Whence all the world derives the glorious Features of beautie, and all shapes select' (12). And Adonis, 'eterne in mutabilitie' and 'transformed oft' (47), ought to be Matter. But is it tolerable that, in defiance of all tradition, Form should be embodied in the feminine image and Matter in the masculine, and even called 'the Father of all formes' (*ibid.*)?

It is hardly tolerable, yet I believe we must tolerate it. Dr Ellrodt thinks (and so do I) that the Sapience of the fourth Hymn must be identified with the Second Person of the Christian Trinity, the Word. I do not at all agree that this image 'can shock only the modern mind' (p. 167). The parallel from a single and audaciously original author (Lady Julian of Norwich) does very little towards palliating the shock. I do not say that this image, if rightly understood, is theologically shocking; it is imaginatively shocking. The intellect can accept it; but on the level of the imagination the masculinity of the Word is almost impregnably entrenched by the sixfold character of Son, Bridegroom, King, Priest, Judge, and Shepherd. Yet all these, apparently, Spenser was prepared to break through. After that, the transference of the sexes between Form and Matter sinks into insignificance.

It is, moreover, most cunningly palliated. The sexual inferiority of Venus to Adonis is heavily compensated by her overwhelming superiority in every other respect. He is mortal (by birth), terrestrial.

She comes from above. She is (probably) Paradigma; certainly goddess, planet, *fortuna minor*. The roles of the sexes are almost reversed in the relation between them. Ordinarily it is the lover who comes to his mistress's bower. But it is Venus who comes to visit Adonis; occasionally, 'when she on earth does dwel' (29). Ordinarily we speak of the male possessing or enjoying the female: but Venus 'when ever that she will'—he has to wait on her will and leisure—'possesseth' Adonis and 'takes her fill' of his 'sweetnesse' (46). He is the flower and she the bee. I do not know where Spenser has shown more delicate art than when he thus secretly restores the traditional relations of Form and Matter at the very point where he has overtly set them aside.

Dr Ellrodt, on the other hand, equates Adonis with Sol, and produces very good evidence that the equation was sometimes made (pp. 82 *seq.*). My dissent from him here involves a principle which may reasonably divide Spenserians in their interpretation of many other passages as well as of this. On my view it is not enough that an interpretation should fit the text logically; it must also fit imaginatively and emotionally. Indeed, if we had to choose, I should prefer a logical to an imaginative and emotional incongruity. This principle of mine can be contested: in the meantime, it is the principle I work by. That is why I cannot accept Adonis as Sol: not because the identification fails to work out conceptually, but because Adonis, as we actually meet him in the poetry, 'feels' or 'tastes' so obstinately unsolar. His garden is on earth (29). It is full of moisture (34). Even within that secret garden he inhabits a still more secret place, a 'gloomy grove', a thicket of 'shadie boughes' (43) where 'Phoebus beams'—his own beams, if he were the sun!—can never reach him (44). He is 'hid from the world' (46). Sweet gums drip about him (43). I cannot feel with Dr Ellrodt that this place 'is obviously reminiscent of Mount Olympus' (p. 86). Its darkness, foliage, dampness, shelter from wind (44), seem to me the antithesis of the shining mountaintop. The statement that the gods 'thither haunt' (49) of itself shows that it is not the gods' home. The verb *haunt* and the adverb of motiontowards (*thither*) mean that it is a place they visit; when they descend, either (mythologically) to take a holiday on earth, or (astrologically) in their influence. Dr Ellrodt's own sugges tion (p. 88 n.) that it has anatomical significance (the *Mons Veneris*) seems inconsistent with his solar theory and far truer to the poetry. I think it is probably right. If so, this is where the profound paradox of Spenser's manipulation of the sexes in this myth reaches its extreme. Adonis is male; yet the Form-giver, approaching his dim bower, is descending to the womb.

To see this paradox in the clearest light we must remember the fruitful tensions and sensitive ambiguities which characterize Spenser's attitude to the sexes elsewhere. His explicit statements are those we should expect from a man of his age. He regards 'soft Silence and submisse Obedience' as proper to women (IV, x, 51). He condemns the breach of natural hierarchy in Radigund (V, v, 25). This is the doctrinal façade. What moves behind it is rather different. He is haunted by the image of the Hermaphrodite (III, xii, old ending; IV, x, 41; VII, vii, 5). His Una, though touchingly unaware of the fact and, in her own eyes, the humblest of forsaken damsels (I, iii, 7), is in reality superior to St George as Grace is to sinful man (I, viii, 1). Britomart defeats Arthegall in the lists (IV, iv, 44) and rescues him from slavery (V, vii, 37 *seq.*). And if, as I think, she becomes Isis in her dream (*ibid.* the 'crowne of gold', vii, 13), then Arthegall is to her as the crocodile is to Isis. She is that Equity (3) or 'clemence' (22) without which his rough 'justise' would be merely *salvagesse sans finesse* (IV, iv, 39). Thus in a sense she rescues or saves him eternally in the Church of Isis as well as at one moment before the Castle of Radigund. But she too, like Una, acts humbly, like a woman in love, paradisially unaware of her high dignity.

Of *The Faerie Queene* in general Dr Ellrodt says 'the scene of the action is on earth' (p. 58). The court of Gloriana is no realm beyond this world; it is Cleopolis, an 'earthly frame' (I, x, 59), utterly distinct from the New Jerusalem. Britomart and Belphoebe are not the two Veneres of Ficino (p. 59). Florimell is not 'true beauty' in any Neoplatonic sense (p. 47). Gloriana is not 'ultimate Platonic truth' (p. 44). There is not a word about Platonism in the Letter to Raleigh; on the contrary, Spenser says he is writing for those who prefer Xenophon (p. 59).

Much of this is welcome. To make Belphoebe a Venus of any sort is, I think, to misunderstand the whole myth to which she belongs. In it Spenser is pacifying the old medieval *débat* between Venus and Diana. Diana's fosterling and the fosterling of Venus are shown to be twin sisters. Both are equally of divine (solar) descent and both immaculately conceived. They are alternative excellences of womanhood between whom there need be no quarrel and no inequality. This and something more—almost, as Cusanus would say, a *coincidentia oppositorum*—is hinted in their grandmother's name, Amphisa—'Both Equal' or 'Equally Both' (III, vi, 4). In more modern terms, they are two archetypes: the Terrible Huntress and the Yielding Bride.

It is doubtful whether Dr Ellrodt's position is much strengthened by the reference to the Letter. This at so many points flatly contra-dicts the text that it is flimsy evidence for anything. And the preference for Xenophon concerns his method, not his doctrine. He is valued for teaching rather 'by example then by rule'.

And has not something of Arthur and Gloriana escaped us? It is very true that their meeting (1, ix, 9–15) is derived from 'fairy lore', from *Lanval* and many other Celtic stories; just as St George's dragon-fight is derived from many other dragon-fights (p. 52). But that tells us nothing about its meaning. It is also true that Arthur declares himself to have been pricked on by 'kindly heat' (1, ix, 9) and subdued by Cupid, 'that proud avenging boy' (12). Of course. No one doubts that the story is *literaliter* erotic. The question whether the erotic images symbolize some supersensuous experience or not remains to be considered on its own merits. (That Gloriana's relation to Elizabeth I is wholly in abeyance at this point, seems to me certain; otherwise the passage would have endangered Spenser's ears, perhaps his head.)

Now the episode is peculiar in two ways. First, we are not allowed to decide whether Arthur's experience was a dream or a reality. At the words 'me seemed' (13) it appears to be a dream; the mention of the 'pressed gras where she had lyen' (15) sounds as if it were very much more. And secondly, we are not given clearly to understand whether, after this night of 'goodly glee and lovely blandishment' (14), the fairy rose (or was dreamed to rise) with her virginity intact.

This double obscurity about both the reality and the result of the *concubitus* is tolerable only on one condition. Suppose it to be real. You can have a story in which two lovers consummate their love, but you must not leave us in doubt. You can also have a story in which they lay together and abstained. It does not matter whether this or that reader thinks such abstinence possible in the real world. It will be poetically possible provided this *tour de force* of chastity is made the main point of the story. What is not tolerable—what is in fact ludicrous—is to pass the thing over as if it were an unimportant detail. Again, you can have a story in which a lover dreams that he has his mistress in his arms. But then the bitter awakening, the disappointment, the realization that it was 'only a dream', must be the catastrophe of that story. Spenser's actual handling is tolerable on one condition only; that we are being shown the sort of experience to which the contrast either between mere 'blandishment' and full fruition or between dream and waking does not strictly apply. But the soul's new-kindled raptures at its first meeting with a transcendental or at least incorporeal object of love, is an experience of that kind. First love of fame, of music, of poetry, of a political 'cause', of a vocation, of a virtue, of God, have this character. To what stage or degree of physical intimacy this spiritual 'embrace' should precisely be compared is a senseless question: you must not ask whether the Queen of Faerie kept her virginity or not. But to doubt whether it was a dream, whether the whole thing, or part of it, and if so what part, was not 'only one's own imagination', is absolutely inevitable.

Gloriana can therefore be glory, in the sense of fame. But I share Dr Ellrodt's reluctance to make her merely the fame that grows on mortal soil (p. 52). She is also, I still believe, Glory in a far more religious sense. I think Spenser avails himself of an equivocation in the word *glory*, as Douglas in his *Palice of Honour* equivocates with *honour*.

For Arthur is certainly neither Aristotle's Magnanimity nor his Magnificence. Dr Ellrodt says that he bears the shield of 'heavenly grace' (p. 51). But in scripture the shield is Faith, not Grace; *scutum fidei* (Eph. vi. 16). And Arthur by uncovering his shield can 'daunt unequall armies of his foes' (I, vii, 34). Had Spenser remembered that by Faith the saints of old *castra verterunt exterorum*

(Heb. xi. 34)? And if Spenser believed, as on one level he certainly did, in salvation by Faith, is it of no significance that Arthur's function in the poem is to save other knights at need? I suspect that Arthur is *inter alia* the knight of Faith, and Gloriana, *inter alia*, that glory beyond the world which Faith pursues.

The reservation *inter alia* is, however, essential. Arthur is also a knight-errant seeking earthly glory (*los*, honour) by deeds of arms. We must repress our impulse to present Spenser with an Either-Or. In the modern criticism of modern poetry the principle of Ambiguity is always assumed; all the possible meanings of any one word are supposed to be in some measure operative. On the verbal level such ambiguity was, in my opinion, undreamed of by sixteenth-century poets and their readers. Its place was taken, I suggest, by icono-graphical ambiguity. It was not felt desirable, much less necessary, when you mentioned, say, Jove, to exclude any of his meanings; the Christian God, the Pagan god, the planet as actually seen, the planet astrologically considered, were all welcome to enrich the figure, by turns or even simultaneously. If more, and more erudite, symbolism than the poet had consciously intended were read into any image, he would not be displeased. If Spenser were a truthful man he might have to agree with Dr Ellrodt that he had never thought of half the allegories his Platonizing critics read into him; whether he would thank Dr Ellrodt for proclaiming the fact is another matter. The closest parallel—it is not a source—to Spenser will I believe be found in the work of the great Italian mythological painters, as Professor Wind[1] has now taught us to interpret them. The aim is to load every inch of the canvas or every stanza of the poem with the greatest possible weight of 'wisdom', learning, edification, suggestion, solemnity, and ideal beauty. Symbols that are on different levels or come from very different sources are not logically harmonized with great care; they are plastically harmonized in the pictorial design or the narrative flow. The inconsistencies we discover in Spenser are perhaps sometimes offences against a sort of consistency he hardly attempted. We are too apt to say of allegory '*A* is *B*' (and there-fore not *C*, *D*, or *E*). But the allegorist was really saying '*A* is like *B*'; therefore quite possibly like *C*, *D*, and *E* as well. Thus

[1] E. Wind, *Pagan Mysteries in the Renaissance* (London, 1958).

B, C, D, and *E* can change and melt into one another, now this predominant, now that, in the fluidity of the poem. Waves at sea are not less beautiful because you cannot represent them in a contour map.

This technique of dissolving views sets a limit (of which he is aware) to the accuracy of Dr Ellrodt's own map. To show that many passages do not, as some thought, demand a Neoplatonic interpretation is not the same as showing that they do not admit it. To show that they do not even admit a strict or technical Neoplatonic interpretation is not to show that they owe nothing to the Florentines at all. Dr Ellrodt often disproves a positive; from the nature of the case, and of logic itself, he cannot equally prove a negative. It can be shown that Spenser never accurately or unmistakably pins Venus down to the place the first Venus holds in their theosophy of emanations. It does not follow that she is never for him the Paradigma and does not carry with her something—just so much as he needed and remembered—of her Neoplatonic associations. It is certain that the court of Gloriana cannot 'be' the archetypal world of Forms. Yet if this place, never actually present in the poem, this so desired place from which nearly everyone has come and to which nearly everyone will return, at some moments suggests another and lovelier world, we need not be sure that the suggestion is wholly unforeseen and fortuitous. If Florimell, lost and bewildered as soon as she leaves that happy realm, and finally captured by the shape-changing Proteus (III, viii), willy-nilly suggests to us the soul lost and imprisoned in the world of matter and change, we cannot be sure that she never suggested this to Spenser. We must not too literally accept the statement that the scene of action is always on earth. Una's country (I, xi) seems to be at least the Earthly Paradise. Mutability's journey is up through the spheres. The garden of Adonis is nowhere and everywhere. The Cave of Despair, the Temple of Venus, Mount Acidale, are within us. But what Dr Ellrodt means is true and important. Spenser is primarily the poet of the *creatura*, the universe.

Chapter XII ('Spenser's religious sensibility') is admirable. Spenser is neither Platonist nor Pantheist nor Puritan. Even his Protestantism is more of the head than of the heart. We must not try to pin him down by such classifications. He himself, through the mouth of Irenius, tells us that he has 'lyttle...to saie of relidgion', having not 'bene much conversant in that callinge' (*View*, ed. Renwick, 1934, p. 104). *Relidgion* had better be glossed as 'technical theology and ecclesiastical polity'. For Spenser was certainly, in his own way, a religious man. And also a religious poet. But the deepest, most spontaneous, and most ubiquitous devotion of that poet goes out to God, not as the One of Plotinus, not as the Calvinists' predestinator, not even as the Incarnate Redeemer, but as 'the glad Creator', the fashioner of flower and forest and river, of excellent trout and pike, of months and seasons, of beautiful women and 'lovely knights', of love and marriage, of sun, moon, and planets, of angels, above all of light. He sees the creatures, in Charles William's phrase, as 'illustrious with being'.

Not, to be sure, that he is a 'nature poet' in the same sense as Wordsworth. He would, in our age, have felt more sympathy with Bergson or even with D. H. Lawrence. His universe dances with energy. In other poets temptation usually summons the will to Titanic action, to the inordinate resolutions of a Tamburlaine, a Faustus, a Macbeth, or a Satan. In Spenser it more often whispers 'Lie down. Relax. Let go. Indulge the death wish'. Yet he is also more Olympian, more tranquil than a modern vitalist. His universe has the vigour not of a battle but of a dance. Here again the parallel is to be sought in the visual arts. *The Faerie Queene* is a verbal, as the Palazzo della Ragione in Padua is a plastic, representation of, and hymn to, the cosmos as our ancestors believed it to be. There has been no delight (of that sort) in 'nature' since the old cosmology was rejected. No one can respond in just that way to the Einsteinian, or even the Newtonian, universe. To excite and satisfy such love the model must be clearly finite yet unimaginably large; patterned and hierarchical; moved in the last resort by love.

I have stressed fully my dissents from Dr Ellrodt precisely because this book seems to me so valuable: it is the *prima facie* case for canonization that demands the Devil's Advocate. I am not certain that I am right and he wrong on any of the disputed points. But I am quite certain that he has often set me right where I had been wrong; and where I was already right he has strengthened my hand.

The Foreword contains apologies for 'controversial eagerness' and for any blemishes that may have resulted from writing in a foreign language. The apologies are gracious, but neither was needed. Dr Ellrodt always treats his opponents—in places I am one of them—with courtesy; and it is much to be wished that all British and American scholars wrote English as well as he.

12

SPENSER'S CRUEL CUPID

Blindfold he was, and in his cruell fist
A mortall bow and arrowes keene did hold,
With which he shot at randon, when him list,
Some headed with sad lead, some with pure gold;
(Ah man beware, how thou those darts behold)
A wounded Dragon under him did ly,
Whose hideous tayle his left foot did enfold,
And with a shaft was shot through either eye,
That no man forth might draw, ne no man remedye.

(F.Q. III, xi, 48)

This stanza provides examples of nearly everything in Spenser which tends to disappoint a modern reader. The movement of the verse is extremely regular: only in the fourth line ('Some headed with sad lead, some with pure gold') is the iambic flow disturbed. The image presented appears banal. We have heard a thousand times before that Cupid is blindfold and that he bears arrows. Even the distinction between two kinds of arrows is not new. We have met it in the *Roman de la Rose* (908 *seq.*) and Ovid's *Metamorphoses* (I, 462 *seq.*). There are no tensions or ambiguities in the language; nothing but literal, sequacious description. The only novelty is the dragon under Cupid's foot. The only puzzle is the shaft that has put out its eyes, and the curious emphasis (in the last line) on the hopeless character of the injury. It sounds almost as if Spenser were pitying the dragon. One does not expect a writer of chivalrous romance to pity dragons.

Such a passage neither demands nor admits the minute verbal explication in which the most vigorous modern criticism excels. There is, however, room for explication of a different sort.

Cupid's arrows, generally banal, are not banal in Spenser.

In the very frontispiece of his poem he has introduced (I, Proem 3) the loves of Mars and Venus. In the *Odyssey* those loves were little

more than a merry tale; by Spenser's time they had come to symbolize the victory of beauty over strength and peace over war;
concord resolving discord. This is what the story meant to Lucretius
and Plutarch; and to Botticelli, in whose picture the profound sleep
of Mars and the waking tranquillity of Venus powerfully present
'the lineaments of gratified desire'—not their desire only but that of
all creation. The disarmament of Mars is emphasized by the fact that
his arms have become toys for infant fawns to play with. But
Spenser adds another detail. He disarms Cupid as well as Mars. It
is a Cupid without his 'deadly Heben bowe' who inspires the
concubitus whereby the goddess Harmony was engendered.

This is not the only place where Cupid is deprived of his weapons.
The Angel in II, viii, 6 is compared not simply to Cupid but to
Cupid sporting with the Graces and 'having laid his cruell bow
away'. Cupid is admitted to the House of Alma (II, ix, 34)
'having from him layd His cruell bow'. Again in the garden of
Adonis he takes his pleasure 'laying his sad darts Aside' (III, vi, 49).

There are, admittedly, places where his arrows are mentioned in
merely rhetorical fashion; as in I, Proem 3 itself or III, ii, 26, or ii, 35,
or vi, 23. They colour the language but barely reach the visual
imagination. When the arrows are included in, or expressly excluded from, a fully realized image, they are usually significant.

Their mention in the stanza we are considering stamps this Cupid
as a particular kind of Cupid.

The bandage on this Cupid's eyes would be banal if we stopped
reading when we had finished the stanza. But it is presently going
to leap into meaning. We shall then see the living Cupid—hitherto
we have been looking at his statue—equally blindfold at first and
then unbinding the bandage to enjoy the sight of Amoret's torture.
At which 'he much rejoiced in his cruell mind' and clapped his
wings (III, xii, 22). He is blind except to the pleasures of cruelty;
to them, gladly attentive.

And what of the dragon? Dragons (or serpents) have various
significances. For modern depth-psychology they mean the *libido* or
even the phallus. In some contexts they have meant wisdom.
Sometimes, if they have their tails in their mouths, they are the
symbol of eternity. But the key to this particular use lies elsewhere.

In Alciati's *Emblematum Liber* (1531)[1] we find the virgin goddess Minerva (or Pallas) pictured with a dragon as her attendant. The verses which follow explain why:

> Vera haec effigies innuptae est Palladis: Ejus
> Hic draco, qui dominae constitit ante pedes.
> Cur divae comes hoc animal? Custodia rerum
> Huic data: sic lucos sacraque templa colit.
> Innuptas opus est cura asservare puellas
> Pervigili; laqueos undique tendit amor.[2]

A long tradition of dragons as guardians lies behind this. The Golden Fleece was guarded by a dragon, and the dragon which guards buried treasure (say, in *Beowulf* and the Volsung story) is as old as *Phaedrus* (IV, xx). More relevant than either is the dragon of the Hesperides. The Hesperides themselves associate it with virginity, and so, more potently and on a deeper level, do the golden apples. For apples often symbolize the female breasts; perhaps, especially, girlish and undeveloped breasts—the *pome acerbe*, the 'unripe' apples, of Ariosto's Alcina in the *Furioso* (VII, 14) or those of Philoclea in the *Arcadia* (1590, I, xiii, 6).

Alciati's book was so well known that we may be sure that it is, directly or indirectly, the source of Spenser's blinded dragon. This is the guardian of chastity mutilated in the very organs which qualified it for guardianship. The same function is allotted to the dragon, with the same emphasis on its eyes, by two other English poets. Thus in Jonson,

> What earthly spirit but will attempt
> To taste the fruite of beauties golden tree,
> When leaden sleepe seales up the dragon's eyes?
>
> (*Every Man in his Humor*, 1601, III, i, 19)

And in Milton,

> But beauty, like the fair Hesperian tree
> Laden with blooming gold, had need the guard
> Of dragon-watch with unenchanted eye.... (*Comus*, 393–5)

---

[1] Although Lewis mentions only the 1531 edition of the *Emblematum Liber*, there are many subsequent editions of this book which Spenser could have used.—W.H.

[2] This is the true likeness of unwedded Pallas. Hers is this dragon, standing at its mistress's feet. Why is this animal the goddess's companion? Its allotted task is to guard things. Thus it cares for groves and sacred temples. Sleepless care is needed to keep girls safe before marriage; love spreads his snares everywhere.

Without going beyond the single stanza, then, we discover that this Cupid is more particularized than he seemed at the first glance. But let us now go beyond it.

He is made of 'massy gold' (stanza 47). Gold of itself could never, I believe, be a symbol of evil to any human poet. But in this particular context Spenser has already contrived to make gold sinister. This statue stands in a room whose walls are covered with tapestries in which

> the rich metall lurked privily,
> As faining to be hid from envious eye;
> Yet here, and there, and every where unawares
> It shewd it selfe, and shone unwillingly;
> Like a discolourd Snake, whose hidden snares
> Through the greene gras his long bright burnisht backe declares.
>
> (28)

Again, if we go forward from the stanza we started with, we discover that this statue is not merely decorative. It is, in the full theological sense, an idol. And its effect on Britomart, through whose eyes we are seeing the whole adventure, is very remarkable. It 'amazed' her; she couldn't stop looking at it; she was 'dazd', dazzled and confused, by its extreme brightness.

Britomart, we know, is the Knight of Chastity. But Chastity, as embodied in her, means for Spenser True Love; that is, constant, fertile, monogamic, felicific love. Though she is, during the action of the poem, a virgin, she is much more like a mother-goddess than a virgin goddess. We are never for long allowed to forget that she is to be the ancestress of kings and heroes—

> For from thy wombe a famous Progenie
> Shall spring, out of the auncient *Trojan* blood. (III, iii, 22–3)

It is love, so conceived, that comes to defeat the cruel Cupid, but is momentarily dazzled by his idol.

The conception of such an enmity between Cupid—one kind of Cupid—and True Love is also found in a passage from Sidney where Cupid is banished from (of all places) the marriage bed. In the Epithalamium sung by Dycus we read

> But thou foule Cupid syre to lawlesse lust,
> Be thou farre hence with thy empoyson'd darte,

Which though of glittring golde, shall heere take rust
Where simple love, which chastnesse doth imparte,
Avoydes thy hurtfull arte.

(*The Poems of Sir Philip Sidney*, ed. W. A. Ringler, Jr.
(Oxford, 1962), p. 92)

The 'arrows' of Cupid in the ancient tradition meant, I believe,
no more than the sweet-sharp stings of bodily desire. It is clear that
they cannot mean this when Spenser or Sidney banishes the arrows
from scenes of what they regard as True Love. If they meant that,
the absence of the arrows could only mean impotence and frigidity.
But in both poets, lawful and unlawful love alike usually seek
fruition; are not, in the cant sense, 'Platonic'.*

13

GENIUS AND GENIUS

Dr Janet Spens, who has done so much in her *Spenser's Faerie Queene* to recall Spenserian criticism to paths unwisely neglected since the seventeenth century, is rightly troubled (p. 22) by the double role of Genius in Spenser's allegory, as the doorkeeper to Acrasia in II, xii, 47 and to Adonis in III, vi, 31 *et seq*. There is a mystery about the first of these two passages which I do not believe that I have solved; but the two-edged use of the name Genius, in general, is explicable by his history.

Mr W. Warde Fowler (in his *Religious Experience of the Roman People*, p. 74) finds the origin of the 'Genius' of early Roman belief in the world-wide conception of a man's spiritual double or external soul which constitutes his higher self. If this were all, the development of the Genius into a familiar δαίμων such as Socrates enjoyed, and thence (under Christianity) into a guardian angel, and so finally into the poetic self of a poet and into all the familiar modern usages, would be simple enough. But Mr Warde Fowler also tells us that for Roman thought the Genius, or higher self, of the *paterfamilias* was specially connected with his function of carrying on the family: in fact, with the reproductive power. Such a peculiar conception leaves the way open for two different developments according as the emphasis is laid on Genius = higher self in general, or on Genius = reproductive power. And the two developments both occurred.

St Augustine (*De Civit. Dei*, VII, 13), criticizing Varro, writes as follows: *Quid est Genius? 'Deus,' inquit [sc. Varro] 'qui praepositus est ac vim habet omnium rerum gignendarum'...alio loco genium dicit esse uniuscuiusque animum rationalem et ideo esse singulos singulorum.* Here we have pretty clearly the two senses developed. Genius *A* is the universal god or spirit of generation. Genius *B* is the higher self, familiar, or δαίμων of any individual man. (It will be clear, of course, that while there is only one Genius *A*, there are as many genii *BB* as there are human beings.) St Augustine, if I follow his argument rightly, regards the double sense as an inconsistency in Varro and so perhaps it was; but in Martianus Capella two separate beings are described. He is speaking of the infra-solar deities whom he distinguishes from the higher gods: *De Nupt. Merc. et Phil.* II, 38, 39 G. *Sed quoniam unicuique deorum superiorum singuli quique* (*i.e.* of the infra-solar gods) *deserviunt, ex illorum arbitrio istorumque comitatu et generalis omnium praesul et specialis singulis mortalibus Genius ammovetur.* Here we might be quite sure that the *generalis praesul* was Genius *A* (as we are that the other is Genius *B*), if Martianus said anything about generation. In fact, he makes his *praesul* provide *gerundis omnibus*, not *gignendis omnibus* as we should expect and are tempted to read. But fortunately later authorities leave us in little doubt. In Bernardus Sylvester's *De Mundi Universitate* we have a descent from heaven to earth, in which the travellers, on reaching the *aplanon*, or sphere of fixed stars, are met by a venerable person described as *Oyarses et genius in artem et officium pictoris et figurantis addictus* (Prosa III *ad fin.*, p. 38 in Barach and Wrobel's ed., Innsbruck, 1876). His pictorial art consists, we are told, in inscribing the Forms, conceived in heaven, upon the phenomenal world, which is precisely what every instance of reproduction does: that, in fact, is why he is called *genius*—Genius *A*. His other name *Oyarses*, as Professor C. C. J. Webb pointed out to me, must be a corruption of οὐσιάρχης; and he had kindly drawn my attention to a passage in Pseudo-Apuleius, *Asclepius* (XIX), where we find an 'Ousiarch' in the sphere of the fixed stars *qui diversis speciebus diversas formas facit*—though he is not here called Genius. Finally we may note that Isidore (a good witness to the accepted usage of any word) explains Genius exclusively in sense *A* (*Genium autem dicunt quod quasi vim habeat omnium rerum gignendarum seu a gignendis liberis unde et geniales lecti dicebantur a gentibus qui novo marito sternebantur. Etymolog.* VIII, xi, 88).

It will readily be seen that Genius *A* counts for much more than Genius *B* in medieval literature. In Alanus, *De Planctu Naturae*, the Genius who appears as the priest of Venus to curse unnatural loves is clearly Genius *A*, who, as the patron of generation and therefore of heterosexuality, has an obvious concern in the matter. He also retains from Bernardus the *officium pictoris et figurantis* and carries a scroll in his left hand and a pen in his right[1] (*De Planct. Nat.* Pros. ix, p. 517 in Wright's *Anglo-Latin Satirists*). From him descend the Genius of the *Roman de la Rose* and the Genius of the *Confessio Amantis*—beings whose association with Venus and Nature is perfectly intelligible when once we have learned of the existence of Genius *A*, though it might perplex a modern reader familiar only with Genius *B*. It is now time to turn to Spenser, but before doing so we must remind ourselves that Genius *B* is itself divided into two classes, the good and evil genius: each man apparently having both the one and the other. Natalis Comes (whom Spenser had almost certainly read) in his *Mythologiae* (IV, iii) writes: *crediderunt singulos homines statim atque nati fuissent daemones duos habere, alterum malum, alterum bonum.* The two angels of Faustus provide a familiar example. The full scheme, therefore, is:

> Genius *A*   God of Generation.
>
> Genius *B*   Second self, individual δαίμων $\begin{cases} \text{I} & \text{Good} \\ \text{II} & \text{Bad.} \end{cases}$

Genius, as I have said, occurs twice in Spenser: in II, xii as the porter of Acrasia, and in III, vi, 32 as the porter of Adonis. The second passage presents no difficulties. It is as clear as can be desired that we have there a portrait of Genius *A*:

> A thousand thousand naked babes attend
> About him day and night, which doe require,
> That he with fleshly weedes would them attire—

which is just what the god of generation ought to do. The whole passage, as Warton* (*ad loc.*) points out, is closely connected with the first-century *Cebetis Tabula*—a popular schoolbook in Spenser's time, mentioned by Milton as an 'easy and delightful book of education'.[2] In it we find a περίβολος, or enclosure, representing Life, and a crowd of the unborn besieging its gate, which is guarded by a γέρων called Δαίμων. His position at the gate of birth and the

---

[1] Is Genius the unnamed 'writer' in Claudian's *De Consolatu Stilichonis*, II, 424 *et seq.*? I owe this suggestion to E. C. Knowlton's 'The Allegorical Figure Genius' (*Classical Philology*, XV, 1920) which, along with the same author's 'Genius as an Allegorical Figure' (*Modern Language Notes*, XXXIX), is the only treatment of the subject I have come across. Mr Knowlton, however, approaches the subject from another angle than mine and does not distinguish Genius *A* from Genius *B*.

[2] *On Education*, Prose Works, ed. Bohn, III, 468.

scroll (χάρτης) which he holds in his left hand leave us in no doubt that he is Genius *A*.[1] The Genius of the garden of Adonis is the god of generation.

It is at the entry to the Bower of Bliss that the trouble begins. Here we read:

> They in that place him Genius did call:
> Not that celestiall powre, to whom the care
> Of life, and generation of all
> That lives, pertaines in charge particulare,
> Who wondrous things concerning our welfare,
> And straunge phantomes doth let us oft foresee,
> And oft of secret ills bids us beware:
> That is our Selfe, whom though we do not see,
> Yet each doth in him selfe it well perceive to bee.
>
> Therefore a God him sage Antiquity
> Did wisely make, and good *Agdistes* call:
> But this same was to that quite contrary,
> The foe of life, that good envyes to all,
> That secretly doth us procure to fall,
> Through guilefull semblaunts, which he makes us see....

What we expect is a contrast between Genius *A* and Genius *B* II: for it must be the god of generation who keeps the gate to the garden of Adonis and it must be a man's evil Genius who ushers him into the garden of Acrasia. What we seem to get is an identification of *A* and *B* I, and a contrast between this composite figure and *B* II. Let us begin with the second stanza. It is certain that the good Agdistes is the good individual Genius (*B* I), for *him* must refer to the subject of the last lines of the preceding stanza; it is tolerably certain that Spenser has got the name Agdistes from Natalis Comes (*loc. cit.*) and from nowhere else—since a further acquaintance with this deity is hardly compatible with the use of the word 'good'. It is certain again, that the 'foe of life' contrasted with Agdistes, is the individual evil Genius: and his activity in 'procuring us to fall' by 'guilefull semblaunts' is in full accordance with the doctrine of *spectra* given by Natalis Comes (see Warton's note). The whole of the second stanza, in fact, is occupied with the contrast between Genius *B* I (= Agdistes) and Genius *B* II. What of the first? It looks, as I have said,

[1] Those interested in the 'hooks and eyes of memory' will be pleased to notice that Acrasia also appears in the *Cebetis Tabula*.

like an account of Genius *A* (the *powre* in charge of *life and generation*) conflated with Genius *B* I (*our Selfe*). This is certainly, I think, how Warton understands the passage, for he begins his quotation from Natalis Comes with the words *Dictus est autem Genius, ut placuit Latinis a gignendo, vel quia nobiscum gignatur, vel quia illi procreandorum cura divinitus commissa putaretur.* It would seem the obvious conclusion that Spenser in fact did not draw, as Natalis Comes does not draw, the medieval distinction between Genius *A* and Genius *B*. Against this conclusion the following considerations, however, may be opposed.

(1) Neither here nor on III, vi, 31 does Warton show himself aware of the medieval double use: he would therefore easily fail to notice it even if it were present.

(2) The proposed interpretation compels us to accept a very odd structure of sentence: the parenthesis beginning at *Not that celestiall powre* is continued for ten lines, and is quite disproportionate to the original statement in one line.

(3) Why is the individual δαίμων (Genius *B* I) called a *celestiall* power? The epithet is not entirely inappropriate to such individual genii, but it is more appropriate to the august 'Oyarses' in the sphere of the fixed stars.

(4) How can Genius *B* possibly be described as providing for the generation of 'all that lives'? There must be as many genii *BB* as there are men (twice as many if we include the evil genii) and each of them, at most, can provide only for the generation of his own charge or his own charge's offspring. I will grant the poetic use of singular for plural: but this will not do. Even if such a collective Genius *B* (*i.e.* the sum of all genii *BB*) can be said to provide for the generation of all human beings, he cannot do so for *all that lives*. In other words, what is said of Genius in the 2nd, 3rd, and 4th lines of the stanza is quite incompatible with what is said of him in the last two lines. The former plainly refer to Genius *A*, the latter as plainly to Genius *B*.

I therefore propose a device by which we can make Spenser consistent at once with himself and with the tradition, at the cost of a sentence no more awkward than the Wartonian interpretation attributes to him. It consists in bracketing lines 2, 3, and 4 of this stanza. These lines would then merely serve to warn the reader that we are not talking of Genius *A* and the whole of the rest of the stanza would refer to Genius *B*. The difference between my inter-pretation and Warton's (or what I suppose to have been Warton's) can be best brought out by a paraphrase.

Warton's: They called him Genius (not the good Genius who is our second self and whom the ancients called Agdistes, but on the contrary) the bad and beguiling Genius.

Mine: They called him Genius (not of course Genius *A*) who is our second self and whom the ancients called Agdistes. But this was the bad and beguiling Genius.

It is needless, I trust, to add that I put forward this suggestion with no claim to certainty. I am certain (by the fourth argument above) that the text as ordinarily punctuated and understood is self-contradic-tory, and I am certain that the Middle Ages distinguished Genius *A* from *B* (or even forgot about *B* in their concentration on *A*) as I have described. The application of this distinction to Spenser, and still more the particular mode in which I have applied it, are naturally much more speculative.

14

A NOTE ON 'COMUS'

The history of *Comus* may be briefly recapitulated as follows. It was written out by Milton—possibly without a previous rough copy—in the book known to us as the *Trinity MS*,* some time before Michael‑mas night 1634. This version may be conveniently called *Trinity* α. From *Trinity* a copy was made, probably by Henry Lawes, still before Michaelmas night 1634. The copying was not very accurately carried out, as the new MS contains fifteen blunders. Some of these show misunderstanding of the text; thus, in 12 (Yet som there be that by due steps aspire), where Lawes reads *with due steps*, it seems probable that he took *steps* to mean 'paces' or 'strides', where Milton was thinking of degrees in a stair or rungs in a ladder (cf. *P.L.* VIII, 591). Other errors affect the metre, as, for example, the unfortunate *enthroned* (for *enthron'd*) in 11, which has penetrated into too many modern editions. From both these considerations it would appear that the copy—which we call the *Bridgewater MS*—was made without any careful supervision by the poet. Besides its errors, *Bridgewater* presents many variations which are intentional: these have long since been explained, and no doubt rightly, as a 'producer's' surgery—the familiar process by which a great poem is whittled into an 'acting version'. The production took place on Michaelmas night 1634: and the first edition appeared in 1637. Before 1637, however, Milton went over his old MS (*Trinity* α) and introduced several new readings, thus producing *Trinity* β. The intermediate position of *Bridgewater* between *Trinity* α and *Trinity* β can easily be shown by the many passages in which *Bridgewater* preserves a reading, still visible in *Trinity*, but now erased or marginally corrected. Thus, in 349 *Trinity* gives *lone dungeon* with *lone* altered in favour of *sad*, which in its turn gives way to *close*; *Bridgewater* reads *lone*. In 384 *Trinity* originally read:

> walks in black vapours, though the noontyde brand
> blaze in the summer solstice.

This is then erased, and in the left-hand margin Milton substitutes

> benighted walks under ye midday sun
> himselfe is his owne dungeon.

Bridgewater preserves the older reading. There are fifteen examples of the same state of affairs; so that in 242, where the words preceding *to all heav'ns harmonies* are (to me) illegibly erased,[1] we can confidently restore them from *Bridgewater's and hold a counterpointe*. The edition of 1637, besides several errors (ll. 20, 73, 131, 417, 443), introduces important novelties. But though Milton did not trouble to copy these novelties into his old, and now very 'un-fair', *Trinity MS*, he kept this MS by him, and made certain further alterations in it after he had sent to the press the new version made for the edition of 1637. Thus, in 214, the old *Trinity* reading, *thou flittering angel*, is marginally altered to read *hovering*; but this alteration was made after the edition of 1637, which preserves *flittering*. The same phenomenon occurs in 956, where the change from *are* to *grow* appears marginally in *Trinity*, but not in 1637. Thus, in addition to *Trinity* α and β, we have a third stratum in the MS—*Trinity* γ, represented by two corrections only. In 1645 *Comus* was again printed in the *Poems both English and Latin*. The period of serious alterations is now over, but some novelties appear. In 1673 the mask appeared, practically unchanged, in the *Poems upon Several Occasions*.

In *Comus*, therefore, we can watch the growth of a poem through the stages:

> *Trinity* α
> *Trinity* β
> 1637
> *Trinity* γ
> 1645.

I neglect *Bridgewater*, whose omissions and rearrangements tell us more of the poet's patience than of his poethood. Confining myself to the remainder, I propose to draw attention to a certain general characteristic of the revision. It will be best to proceed inductively.

> 242. *Trin.* α. *Bridg.* and hold a counterpointe.
> *Trin.* β. 1637. 1645. 1673. and give resounding grace.

[1] I work from Aldis Wright's facsimile. Possibly in the original the old reading may be more easily deciphered; but it must differ considerably from most of the erasures. It is not a mere 'crossing-out', but an attempt at real obliteration.

Whether the change here is, or is not, from worse to better, it is certainly from the more striking and remarkable to the more ordinary. The rejected reading is more *unexpected*: it has that species of 'originality', that power of drawing attention to itself, which would attract a 'metaphysical', or a modern, poet. For the moment I will confine myself to reminding the reader that this is almost the one rejected reading in *Trinity* which Milton took the trouble to scratch out illegibly—one might almost say vindictively.

359 *et seq.* Trin. Bridg.

> Peace brother peace
> I doe not thinke my sister so to seeke etc.

1637. 1645. 1673.

> Peace Brother, be not over-exquisite
> To cast the fashion of uncertain evils;
> For grant they be so, while they rest unknown,
> What need a man forestall his date of grief,
> And run to meet what he would most avoid?
> Or if they be but false alarms of Fear,
> How bitter is such self-delusion?
> I do not think my sister so to seek, etc.

Here there can be no question that the alteration is undramatic. The passage on the self-sufficiency of virtue which follows is, in any case, a long and improbable suspension of action; but in *Trinity* and *Bridgewater* at least we hasten to it, and, if the main action is delayed, the temperamental conflict between the brothers is given some liveliness by the impatient repetition 'peace brother peace'. In 1637 even this semblance of drama has disappeared; the Elder Brother lectures rather than argues. Milton is altering his poem so as to make it even less dramatic and more gnomic than it was before.

384. Trin. α. Bridg.

> walks in black vapours, though the noontyde brand
> blaze in the summer solstice

Trin. β. 1637. 1645. 1673.

> Benighted walks under the mid-day Sun;
> Himself is his own dungeon.

Both readings appear to me excellent, but with different kinds of excellence. Neither, of course, is a close copy of the speech of real men; but the earlier, with its natural syntax, and its more highly-coloured pictorial quality—which could be made to seem as if it grew while the brother spoke—might well be thrown off by a good actor with an appearance of realism. The second reading is, from the actor's point of view, vastly inferior. The Latin syntax of 'benighted walks' removes it at once to a different plane. 'Himself is his own dungeon' is imaginative, but with the moral imagination; there is no *picture* in it to compare with the blaze of the solstice. Again, the contrast, which the earlier reading makes audible in a 'though'-clause, is purely intellectual in the later. Milton is moving further from naturalism; exchanging a sweeter for a drier flavour; becoming (in one of the senses of that word) more classical.

409 *et seq. Trin.* α. *Bridg.*

  secure wthout all doubt or question, no
  I could be willing though now i'th darke to trie
  a tough encounter wth the shaggiest ruffian
  that lurks by hedge or lane of this dead circuit
  to have her by my side, though I were sure
  she might be free from perill where she is
  but where an equall poise of hope & fear, etc.

1637. 1645. 1673.

 Secure without all doubt, or controversie:
 Yet where an equal poise of hope and fear, etc.

In this passage *Trinity* α itself is already the correction of a pre-α stage which read *Beshrew me but I would* instead of *I could be willing*, and *passado* instead of *encounter*. The two most racy, and least Miltonic, expressions, had therefore gone the way of *counterpointe* in 242, before Lawes made his copy: something of energy and facile 'point' had already been sacrificed to the unity of Milton's style. What remained, however, was still good theatre; the boyish and noble actor, waving his little sword, with his colloquial *i'th darke* and his picturesque shaggy ruffians and dead circuits, all to be faced in defence of his sister, would to this day be snatched at by any producer anxious to 'brighten up' the dialogue at this point. But Milton, as is becoming apparent, did not desire, though he could provide, good theatre. He drops the whole passage. One concession to drama remained: an actor could still make something lively out of *without all doubt or question—No!* And Milton could have kept this consistently with the omission of the shaggy ruffians. But he did not; once again the final version, *secure without all doubt, or controversy,* gives the Elder Brother the purely didactic tone. Instead of the dramatic break we have the purely metrical break of a feminine ending.

605. *Trin. Bridg.* 1637. monstrous buggs.
1645. 1673. monstrous forms.

We must naturally remove from our minds the ludicrous associations which the earlier form has for a modern reader. These are the 'bugs to frighten babes withal' of Spenser. When this has been done, the passage falls into line with the general trend of the alterations. The more forcible, native word, the word that draws attention to itself, is erased in favour of the comparatively colourless loan word. Not so would Donne or D. H. Lawrence have chosen.

608. *Trin. Bridg.* 1637. by the curls & cleave his scalpe
downe to the hips
1645. 1673. by the curls, to a foul death,
Curs'd as his life.

There is no question which reading has the more 'punch' in it. Both are full of energy; but the one is physical energy, demonstrable by the actor, the other is moral. Again Milton moves away from the theatre.

779 *et seq.* In this passage, which is too long to quote in full, the whole of the Lady's exposition of the sage and serious doctrine of virginity appears for the first time in 1637, with a consequent addition to Comus's reply. The original version read

cramms & blasphems his feeder. Co. Come no more

This constitutes the most important single addition made in the composition of *Comus,* and it is one without which the tone of the mask would be different. Characteristically, it is an alteration not in the dramatic, but in the gnomic and ethical direction.

847. *Trin.* α. and often takes our cattell wth strange pinches
Ceteri omit.

The first version might have come out of *A Midsummer Night's Dream.* It belongs to the fairy world of real popular superstition; it breathes a rusticity which has not been filtered through Theocritus and Virgil, and a supernatural which is homely—half comic, half feared—rather than romantic. But Milton has gone as near that world as he chooses to go, in the preceding lines; anything more would be out of the convention in which he is writing. He can just venture on the 'urchin blasts'; 'pinches' oversteps the line drawn by literary decorum. He therefore cancels the verse.

975 *et seq.* The alterations in the concluding song are probably familiar to most readers and need not be dealt with in detail. It is enough to say that *Trinity* α and *Bridgewater* both lack what *Trinity* β gives; the contrast, beautifully emphasized by a change of metre (Celestial Cupid her fam'd son advanc't), between terrestrial and celestial love. The new passage, addressed to 'mortals' only if their 'ears be true' (like its counterpart in the *Apology for Smectymnuus*),[1] falls in naturally with the change at ll. 779 *et seq.* and sums up the increasing gravity of the work in its progress towards the final text. It throws light, moreover, on the famous excised passage which *Trinity* gives us in the prologue. It is true that a sensitive reader can find ample justification for that excision without looking beyond the prologue itself. In the present text we begin with six of the most impressive verses in English poetry; impressive because we pass in a single verse from the cold, tingling, almost unbreathable, region of the aerial spirits[2] to the *smoak and stirr of this dim spot.* Each level, by itself, is a masterly representation: in their juxtaposition ('Either other sweetly gracing') they are irresistible. The intrusion of an intermediate realm, as serene as the air and as warmly inviting as the earth, ruins this effect and therefore justly perished. But its erasure becomes all the more necessary when the poet, with his Platonic stair of earthly and heavenly love, has found the real philosophical intermediary and, with it, the real use for his Hesperian imagery. Having found the true reconciliation he knows that it must come at the end; we must begin with the contrast. Nothing that blurs the distinction between the region of the Spirit and the region of Comus must be admitted until we have passed the 'hard assays'; then, and

---

[1] *Prose Works*, ed. St John, vol. III, p. 117, 'Let rude ears be absent'.

[2] It is an interesting question how far Milton regarded them with something more than poetic faith. Certainly his Attendant Spirit, who appears as a *Daemon* in *Trinity*, has several features in common with the 'aerial demons' in Milton's fellow collegiate, Henry More.*

not till then, the more delicious imagery, which had been mere decoration in the opening speech, may be resumed and called into significant life.

In tenui labor. It may seem rash, on the strength of a few alterations, and those minute ones, to speak of a general characteristic in Milton's revision. Yet it is just on such apparent *minutiae* that the total effect of a poem depends; and that there is a common tendency in the alterations I have discussed, few readers will probably dispute. The tendency is one easier, no doubt, to feel than to define. The poet cuts away technical terms and colloquialisms; he will have nothing ebullient; he increases the gnomic element at the expense of the dramatic. In general, he *subdues*; and he does so in the interests of unity in tone. The process is one of conventionalization, in this sense only—that the poet, having determined on what plane of convention (at what distance from real life and violent emotion) he is to work, brings everything on to that plane; how many individual beauties he must thereby lose is to him a matter of indifference. As a result we have that dearly bought singleness of quality—

> smooth and full as if one gush
> Of life had washed it—

which sets *Comus*, for all its lack of human interest, in a place apart and unapproachable.

Whether Milton's aim was a good one—whether he paid too high a price for it and sacrificed better things for its sake—these are questions that each will answer according to his philosophy. But if we blame *Comus* for its lack of dramatic quality, it is, at least, relevant to remember that Milton could have made it—nay, originally had made it—more lively than it is; that he laboured to produce the quality we condemn and knowingly jettisoned something of that whose absence we deplore. It is arguable that he chose wrongly; but the example of what may be called poetic chastity—an example 'set the first in English'—deserves attention.

ADDITIONAL EDITORIAL NOTES

page 4, line 20. George Herbert, *The Elixir*, 9–12.

page 6, line 12. By John Skelton.

page 8, line 22. By Thomas Dekker.

page 10, line 3. An Old High German lay sometimes spelt *Hildebrandslied* or *Hildebrand*.

page 16, line 22. Lewis's fullest and most interesting discussion of the Jungian archetypes is found in his essay 'Psycho-analysis and Literary Criticism', *Essays and Studies by Members of the English Association*, XXVII (1942), pp. 7–21.

page 21, n. 1. Laʒamon's *Brut* is extant in two manuscripts, Cotton Caligula A ix and Cotton Otho C xiii, both of which are printed in Madden's edition. Lewis is following Cotton Caligula A ix and writes two half-lines as one. Lewis, obviously, wanted the text to be as readable as possible and, besides departing from a few scribal conventions (such as expanding the contractions), supplies his own punctuation of the text. Because of this, I have followed the present-day usage of beginning each new sentence with a capital letter.

page 32, line 18. This word added by Lewis.

page 32, line 33. Lewis is here correcting Madden's edition, which reads *al se cunes*.

page 34, n. 1. Wilson's edition contains three separate texts of *Sawles Warde*, MSS Bodley 34, Royal and Cotton. Lewis's references are to MS Bodley 34. Printed in this same volume are the corresponding chapters (XIII, XIV, XV) of Hugo of St Victor's *De Anima*. The entire *De Anima* is found in Migne's *Patrologia Latina* (1854), vol. 177.

page 41, line 17. Laʒamon, 15774–9 (Madden's edition).

page 42, line 13. Guillaume Deguileville, *Pèlerinage de l'Homme*. In Lydgate's trans. (E.E.T.S., Extra Series LXXVII, ed. F. J. Furnivall, 1899), 3415 *seq*.

page 42, line 25. *De Gen. Animalium*, 778 *a*; *Polit.* 1255 *b*.

page 46, line 24. *Metaphysics*, 1072 *b*; cf. *Paradiso*, XXVIII, 41–2.

page 47, line 13. Giacomo Leopardi, 'L'Infinito', *Canti*, ed. Giuseppe de Robertis (Firenze, 1960), p. 124, l. 15.

page 49, line 14. *Il Penseroso*, 69–70.

page 51, line 1. *Metaphysics*, 1072 *b*.

page 52, line 6. 'The silence of those eternal spaces frightens me' is a translation of Pascal's *pensée*: 'Le silence éternel de ces espaces infinis m'effraie': Brunschvicg No. 206 (II, p. 127).

The indirect quotation, 'that though we are small and transitory as dew-drops, still we are dew-drops that can think', does, I feel, require a comment. Lewis has confused (or is it an inspired misreading?) Pascal's original *roseau* (reed) with *rosée* (dew). Although Pascal really compares man to a reed, I feel that I should preserve what Lewis wrote. This is because his image of the 'dew-drop' strikes me as the superior image, and it quite obviously serves his purpose best. The complete text of the *pensée* to which he is referring is: 'L'homme n'est qu'un roseau, le plus faible de la nature; mais c'est un roseau pensant. Il ne faut pas que l'univers entier s'arme pour l'écraser: une vapeur, une goutte d'eau, suffit pour le tuer. Mais, quand l'univers l'écrase-rait, l'homme serait encore plus noble que ce qui le tue, parce qu'il sait qu'il meurt, et l'avantage que l'univers a sur lui; l'univers n'en sait rien. Toute notre dignité consiste donc en la pensée. C'est de là qu'il faut nous relever et non de l'espace et de la durée, que nous ne saurions remplir. Travaillons donc à bien penser: voilà le principe de la morale': Brunschvicg No. 347 (II, pp. 261–3).

page 53, line 7. *Comus*, 976–8.

page 56, line 8. Cf. C. S. Lewis, *The Abolition of Man* (Oxford, 1943), chapter III, p. 52, especially: 'The fact that the scientist has succeeded where the magician failed has put such a wide contrast between them in popular thought that the real story of the birth of Science is misunderstood. You will even find people who write about the sixteenth century as if Magic were a medieval survival and Science the new thing that came in to sweep it away. Those who have studied the period know better. There was very little magic in the Middle Ages: the sixteenth and seventeenth centuries are the high noon of magic. The serious magical endeavour and the serious scientific endeavour are twins: one was sickly and died, the other strong and throve. But they were twins. They were born of the same impulse. I allow that some (certainly not all) of the early scientists were actuated by a pure love of knowledge. But if we consider the temper of that age as a whole we can discern the impulse of which I speak. There is something which unites magic and applied science while separating both from the 'wisdom' of earlier ages. For the wise men of old the cardinal problem had been how to conform the soul to reality, and the solution had been knowledge, self-discipline, and virtue. For magic and applied science alike the problem is how to subdue reality to the wishes of men.'

page 57, line 19. *The Extasie*, 57–8.

page 57, line 33. *Sancti Dionysii...opera omnia...studio Petri Lanselli...Lutetiae Parisiorum* (MDCXV).

page 61, line 16. *De Caelo, 279 a.*

page 65, line 32. William Kinglake, 'The Troad', *Eōthen, or Traces of Travel Brought Home from the East* (London, 1844), p. 58.

page 67, line 32. 'Milton', *The Edinburgh Review*, XLII (August 1825), p. 316.

page 71, line 29. 'Light', *Symbolism and Belief* (London, 1938), pp. 125–50.

page 78, line 17. *Shakespeare's Imagery and What it Tells us* (Cambridge, 1935).

page 85, line 9. Lewis was quoting from memory. Patmore says in *The Wedding Sermon*, X, 87–9:

> Spirit is heavy nature's wing,
> And is not rightly anything
> Without its burthen, etc.

page 88, line 30. *The Faerie Queene*, I, i, 6.

page 105, line 5. Lewis wrote an article on Sir Ector's lament in which he says 'The ideal embodied in Launcelot is "escapism" in a sense never dreamed of by those who use that word; it offers the only possible escape from a world divided between wolves who do not understand, and sheep who cannot defend, the things which make life desirable'. 'Notes on the Way', *Time and Tide*, XXI (17 August 1940), p. 841.

page 108, line 6. *Paradise Regained*, II, 359–60.

page 108, line 22. For Lewis's own criticism of *Taliessin through Logres* and *The Region of the Summer Stars*, see *Arthurian Torso: Containing the Posthumous Fragment of 'The Figure of Arthur' by Charles Williams and a Commentary on the Arthurian Poems of Charles Williams by C. S. Lewis* (1948); see also Lewis's reviews of *Taliessin through Logres* in *Theology*, XXXVIII (April 1939), pp. 268–76, and *The Oxford Magazine*, LXIV (14 March 1946), pp. 248–50.

page 110, line 35. See also Lewis's essay on 'The English Prose *Morte*' in *Essays on Malory*, ed. J. A. W. Bennett (Oxford, 1963), pp. 7–28. In this essay Lewis expands some of the paradoxes—touched on in 'The *Morte Darthur*' of this volume—which, as he says, 'have been thrown up by the remarkable discoveries made in the last fifty years about Malory and the book (or books) which he translated, with modifications, from the French and which Caxton printed in 1485'. 'The English Prose *Morte*' is followed, in the same volume, by 'On Art and Nature: A letter to C. S. Lewis' by Professor Vinaver.

page 111, line 31. *Gabriel Harvey's Marginalia*, ed. G. C. Moore Smith (Shakespeare Head Press, Stratford-upon-Avon, 1913), p. 168.

page 112, line 1. In *A Preface, or rather a Brief Apologie of Poetrie* prefixed to the translation of *Orlando Furioso in English Heroical Verse* (1591).

page 113, line 19. Sir William Davenant in his preface to *Gondibert* (1650).

page 113, line 34. All the quotations from Thomas Rymer come from his preface to the translation of R. Rapin's *Reflections on Aristotle's Treatise of Poesie* (1674).

page 114, line 1. In his dedication to *King Arthur: or, The British Worthy. A dramatick Opera* (1691), Dryden speaks of 'that Fairy kind of writing, which depends only upon the Force of Imagination'. It may be that Addison is misquoting Dryden when, in *The Spectator* (1 July 1712), no. 419, he says 'This Mr Dryden calls the Fairy Way of Writing'.

page 115, line 7. Vernon Lee (pseudonym for Violet Paget), 'The School of Boiardo', *Euphorion: Being Studies of the Antique and the Mediaeval in the Renaissance*, II (London, 1884), p. 113.

page 116, line 10. Professor J. R. R. Tolkien's Andrew Lang Lecture was delivered at St Andrews in 1940. It was expanded and published under the title 'On Fairy-Stories' in *Essays Presented to Charles Williams* (Oxford, 1947). Lewis is thinking of a passage in 'On Fairy-Stories' in which Professor Tolkien says (p. 79): 'It is part of the essential malady of such days—producing the desire to escape, not indeed from life, but from our present time and self-made misery—that we are acutely conscious both of the ugliness of our works, and of their evil. So that to us evil and ugliness seem indissolubly allied. We find it difficult to conceive of evil and beauty together. The fear of the beautiful fay that ran through the elder ages almost eludes our grasp. Even more alarming: goodness is itself bereft of its proper beauty. In Faerie one can indeed conceive of an ogre who possesses a castle hideous as a nightmare (for the evil of the ogre wills it so), but one cannot conceive of a house built with a good purpose—an inn, a hostel for travellers, the hall of a virtuous and noble king—that is yet sickeningly ugly. At the present day it would be rash to hope to see one that was not—unless it was built before our time.'

page 117, line 4. *Gerusalemme Liberata*, XVI, ix, 7–8.

page 118, line 11. 'Milton and Poussin', *Seventeenth Century Studies Presented to Sir Herbert Grierson* (Oxford, 1938), p. 195.

page 118, line 35. *Paradise Lost*, I, 16.

page 118, line 37. *Orlando Furioso*, I, ii, 2.

page 153, line 33. Josephine Waters Bennett, 'Spenser's Garden of Adonis', *Publications of the Modern Language Association of America*, XLVII (1932), pp. 46–80.

page 168, line 12. For Lewis's other studies in Spenser see: 'Spenser's Irish Experiences and *The Faerie Queene*', *The Review of English Studies*, VII (Jan. 1931), pp. 83–5; chapter VII, '*The Faerie Queene*', in *The Allegory of Love* (Oxford, 1936), pp. 297–360; Book III, chapter I, 'Sidney and Spenser', in *English Literature in the Sixteenth Century, excluding Drama*, The Completion of 'The Clark Lectures', Trinity College, Cambridge, 1944 (*The Oxford History of English Literature*, vol. III; Oxford, 1954), pp. 318–93.

page 171, line 25. Thomas Warton, *Observations on the 'Faerie Queene' of Spenser* (London, 1754), section III, pp. 57–60.

page 175, line 3. After comparing Lewis's quotations from William Aldis Wright's facsimile of the *Trinity MS*, I have needed to correct a number of scribal errors which appeared in the original issue of this essay.

page 180, n. 2. Cf. C. S. Lewis, 'Above the Smoke and Stir', *The Times Literary Supplement* (14 July 1945), p. 331; B. A. Wright, *ibid.* (4 August 1945), p. 367; C. S. Lewis, *ibid.* (29 September 1945), p. 463; B. A. Wright, *ibid.* (27 October 1945), p. 511.

INDEX

Abrabanel, 149, 151

Achilles (in Homer), 114

Acrasia (in Spenser), 117, 138–40, 141, 142, 169, 171, 172

Adam, 85, 86, 91, 117

Addison, 137, 185

Adonis (in Spenser), 153, 155, 156, 157, 161, 169, 171, 172, 185

Ælfwald (in Laȝamon), 21

Aeneas, 16, 112

aether, 48, 56

Agamemnon (in Homer), 112

Agatone, 94

Agdistes (in Spenser), 172, 174

Agrican (in Milton), 119

Ahab, Captain, 135

air (its realm), 48

Alanus ab Insulis, *De Planctu Naturae*, 59, 170; mentioned, 96

Alberich, 116

Albracca, 119

Alciati, 166

Alcina (in Ariosto), 166

Alcmena (in Ovid), 100

Aldolf (in Laȝamon), 24

Alexander, William, 112

alfene, 28

allegory, in *Sawles Warde*, 34; in Spenser, moral and historical allegory in *The Faerie Queene*, 136–7; broad outlines, 137–8; abstract puts on flesh and blood, 138; contrast between Bower of Acrasia and House of Busirane, 138–40; moral, 140–1; obstacles to reading, 141–2; consciousness of moral allegory, 148; read into him by Platonizing critics, 160; mentioned, 133

Alma, in Dryden, 114; in Spenser, 165

Amadis of Gaul, 114

Amor vitae aeternae et Desiderium coelestis patriae (in *De Anima*), 34

Amoret (in Spenser), 165

Amphiaraus (in Dante), 95

Amphisa (in Spenser), 158

Anderson, Lady Flavia, 13 n. 1

Androgeus (in Laȝamon), 28

Angelica (in Milton), 119

angels, the nine classes, 53–4; in Pseudo-Dionysius, 57–8; in Dante, 81; in Spenser, 144, 165; guardian angel, 169

Animus, 34

Annunciation, the, why made by an archangel, 54

Antigone (in Dante), 95

Antipodes, the, 49

Apocalypse, the, 71

Apollo, in Statius, 98, 99; mentioned, 122

Apollonius Rhodius, 113

Apuleius, 41

Apuleius, Pseudo-, 170

Aquinas, 44

Arabian Nights, the, 12

Arcadia, the, 166

Argante, in Laȝamon, 28; in Tasso, 120

Argia (in Dante), 95, 101

Argo, the, 83

Argos, 98

Ariosto, 111, 112, 113, 114, 118, 131, 133, 166, 185

Aristotle, on Moon as boundary, 42; his logic, 44; Latin translations, 45; perceptible world as part of the whole, 46; Unmoved Mover, 50–1, 62, 74; *Metaphysics*, 56–7, 182, 183; mentioned, 29, 34, 50, 71, 112, 159

Arlo, 125

Armagh, 124

Armida, 117

Arnold, Matthew, 10, 64

Artaban (in Calprenède), 114

Arthegall (in Spenser), 157

Arthur, in Geoffrey of Monmouth, 19; in Laȝamon, 21, 23, 26–8, 30, 32–3, 37; his Celtic origin, 24; in Wace, 27; in Malory, 103, 106; in Spenser, 131, 133, 134, 137 n. 1, 144–5, 158, 159, 160; mentioned, 24

Asclepius, 170

Assumption, the (as parallel), 100

astrology, 55–6, 91, 141

Athens, 45
Augustine, St, 71, 149, 153, 169–70
Austen, Jane, 36
Authorised Version, the, 3
Avalon, 28
Avon, the, 33

Ballads, 38, 43–4
Barach, Carl Sigmund, ed. *De Mundi Universitate*, 170
Barclay, Alexander, 128
Bartas, du, 111
Bayeux, 19
Bede, 20
Beethoven, 49
Belphoebe (in Spenser), 136, 157
Bennett, J. A. W., 184
Bennett, Josephine Waters, 153, 185
Beowulf, 22, 25, 28, 166
Bercilak, Sir, 11
Bergson, 162
Bernardus Silvestris (or Silvester), 96, 170
Bevan, Edwyn, 71, 184
Bladud, King, 25
Bliss, A. J., ed. *Sir Orfeo*, 5 n. 1
Boccaccio, 21, 37, 115
Boethius, 45, 149, 151, 152
Boiardo, 111, 119, 131, 133, 143, 185
Boileau, 113
Borst, William, viii
Bossu, le, 112
Botticelli, 165
Bouge of Court, the, 6, 182
Bower of Bliss, the, 138–40, 141–2, 172
Boyle, Elizabeth, 123
Brennes, in Geoffrey, 24; in Laʒamon, 27
Br'er Rabbit, 135
Bridges, Robert, 65
Bridgewater MS, see Milton
Britomart (in Spenser), 139, 157, 167
Broceliande, 20
Brook, G. L., 18 n. 1
Brooke, 127
Browning, 132
Brunschvicg, Léon, ed. *Pensées*, 183
Brut, viii, x, 18, 20, 21, 22, 23, 24, 25, 26, 27, 41, 182
Bunyan, 68, 147
Burke, Edmund, 142
Busirane, House of, 139–40, 141

Byron, 131

Cador (in Wace), 26, 28
Caelia, House of, 141
Caliban, 135
Calprenède, 114
Calvin, 121
canzone, 130
Capaneus (in Dante), 95
Carlyle, 48
Cassibelaune, in Geoffrey, 24; in Laʒamon, 28
Castelvetro, 112
cathedral, comparison with medieval books, 39
Catiline, 111
Cato (in Dante), 97
Caxton, 103, 104, 105, 106, 107, 109, 110
Cebetis Tabula, the, 153, 171, 172 n. 1
Ceres, 108
Cézanne, 68
Chalcidius, 91, 96, 149, 151
chansons de geste, 113
Charlemagne, in Milton, 119; in Boiardo and Ariosto, 131
Chaucer, *Book of the Duchess*, 129; Prologue and links in *The Canterbury Tales*, 38; *Clerkes Tale*, 6; *Knights Tale*, 1, 37; *Monks Tale*, 8; *Phisiciens Tale*, 7; *Troilus*, 8, 9, 37, 38, 39, 151; use of the word *dim*, 5 n. 2; mentioned, 18, 21, 33, 37, 39, 115, 130
Childric (in Laʒamon), 29
Chrestien de Troyes, 39
Christianity, dislike of, 13; reverence for, 15; in Middle Ages, 50; Dante attributes to Statius, 94, 95; human soul sought, 144; mentioned, 99, 151, 169
Cicero, 45, 76
Cinderella, 1
Claude, 147
Claudian, 23, 171 n. 1
Clementia, 99
Cleopolis (in Spenser), 151, 157
Clorinda, 120
Coleridge, 33
Colgrim (in Laʒamon), 32
Colin Clout, 125, 126, 142
Coloneus, 2
Comes, Natalis, 171, 172–3

Confessio Amantis, the, 171
Constance, King, 21
Convivio, the, 95, 101
Corineus (in Laȝamon), 29
Coroebus (in Statius), 98, 99
Correggio, 147
Cory, 4
Cotton Caligula MS (of Laȝamon), 182
Cotton Otho MS (of Laȝamon), 27 n. 4, 182
Crotopus, 98
Cupid, in Spenser, 142, 158, 164–5, 167–8; in Milton, 180
Cusanus, 153, 158

daemons, in Laȝamon, 32, 41–2; between Moon and Earth, 53; do good or evil, 56; in More's *Immortality of the Soul*, 154, 180 n. 2, 186; in Milton, 180 n. 2, 186
Dame Heurodis, *see* Heurodis
Dante, his angels, 54; his similes, 64, 66–76; poetic excellence, 76–7; imagery in last eleven cantos of *Comedy*, 78–93; *Convivio*, 95, 101; belief that Statius was not far from Christian faith, 94–6; agreement about Fall and nature of man, 96–102; mentioned, viii, 7, 44, 49, 51, 61, 62, 182
Davenant, William, 113, 185
Day of Judgement, the, 33
De Anima, *see* Hugo of St Victor
Deaðes Sonde (in *Sawles Warde*), 35
Deguileville, Guillaume, 42, 182
Deipyle (in Dante), 95, 101
Dekker, Thomas, 8, 182
Desmonds, the, 124
Devil's Advocate, the, 162
Diana, 102, 158
Dickens, 132
Diomede (in Dante), 95
Discorsi, the, 112
Dolman, John, 127
Domitian, 96
Donne, *Aire and Angels*, 7–8; *The Extasie*, 57, 183; similes, 72–3; mentioned, 132, 142, 143, 151, 179
Douglas, Gavin, 159
dragons, in Spenser, 164, 166; various significances, 165; in Alciati, *Beowulf*,

the Volsung story, *Phaedrus*, Jonson and Milton, 166
Drayton, 128, 129
Dryden, 113–14, 136, 185
Dublin, 123
Duessa (in Spenser), 136
Dunbar, 18
Dycus (in Sidney), 167

E. K., 122, 147
Earth, scene of generation and decay, 42; size, 48; Dante's understanding of gravitation, 49; Plutarch's 'orchard' between Earth and Moon, 155; mentioned, 84
East Anglia, 21
Ector, Sir (in Malory), 105, 108, 184
Eddington, 75
Edinburgh Review, The, 184
elfes, 122
Elizabeth I, 125, 132, 136, 145, 158
Ellrodt, Robert, *Neoplatonism in the Poetry of Spenser*, ix, 149–63
Emblematum Liber, 166, 166 n. 1
Empyrean, as boundary of the *mundus*, 45; region beyond outermost sphere, 59; as centre, 62; mentioned, 53, 61, 78, 85
Engle, the, 20, 23, 24
Eniautos Daimon, 10, 11
Eriphyle (in Dante), 95
Erminia (in Tasso), 120
Ernleȝe, 20
Essay on Man, The, 68
Eteocles (in Statius), 95
Ethelbald (in Laȝamon), 21
Euclid, 49
Europa, 81
Eurydice, 77
Eve, 117

fairies, 122, 147, 148, 158
Fall, the, 96
Farrer, Dr and Mrs Austin, x
Fates, the, 99
Faustus, 162, 171
fays, 20, 107, 116, 185
fées, 28
ferlies, as 'sports of fancy', 12; evoke mystery, 13; affect us, 14–15, 16, 17; mentioned, 13

Ficino, 149, 150, 152, 157
Fifteen Poets, ix
Filostrato, Il, 21
Firbolgs, 126
Firenze, 182
Florimell (in Spenser), 144, 157, 161
Fortitudo (in De Anima), 34
Fortune, 48, 82
Fowler, Alastair, ix, x
Fowler, W. Warde, 169
Francesca, see Paolo and Francesca
Fraunce, Abraham, 111
Freud, 137
Froissart, 120
Furnivall, F. J., 182

Gabriel, St (in Milton), 118
Galahad, Sir (in Malory), 108
Gallaphrone, 119
Gareth, Sir (in Malory), 109
Gawain, Sir, in Malory, 9, 10, 39; in Wace, 26, 28; in Laȝamon, 26; in Tennyson, 10
Gawain and the Green Knight, 11, 14, 18
Genius, as doorkeeper to Acrasia and Adonis, 169; as higher self and as reproductive power, 169; in Augustine, 169–70; in Martianus Capella, Bernardus, Pseudo-Apuleius, Isidore and Alanus, 170–1; in Roman de la Rose and Confessio Amantis, 171; connexion of Genius in Spenser to Natalis Comes and to Cebetis Tabula, 171–4
Geoffrey of Monmouth, 19, 21, 24, 27, 28, 37, 41
George, St (in Spenser), 144, 157, 158
Gerusalemme Liberata, 111, 112, 113, 114, 115, 117, 118, 119, 131, 185
Gibb, Jocelyn, ed. Light on C. S. Lewis, vii
Gigadibs, 28
Gille Callæt (in Laȝamon), 21
Gloriana, as Elizabeth I, 136, 145; as Glory, 136, 144–5, 159, 160; as Queen of Faerie, 159; mentioned, 137 n.1, 152, 157, 158, 161
Godfrey of Bouillon, 112, 131, 185
Godlac (in Laȝamon), 29
Goffredo, see Godfrey of Bouillon
Golden Bough, The, 13, 16
Golden Fleece, the, 166

Golding, Arthur, 153
Gondibert, 185
Googe, 127
Goswhit (in Laȝamon), 21
Gower, use of word dimme, 5 n.2; Genius in Confessio Amantis, 171; mentioned, 33
Grail, the, 13, 14, 39, 108, 109
Grey of Wilton, Lord, 123
Grierson, Herbert, 185
Griffin (in Laȝamon), 21
gryphon, 54
Guillaume de Lorris, 17
Guinevere (in Malory), 105, 108, 109
Guyon, Sir (in Spenser), 133, 138–9, 144

Hades, 97
Hamlet, 8
Hardie, Colin, x
Hardy, Thomas, 128
Harington, John, 111–12, 185
Harvey, Gabriel, 111, 115, 122, 184
Harvy Hafter, 6
Hawes, Stephen, 131
Hebrews, the Epistle to the, 100, 141, 160
Heliodorus, 114
Hellenore (in Spenser), 138 n.1
Hengest, 21, 24
Hennebont, the siege of, 120
Henry II, 19
Henry VII, 131
Heraclitus, 4
Herbert, George, 4, 182
Hercules (in Ovid), 100
Hermes (in Cusanus), 153
Hermetica, the, 149
Hero and Leander, 147
Hesperides, the, 166
Heurodis, Dame, 5
Hiltebrantslied, 10, 182
Hobbes, Thomas, 113
Homer, Homeric similes in Laȝamon, 31; primeval conversational usage of simile, 64–5; 'long-tailed' simile, 65; similes compared with Virgil's, 65–6; similes compared with Dante's, 69–70; mentioned, 32, 72, 73, 76, 90, 110, 111, 112, 114, 132, 164
Hopkins, 4, 75
Hrothgar, 23

Huckleberry Finn, 128
Hugo of St Victor, 33–6, 182
Hurd, Richard, 114
Hypsipyle, in Dante, 95; in Statius, 98

imagery, in the last eleven cantos of Dante's *Comedy*, viii, 78–93
Imitation, the, 92
Incarnation, the, 86, 100
Innsbruck, 170
Intelligences, 51, 53, 54, 56
Irenius (in Spenser), 162
Isaiah, 57
Isidore, 170
Isis, 157
Ismene (in Dante), 95

Jack in the Green, 11
Jack the Giant-Killer, 135, 147
James, St, 79, 87, 88
James I, 136
Jean de Meung, 96, 152, 153
Jeans, 75
Jersey, 19
Jerusalem, 131
Job, 112
Jocasta (in Dante), 95
Johan, see *Sawles Warde*
Johnson, Dr, 126, 137, 154
Jonson, Ben, 124, 166
Jove, as planet, 54; in Statius, 99; in Ovid, 100; in Spenser, 88, 152, 160
Joyous Gard, 105
Jugurtha, 111
Julian of Norwich, Lady, 155
Julius Caesar, 27, 28
Jung, 13, 16, 137, 182
Jupiter, the planet, 45; the god, 98, 99, 100
Justitia (in *De Anima*), 34
Juvenal, 94, 95

Karamazov, 135
Keats, 107, 136
kenningar, 23
Kilcolman, 123, 124, 126
King Solomon's Mines, 12 n. 2
Kinglake, William, 65, 184
Knowlton, E. C., 171 n. 1
Knox, 121
Kupris (= Venus), 54

Lancelot (Chrestien's), 39
Lang, Andrew, 185
Langland, on the Incarnation, 5–6; premise that *Piers Plowman* is great sermon, 9; mentioned, 4, 33
Lanval, 158
Launcelot, Sir (in Malory), 105, 108, 109, 110
Lawes, Henry, 175, 178
Lawrence, D. H., 162, 179
Laȝamon, few readers, 18; purpose, 20; sources, 20; debt to Wace, 20–1; Arthurian names, 21; agreement with Geoffrey against Wace, 21; his MS of Wace, 22; metre, 22–3; Anglo-Saxon in style, 23; British in sympathy, 24; comparisons with Wace, 24–8; love of supernatural, 28; peculiarities, 29–30; similes, 31–3; as author of *Brut*, 36–9; extant in two MSS, 182; mentioned, viii, x, 41, 182
'Lee, Vernon', 114–15, 185
Leopardi, 47, 182
Leslie, R. F., ed. E.E.T.S. edition of *Brut*, 18 n. 1
Lewis, C. S., *The Abolition of Man*, 183; 'Above the Smoke and Stir', 186; *The Allegory of Love*, 186; 'The Anthropological Approach', vii; *Arthurian Torso*, 184; *The Discarded Image*, vii, viii; *English Literature in the Sixteenth Century*, 186; 'The English Prose *Morte*', 184; 'Notes on the Way', 184; 'Psycho-analysis and Literary Criticism', 182; Introduction to *Selections from Laȝamon's 'Brut'*, 18 n. 1; 'Spenser's Irish Experiences and *The Faerie Queene*', 186; reviews of Charles Williams's *Taliessin through Logres*, 184
Lewis, W. H., vii, x
Light on C. S. Lewis, see Gibb, Jocelyn
Liverpool Cathedral, 110
Loch Lomond, 28
Locrin (in Laȝamon), 29
Logres (in Milton), 108
Loomis, R. S., 9, 15, 16
Lucan, 95
Lucretius, 75, 96, 165
Luke, St, 34

Lydgate, 182
Lyonesse (in Milton), 108

Macaulay, 67, 68, 184
Macbeth, 162
Macbeth, Lady, 97
Macrobius, 149, 153
Madden, F., viii, 18 n.1, 21 n.1, 182
Malbecco (in Spenser), 138 n.1
Maldon, 22
Malory, discovery of Winchester MS, 103; Malory's literary career, 103–4; private life, 104; ethical tone of *Morte*, 104–5; lawyers' evidence, 105; eight separate romances, 105; similarities between the Winchester MS and Caxton, 106–7; style, 107; as realist, 107–8; attitude to the story of the Sangreal, 108–9; human relationships of the Arthurian world, 109–10; *Morte* as occupying position half-way between works of art and nature, 110; mentioned, viii, 37, 38, 130, 133, 147
Manto (in Dante), 95, 97
Marhaute, Sir (in Malory), 103
Mark, King, 105
Mars, the planet, 45, 54; in Spenser, 164–5
Martianus Capella, 76, 170
Mary Queen of Scots, 136
Mason, Eugene, 18 n.1
Matthew, St, 34
Mead (in *Sawles Warde*), 34
Melanippus (in Statius), 95
Menelaus, x, 64
Menoeceus (in Statius), 100, 101
Mercury, the planet, 45
Merlin, 16, 19, 30, 32, 41
Michael, St (in Milton), 118
Michael's Mount, St, 103
Migne, J. P., ed. *Patrologia Latina*, 182
Milton, *Apology for Smectymnuus*, 180; *Comus*, ix, 49, 53, 117, 166, 175–81, 183, 186; *Lycidas*, 75, 128; *On Education*, 171 n.2; *Paradise Lost*, 49, 118, 119, 175, 185; *Paradise Regained*, 108, 184; *Poems both English and Latin*, 176; *Poems upon Several Occasions*, 176; *The Reason of Church Government*, 112; on *space*, 7; on *influence*, 8; influence of Tasso and Boiardo, 118–19; use of *Cebetis Tabula*,

171; *Trinity MS* of *Comus*, 175; *Bridgewater MS*, 175; *Trinity* α and β, 175; both differ from *Bridgewater*, 175–6; comparison of *Trinity MSS*, *Bridgewater* and printed versions of 1637, 1645 and 1673, 176–81; mentioned, 35, 64, 66, 68, 72, 75, 99, 104, 132, 142, 184, 185
Minerva (in Alciati), 166
Mirror for Magistrates, 127, 128
Moon, as great boundary, 42; smallest sphere, 45; Milton's description, 49; character, 54; the city wall, 59; nearest Earth, 62; Plutarch's 'orchard' between Earth and Moon, 155; mentioned, 46, 48, 52, 53, 69
More, Henry, 154, 180 n.2
Morris, William, 104
Morte, the English alliterative, 106
Morte, the stanzaic English, 107
Morte Darthur, the, viii, 38, 103, 104, 105, 108, 110
Mozart, 68, 116
Mulcaster, Richard, 121
Munchausen, Baron, 12, 107
Munera, Lady (in Spenser), 138
Munster, 124
Murray, Gilbert, 110
music, of the spheres, 52

Nature, as personified in *Pèlerinage de l'Homme*, 42; in Bernardus, Alanus, Jean de Meung and Statius, 96; in Spenser, 152–3; in Cusanus, 153; in Macrobius, 153; in Gower, 171
Nausicaa, 1
Newtonian model of the universe, 47, 48, 49

Oakeshott, W. F., 103
Odysseus (in Homer), 112
Oedipus (in Dante), 95
Olindo (in Tasso), 113
Olympus, Mount, 156
Orfeo, Sir, 5, 6
Orlando (in Ariosto), 112
Orlando Furioso, 111, 112, 118, 131, 166, 185
Orlando Innamorato, 111, 119, 131
Orpheus, 16, 72, 77
Orphism, 149

ottava rima, 131
Ovid, 100, 133, 153, 164
Oxford Dante Society, viii
Oyarses (= οὐσιάρχης), in Bernardus,
  170, 173

Padua, 162
Paget, Violet, *see* 'Lee, Vernon'
Palazzo della Ragione, 162
Pallas, 102; in Alciati, 166, 166 n.2
Pantolaus (in Laȝamon), 29
Paolo and Francesca, 3
Pascal, 52, 183
Patmore, 85, 184
Patrologia Latina, 182
Paul, St, 36, 45, 101, 159
Pearl, 7, 18
Pèlerinage de l'Homme, Nature and Grâce-
  dieu, 42; mentioned, 182
Penia, *see* Poros and Penia
Persuasion, 36
Peter, St, 85, 90
Petrarch, 115
Phaedrus, 166
Philistines, 13
Philoclea (in Sidney), 166
Picasso, 68
Pico, 149
Pietas, 98, 99
Pindar, 130, 132
planets, the, 45, 54, 55, 62, 152, 155, 160
Plato, his pneumatology reproduced by
  Apuleius, 41; *Timaeus*, 44; mentioned,
  58, 74, 96, 144, 149, 150, 154
Plotinus, 149, 162
Plutarch, 36, 154, 155, 165
Polynices (in Statius), 95
polyphonic narrative (and technique),
  133–5
Poros and Penia, myth of, 150
Porphyry, 149
Pound, Ezra, 68
Poussin, 185
Praz, Mario, 118, 185
Prelude, The, 68, 83
Pridwen (in Laȝamon), 21
Primum Mobile, the, 48, 50, 61, 62, 72, 74
principalis fur (in *De Anima*), 33
Proserpine, 72
Proteus (in Spenser), 161

Prudentia (in *De Anima*), 34
Pseudo-Dionysius, *Celestial Hierarchies*,
  57–8, 184; mentioned, 149
Ptolemy, Ptolemaic cosmos, 49, 51; men-
  tioned, 46, 76
Punch, 44

Queen of Night, the (in Mozart), 116
Quellenforschung, 149

Rabelais, 115
Radigund (in Spenser), 157
Raleigh, Walter, 123, 136, 157
Raphael, 54
Rapin, 185
Reason, which governs the Appetites, 58
Redcrosse Knight, the, 141
Renwick, W. L., ed. *A View of the
  Present State of Ireland*, 162
Reverentia, 98
Reynard the Fox, 129
Rhipeus (in Dante), 97
Ridwathlan (in Laȝamon), 31
Rime of the Ancient Mariner, The, 107
Rinaldo, in Spenser, 111; in Boiardo,
  111; in Tasso, 112, 114, 120
Ringler, W. A., Jr., ed. *The Poems of
  Sir Philip Sidney*, 168
Robertis, Giuseppe de, ed. Leopardi's
  Canti, 182
Rochester, Bishop of, 122
Roland, Chanson de, 20, 100
Roman de la Rose, 152, 153, 164, 171
Romance, not typical of Middle Ages,
  43–4; in *Paradise Lost*, 119; chivalrous
  romance, 130; metrical, 148; men-
  tioned, 122, 131
Ronsard, 131
Round Table, the, 108, 109
Ruggieri (in Dante), 95
Rymer, Thomas, 113, 185

Sackville, Thomas, 127
St Andrews University, 116, 185
Salisbury Cathedral, 44
Sallust, 111
Sangreal, the, *see* Grail
Sankgreall, the, *see* Grail
Sannazaro, 128
Sarastro (in Mozart), 116

Saturn, the planet, 45, 54

Sawles Warde, New Testament source, 33–4; relation to Hugo of St Victor's De Anima, 33–6; Johan, the author, 34, 35, 36; allegory, 34; compared with De Anima, 34–5; MSS, 182

Scaliger, 114

Second Coming, the, 33

Seneca, 45, 95, 127

Senlac, 20

Seven Champions, The, 147

Severn, the, 20

Shakespeare, Henry VI, 10; A Midsummer Night's Dream, 179; Venus and Adonis, 147; mentioned, 36, 77, 78, 129, 132, 142, 143

Shelley, 85, 131, 144

Sidney, Philip, 111, 114, 123, 127, 138, 166, 168, 186

similes, in Laȝamon, 31–3; three classes, 64; Homeric type, 64–5; in Virgil, 65–7; mentioned, viii, 69, 78, 82

Simonide, 94

Sins, the Seven, 60

Skelton, John, 6, 182

Smith, G. C. Moore, ed. Gabriel Harvey's Marginalia, 184

Socrates, 169

Sophocles, 2

Spens, Janet, 169

Spenser, Amorettt, 124, 129, 150; Colin Clouts Come Home Again, 124, 125, 129; Complaints, 124, 128; Daphnaida, 129; Epithalamion, 124, 129, 130, 146, 151; Faerie Queene, 111, 112, 113, 115, 116, 122, 123, 124, 125, 126, 129, 132, 136, 137, 138, 140, 141, 142, 143, 146, 147, 153, 157, 162, 164, 184, 186; Foure Hymnes, 130, 150, 151; Mother Hubberds Tale, 129; Muiopotmos, 129, 132; Prothalamion, 130; Shepheards Calendar, 122, 124, 128, 147; View of the Present State of Ireland, 123, 125, 162; Bower of Bliss copied from Tasso, 116–17; difference between Spenserian and Italian stanza, 118; school and university career, 121; attitude to Puritanism and Humanism, 122; temporary employment, 122–3; relations to Ireland, 123–6; visits to England, 124–

6; English poetry when Spenser began to write, 127; strong impulse to continue and develop the medieval tradition of chivalrous romance, 130; genesis of Faerie Queene, 130–2; its narrative technique, 133–6; its allegory, 136–42; language, 142–3; as Christian and Platonist, 144–5; entering Spenserian world for first time, 146–7; first romantic medievalists, 147–8; distinction between diffused and Christianized Platonism and a more aesthetic Platonism, 149–50; chronology and Ovidian, medieval and Petrarchan strains in first two hymns, 150–1; relation between first and second pair of hymns, 151; Mutability fragment as baptized Platonism of Middle Ages, 151; Nature, 152–3; cryptic image of garden of Adonis, 153; Time, 153–4; souls undergoing reincarnation, 154; Spenser's garden cannot be located, 155; Venus and Adonis, 155; Sapience of fourth hymn identified with Second Person of Trinity, 155; Venus and Adonis as Form and Matter, 155–6; identification of Adonis with Sol, 156–7; medieval débat between Venus and Diana, 158; meeting of Arthur and Gloriana, 158–9; meanings behind Gloriana and Arthur, 159–61; religious sensibility, 161–2; Cupid as blindfold with dragon under his foot, 164; loves of Mars and Venus, 164–5; Cupid deprived of his weapons, 165; as blind, 165; significance of dragon, 165–6; gold as sinister, 167; effect of Cupid's statue on Britomart, 167; contrast between Cupid and True Love, 167–8; double rôle of Genius as doorkeeper to Acrasia and to Adonis, 169, 171–4; mentioned, 31, 64, 88, 114, 117, 179, 185, 186

Speranza (in Spenser), 141

Speroni, Sperone, 112, 120

Spiers, J., Medieval English Poetry: The Non-Chaucerian Tradition, 1, 4, 9 n. 2, 12, 13, 15, 17, 39 n. 1

Spinoza, 49

Spurgeon, Caroline, 78, 79, 184

stars, 52

Statius, in the *Purgatorio*, 94; Christian elements in *Thebaid*, 95; figure of *Natura*, 96; conception of man, 96; of sin, 96–8; Olympians as devils, 98–9; ethical personifications, 99; Jupiter as transcendent Creator, 99; gods as good powers, 100; attitude to sexual life, 101; anticipation of elements in Christianity, 102; mentioned, viii

Stevens, J. E., x

Stonehenge, 30

Stratford-upon-Avon, 184

Styx, the, 98, 100

Surrey, Henry Howard, Earl of, 127

Taillefer, 20

Tamburlaine, 162

Tasso, reputation in England, 111; one of the great masters, 111–12; criticism in the seventeenth century, 112–14; revival in the eighteenth century, 114–15; influence on English poets, 115–19; abiding merit, 119–20; mentioned, vii, viii, 68, 131, 133, 134, 185

Taulard, 103

Teiresias (in Dante), 95, 97

Temperantia (in *De Anima*), 34

Tennyson, 10, 64, 104

Testament of Beauty, The, 68

Thebaid, the, 94–101

Thebes, 100

Theocritus, 179

Theseus (in Chaucer), 1

Timaeus, the, *see* Chalcidius

Timias (in Spenser), 133

Timor Mortis (in *De Anima*), 34, 35

Tintoretto, 147

Titan (in Spenser), 152

Tolkien, J. R. R., 116, 185

Toser, 91

Tottel's Miscellany, 127

Treasure Island, 12 n. 2

Trinity MS, *see* Milton

Tristram, Sir, 105

Trojans, the, 24

Turberville, 127

Tweedsmuir, Lord, 68

Tydeus, in Statius, 95; in Dante, 95

Tyrone, Earl of, 124

Ugolino (in Dante), 95

Ulysses (in Dante), 3, 95

Una (in Spenser), 144, 157, 161

Unmoved Mover, in Aristotle, 50–1, 62, 74; mentioned, 86

Urry, Sir (in Malory), 109

Ursula (in Laȝamon), 29

Uther (in Laȝamon), 28, 30

Varchi, 151

Varro, 169–70

Venus, the planet, 45; in Spenser, 142, 150, 155, 156, 158, 161; in Alanus, 170; in Gower, 171

Venus and Adonis, 147

Verne, Jules, 68

'Vernon Lee', *see* Lee

Veronica, 88–9

Vida, 118

Villon, 3

Vinaver, Eugène, ed. *Works of Sir Thomas Malory*, viii, 103, 104, 105, 106, 107, 108, 109, 110; 'On Art and Nature: A letter to C. S. Lewis', 184

Virgil, his Fourth Eclogue, 4; similes, 65–7, 69, 72, 73, 75; discipleship of Statius, 94; influence of *Aeneid* on Statius, 100–1; mentioned, 31, 34, 49, 64, 76, 95, 96, 97, 102, 111, 112, 113, 128, 131, 180

Virtues, the Seven, 60

Virtus, 99

Volsung story, the, 166

Vortigern, 21

Vortimer (in Laȝamon), 27

Vulgate Version of the Arthurian Romances, The, x

Wace, *Geste des Bretons*, 18 n. 1, 20, 24, 25, 26–30; *Roman de Rou*, 20; *Roman de Brut*, 20; mentioned, 19, 21, 25, 32, 36, 37

Wagner, 116

Warton, Thomas, 147, 171–4, 186

Wartons, the, 147

Water Babies, The, 115

Waverley, 114

Webb, C. C. J., 170

Wells, H. G., 68, 75

Wells Cathedral, 110

Weston, Jesse, 15, 16
Wil (in *Sawles Warde*), 34
William the Bastard, 20
Williams, Charles, his *Taliessin through Logres* and *The Region of the Summer Stars*, 108, 184; quoted, 162; *Arthurian Torso*, 184; mentioned, 89, 185
Williams, Daryl R., x
Wilson, R. M., ed. *Sawles Warde*, 34 n. 1, 182
Winchester College, 103
Winchester MS, the, 103, 106, 107, 108, 109
Wind, E., *Pagan Mysteries in the Renaissance*, 160 n. 1
Wit (in *Sawles Warde*), 34
Witch of Edmonton, The, 8, 182
Wordsworth, 33, 48, 64, 68, 75, 83, 104, 124, 147, 162

Works of Sir Thomas Malory, The, viii, 103, 105, 110
Worthies, the Nine, 60
Wright, *Anglo-Latin Satirists*, 171
Wright, B. A., 186
Wright, William Aldis, 176 n. 1, 186
Wrobel, Johann, ed. *De Mundi Universitate*, 170
Wyatt, Thomas, 127
Wygar (in Laȝamon), 28

Xenophon, 157, 158

Yeats, W. B., 10, 148
Ygærne (in Laȝamon), 28
ylfe, 28

Zodiac, the, 60
Zoroaster, 14